GREAT LAKES
SALMON & TROUT FISHING

ESSENTIAL TACTICS AND SEASONAL STRATEGIES

Captain Dan Keating

TWO FISH PUBLISHING

TWO FISH PUBLISHING
Great Lakes Salmon and Trout Fishing: Essential Tactics and Seasonal Strategies
Copyright © 2015 by Dan Keating

All rights reserved. No part of this book may be reproduced, stored or transmitted in any form or by any means—mechanical, electronic, recording, photocopy or other means—with out the written permission of the author.

Manufactured in the United States of America

ISBN 978-0-9774273-4-5

Interior design by Angie Messinger
Cover design by Josh Visser
Edited by Dave Mull

Diagrams by Duke Janssen, Lucky Lou Fishing

To Mom and Dad
*Thank you for giving me the opportunity to pursue my passion.
You watered my love of fishing with your time, patience, and love.*

CONTENTS

1 **Essential Tactics—Why We Go Trolling**........................ 1
   Big Picture Thinking................................... 3
   Putting it all Together—The Group Dynamic 7
2 **Downrigger Techniques That Will Shake the Depths**......... 15
   Downrigger Basics................................... 18
   Aggressive Downrigger Tactics........................ 23
   Stealth Downrigger Tactics 29
3 **Diving Planers—Down and Out on the Great Lakes**.......... 43
   The Basics 45
   Think About the *Where* Factor 49
   Stealth Divers—Slide Divers and Torpedoes 56
4 **Wire Line Strategies—The Old and the New** 59
   Wire Line Properties—Traditional Wire vs. Copper 61
   Wire Line Tactics................................... 63
5 **Copper Line Tactics—Stealth, Versatility and More**......... 73
   The Mechanics of Fishing Copper...................... 74
   Navigating Tangles.................................. 77
   Running Copper on Side Planers 79
6 **Lead Core Madness**....................................... 85
   Why Fish Lead Core?................................. 87
   Lead Core Basics 90
   Running Lead Core on Side Planers 92
   The Torpedo SWR—Ultimate Stealth, Maximum Versatility ... 98
7 **Coho—Silver Fun** 103
   Spring Coho 103
   Spring Trolling Secrets.............................. 108
   Summer Coho....................................... 115
8 **All Day Kings** 121
   Early Morning Kings................................. 123
   Listen to the Fish—Make Adjustments................. 130

	Mid Morning Blues.................................. 133
	Tactics and Strategies Option 1 136
	Tactics and Strategies Option 2 140
	Tactics and Strategies Option 3 144
	Afternoon and Evening Strategies 146
9	**Steelhead—Chrome Thunder Near and Far** **148**
	Steelhead Basics 150
	Spring Steelhead A-Z............................... 152
	Tricks and Tactics to Catch Spring Steelhead.......... 161
	Summer Steelhead 167
10	**Lake Trout Wisdom** **173**
	Lake Trout Characteristics 174
	Locating and Catching Spring Lake Trout............. 175
	Summer Laker Tips 180
11	**Brown Trout Logic** **189**
	The Basics 191
	How to Find Browns............................... 193
	Strategies and Tactics for Brown Trout............... 195
12	**Fishing With Meat—Lessons from Uncle Bud** **205**
	Bait World.. 207
	Running the Bait.................................. 212
13	**Currents—Listen to the Lake** **217**
	The Basics 218
	Measuring Currents................................ 229
	Boat Control—Learning How to Deal With Waves and Currents.................................... 233
	Impact of Currents on Trolling Presentations and Lure Selection 236
	How the Weather Can Help You Locate Fish—A New Way of Thinking 240
A Final Word from Captain Dan: Powerful Fishing.............. **245**	

CHAPTER 1

Essential Tactics— Why We Go Trolling

Trolling is the most popular fishing method for Great Lakes salmon and trout because it is the most productive technique we've found so far. The handy on-line dictionary defines trolling as "to fish by trailing a baited line behind a slowly moving boat." Let's get something straight, I've trolled to the moon and back and I've never quite understood trolling in those words. The dictionary makes trolling sound so random, so—let's be honest—boring! Trolling is an art that blends hunting, imagination, and experience. Far from being the lazy way to fish, it's hard work as we seek to understand the water and interpret the moods of a local fish population. It is never random and, when properly executed, never boring!

Trolling is *the* most effective method to locate and catch open water salmon and trout. A well-executed trolling strategy allows us to systematically cover water, locate fish, and then catch them. Trolling lets us fish multiple lines simultaneously, which lets us experiment aggressively with lure and bait selection and dial into what the fish want faster, as well. When we're not adjusting lines or reeling in fish, trolling allows us to study the sonar and map out the bottom topography below. Savvy anglers closely analyze structure and, over time, isolate which areas hold fish.

Plus, trolling is a fun, relaxing way to spend time with friends and family. We can eat a sandwich and enjoy a beverage while we do it, too.

Modern trolling techniques allow us to strategically target multiple layers of the water column. On the Great Lakes, anglers commonly run a wide variety of spreads from 2 to 12 lines. Some larger charter boats routinely run more than 15 lines at a time. To be honest, many days you only need three to six lines to make a great catch. Ultimately, boat size, state laws, experience, waves, and weather will dictate the number of lines you can run.

Trolling is far from a new technique. Anglers around the world have been trolling for ages: from simple hand lines dragged behind a wind-driven skiff to million-dollar battle wagons loaded with state-of-the-art electronics and sprouting multiple, expensive rod-and-reel combos. Men and women have trolled to catch everything from pan fish to saltwater giants such as tuna and billfish. What makes trolling on the Great Lakes so special is that anglers have developed and refined a variety of techniques to catch our salmon and trout.

The goal of the group dynamic is draw fish into your spread and trigger strikes. This is what it's all about!

Fishing on the Great Lakes requires anglers to target vast stretches of the water column. On any given day, we might find salmon and trout suspended from just below the surface down to the bottom, and anywhere in between. To catch fish, anglers have developed a variety of techniques to present their lures in a natural way to fish that can be as deep as 200 feet or more.

These presentations and tactics have been developed in response to the nature of how Mr. Salmon and Mr. Trout move. They are not ambush predators who patiently hide behind a rock or weed line, waiting for an unwary victim to swim by. They are pelagic species that are constantly on the move. They make seasonal and daily movements. Seasonal movements or migrations are fairly predictable and dictated by biological factors such as the fish's instinct to spawn. Environmental factors, macro-weather patterns, currents, and the seasonal warming and cooling of the lake also influence their migrations.

What we've only recently started to understand are the daily horizontal and vertical movements of these predators. Horizontally, they move between shallow and deep water, perpendicular to the shoreline. They also make daily vertical movements in the water column. Many experienced tournament anglers and charter captains believe kings make the biggest vertical moves. Some have observed kings move up 100 feet or more in the water column to feed and then drop back down again. Daily horizontal and vertical movements are influenced by environmental factors including weather, light penetration, water clarity, wave texture, currents, structure, water temps, forage availability, and boat pressure.

Seasonally and daily, these fish move around more than we ever realized. Are these movements random? Or can we, the ever-inquisitive fishermen that we are, anticipate these movements? The answer is a resounding *YES!* Movements are predictable and a thorough understanding of the interplay between species and external factors, and keen observation skills will lead us to fish. With time and experience you will learn to pattern their movements and make highly educated guesses that will help you target fish. You can learn how to read the environment and adjust your presentations based on the clues the weather and water provide. This will save you valuable time, not to mention a load of fuel, and lead to more time on the reel and less time wondering if you should be fishing somewhere else.

BIG PICTURE THINKING

Some of my favorite childhood fishing memories flow from the shore of Besser's Pond. This was a tiny body of water that was a short walk from my home in Wheaton, Illinois. Besser's was my favorite spot to hang out at after school—winter, spring, summer or fall. When I first started fishing there, I used only one rod. My favorite bait was a juicy night crawler, preferably one I found in my yard. As I gained experience, I graduated to tossing spinners, flies, and crankbaits. One day I had the bright idea that I should fish with two lines: one with a worm and the other with an artificial. It took a little more effort to manage two lines, but before I knew it, I was catching twice as many fish! Fishing two lines simultaneously allowed me to gather valuable information. I made adjustments and dialed into the fish faster than ever, and I caught more fish!

Fast-forward several years to when I found myself on the open waters of Lake Michigan with my dad. We started trolling with only a few lines but gradually progressed to running four, then six rods. Several years later, I found myself at the helm of a charter boat that resembled a minesweeper going through the water!

When my dad and I first started fishing, tangled lines and fruitless outings were the norm. Some days just keeping our boat trolling in a straight line was a challenge, and I'm pretty sure that I was probably a bit rough on my dad's driving skills. Despite the lack of success, we learned many valuable lessons. One of the most important of those lessons from our early adventures was to look at the *big picture*. This was paramount to success. Our ability to locate fish and run a spread of lines, tangle free, and dial into a hot bite is enhanced when a comprehensive view of the environment and our tactics informs our decisions.

Back in the '70s, we didn't have sub-surface probes. I remember one hot August day out of Waukegan, Illinois. The reports were dismal, but we still tried. We had one of those temp probes that is attached to a coated wire and wound on a wheel. We left the harbor, and every half-mile or so, we stopped, taped the probe to a downrigger weight, and dropped the rig down. This was primitive fishing by today's standards, but we were trying to understand the temperature stratification of the water and to locate any currents. Merely looking across the surface of the water and trying to analyze other people's fishing reports was not enough. We were learning to read the water and make decisions based on what we could see!

After taking a temperature profile of the water column on this particular August day, we were surprised that the coldest water we found was on the bottom in 20 feet. As we moved out into the lake, we found only warm water. At this point in our salmon fishing career, we knew nothing about upwellings. We didn't understand how cold water off Waukegan would *roll* in from the deeps on a southerly wind, but we did realize that we had a band of cold water tight to the bottom in 20 feet of water. Finding nothing out deep, we ran back toward shore, set up south of the harbor, and worked from 10 to 30 feet of water. To our surprise, the water continued to cool off, and we caught some very nice staging kings! The other boats? They were out deep fishing where the fish were yesterday. On this day, the fish had just moved in, and we found them. Fish move every day, and the goal of this book is to teach you how to react to changes and find fish—wherever you fish!

Trolling requires anglers to visualize the world beneath the waves from a three-dimensional perspective. This vision helps us to understand the environment and the interplay between currents, structure, and weather. When we set lines, we are invading the fish's world. We want to enter their environment as naturally as possible. A three-dimensional perspective gives us more control over our trolling spread, minimizes tangles, and helps us to dial into the fish. With experience, we can learn to anticipate where fish move when conditions change. Being able to visualize the world beneath the waves is the foundation of success.

How do we put our lures in the strike zone? On any given day, we may catch fish on the surface, on the bottom or suspended anyplace in between. For this reason, a thorough understanding of all available tactics will give us the flexibility to catch fish throughout the day.

Weaving a productive trolling spread is a blend of art, science, and a *healthy dose of experience.* If we randomly assemble a collection of lines and lures and just throw them behind the boat, we might as well plan on a Filet-O-Fish sandwich for dinner. Our goal as educated anglers is to attract maximum attention to our spreads and trigger these fish to strike! When we build a well-thought-out trolling spread, we catch more fish.

To simplify, we will divide all presentations into two basic categories: aggressive and stealth. The mood of the fish and external or environmental factors will determine which type of tactics will produce best on any given day. Some days, a stealth spread may be best. At times, an aggressive spread will dominate. Most days, however, a blended spread of stealthy and aggressive presentations will be most productive.

One of many unsolved mysteries in the world of fishing is why the delivery device impacts lure action and the lure's *signature*—the vibrations the lure produces and how much water it displaces. For whatever reason, on some days, fish will only strike lures presented on one method. This may change hourly. For example, fish often aggressively strike baits behind a big old downrigger cannonball early in the morning as this 12-pound hunk of lead comes through, displacing water right under the boat. But once the sun rises, they often prefer lures behind stealthier copper and lead core lines and Torpedo weights. A heavy current may play into this, but more times than not, it is a reflection of the temperament of the fish. Fish can be moody!

A combination of tactics may produce best when woven together. For example, a multi-dimensional spread consisting of a few riggers, two divers, a copper line, and a seven-color lead core line might produce more action than a spread consisting of only coppers or only lead core. Obviously, the depth you are targeting will influence which presentations you will want to run.

Another reason to run a mixed spread is that it helps us to *listen* and learn. We listen to the fish and learn what they want so we can dial in the rest of our spread. If we start with four or five different types of presentations and the fish are hitting only one or two of them, we can adjust our other lines. Often, it is a matter of identifying whether the fish want stealthy or more aggressive presentations. Keep in mind that hot combinations may look very different from one season to the next, as well as from shallow water to deep water. Every boat fishes slightly different, as do individual anglers. We all need to identify what works best off our own boats. In other words, pay attention to everything that is going on in the stern of your boat, both above the surface and below. This is intuitive fishing.

1. Aggressive vs. Stealth—nature of fish/external factors.
2. Presentation impacts lure action/signature—some days fish only strike one method.

3. Delivery device impacts location/relationships within your spread.
4. Combination of tactics may produce best (weave them together).
5. Multiple presentations will help you dial into the fish faster.
6. Listen to the fish. Intuitive fishing.

Before looking at the inner workings of a well-engineered trolling pattern, we need to understand the one variable that impacts the entire spread—trolling speed. Determining the right trolling speed and trolling angle each day is critical to success. While the faster one trolls, the more water they cover, we must always match our trolling speed with the lures, bait, and attractors we are pulling.

Trolling speed is greatly influenced (and sometimes complicated) by wind, waves, current, and lure selection. While every boat fishes different, the general trolling range is from 1.2 to 3.0 kts. (1.5 to 3.6 mph). A sub surfaces probe or GPS can be used to monitor trolling speeds. Each day you must match the correct speed with the proper angle to be successful. Frequently, you will need to adjust trolling speeds every time you change direction.

PUTTING IT ALL TOGETHER—THE GROUP DYNAMIC

Trolling is the art of running multiple lines and delivery devices as you systematically eliminate unproductive water. If you want to maximize the impact of your trolling spread, you need to think collectively. You are not running an *individual* downrigger, an *individual* directional diver or sinker, an *individual* side planer, copper, lead core, or wire line. You are running a team of lures and delivery devices. Each team of lures will consist of multiple parts, moving through the water column together. This is what we refer to as the *group dynamic*.

Our group dynamic will do one of two things: either it will attract fish into our spread and trigger strikes, or it will repel fish. Our goal is to attract maximum attention and convert these fish to strikes! From there, it is all up to the angler on the rod to boat the fish.

Two types of fish will be drawn into our spread: aggressive fish and

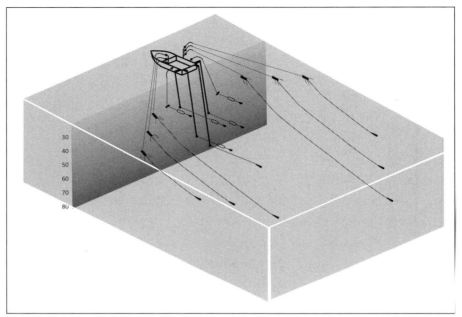

Great Lakes anglers systematically troll a variety of presentations to catch salmon and trout. When setting a spread of lines, think about the relationships created between all the individual lures and delivery devices. Learn to fish your spread as a team of lures.

those that are merely curious. The former are either hungry or just ticked off and looking to pick a fight with the next guy in the food chain. These are often the early morning fish that make life exciting!

Negative or curious fish, which we often encounter throughout the day, are a different creature. Their stomachs are full, or they may be overly cautious and just floating around, daydreaming about the early morning buffet they enjoyed. Understanding the temperament of the fish will help us determine lure selection. It will also inform our choice of which delivery methods to deploy. As we make adjustments throughout the day, we must ask, "are the fish aggressive or are we trying to catch negative fish?"

Some of you may be asking, "But what about the fish that run from the boat? The super turned off fish? The ghost fish that we don't even know are there?" These are the fish that will often take properly presented lures on super stealth presentations such as Torpedo Secret Weapon Rigs, copper hybrids, and wire divers set out on long lines, diving deep, and off to the side of the inner group dynamic.

Our world and our lives are defined by relationships. It's no different when we are fishing. Every time we troll more than one line, we need to consider the vertical and horizontal relationships created between our lines, delivery devices, attractors, and lures. These relationships are as important as the lures and trolling speed. Everything is impacting everything else around it. Every lure you troll has a relationship to the boat and other lures, attractors, and delivery devices (planer boards, downrigger weights, etc.) that are in the spread. The right bait run in the wrong location or on the wrong delivery device usually won't catch a fish.

Let's unpack the strategy for weaving an irresistible trolling spread. Think of yourself as a coach. Not only are you choosing lures or baits for your lineup, you are also determining where and how to run them. What type of line you use them on and how you insert them into your trolling spread are as important as the lures themselves. As you change baits, you want to think about *where* individual lures are in relation to each other and the boat. It is the combined impact of your group dynamic that will draw fish into your spread and trigger strikes—or repel fish.

Before setting lines, you need to envision your trolling spread from the fish's perspective. You need to think three-dimensionally. This is a core lesson that I teach at fishing seminars.

Before dropping the first line, create horizontal and vertical boundaries that will determine where to set your riggers, coppers, divers, etc. To do this, determine what layers of the water column may hold fish. Water, temperature, depth, current, light penetration, wave texture, baitfish, number of anglers on board, and most importantly, fish temperament help us isolate productive vertical boundaries. Horizontal relationships extend laterally to the side and behind your boat. Trolling boards, directional divers, Torpedoes, and pancake-shaped downrigger weights allow you to send lures out to the sides of your boat.

Establishing the horizontal dimensions is an art form. First, we have the horizontal boundary that extends at a 90-degree angle port and starboard from the center of our boat. Secondly, the horizontal layer extends linearly on a horizontal plane behind the boat. This is referred to as *lead length* and sometimes as *stretch*. Although many anglers ignore this second horizontal relationship, it is often the most important factor of the day. Always consider these two horizontal dimensions as you set lines and make adjustments.

What does all of this look like? Let's unpack the vertical dimensions first. Let's say we're targeting a mixed bag of kings and steelhead. Kings like cold water, 42 to 48-degrees. Steelies often are found in the thermocline or just above it. On this theoretical day, we're trolling in 140 feet of water, and the 42- to 48-degree band of water stretches from 80 feet down to 120 feet. This is "Strike Box Number 1."

On this day, the thermocline is between 50 and 60 feet. We therefore want to create a second strike box from about 40 feet down to 60 feet. That will be "Strike Box Number 2." As we deploy our rigs, we want to intentionally target both of these vertical layers. Let me just say, I love days like this. We can spread out our lines and really catch a load of fish!

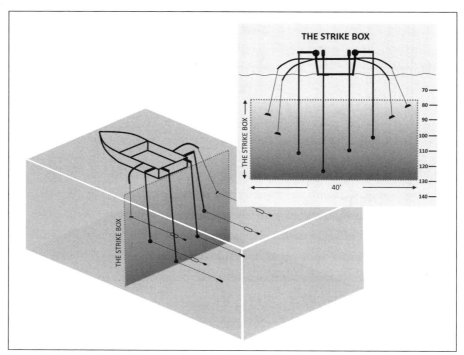

Determining what levels of the water column hold fish will help you effectively set lines.

Fish temperament, target depth, sea conditions, currents, and our ability to mix multiple presentations will dictate horizontal relationships. If the fish are aggressive, we'll want to pack the lures in close together and create maximum noise. At times, coho and steelhead are drawn to a squadron of spoons and flasher/fly combos 20 to 50 feet below a spinning propeller—lures with short lead lengths behind the boat work best. At times, running our lures with only 10 to 20 feet of vertical separation will trigger maximum action. When fish are in a bad mood, we will want to keep our lures spread out with at least 20 to 50 feet of vertical separation. Some days the best rod is a lone rigger set well below all the other lines. If we place a second rod in the basement, neither works.

Negative fish need a stealthier spread. On calm, sunny days, or when the fish are suspending in clear water 20 to 40 feet down, we want to spread our lines out horizontally, away from the boat, creating maximum distance between individual lines. I remember a day when the best rods were segmented leads, and I had to run the Church Boards a country mile off the sides. Yes, it was a pain! There was boat traffic, and I was reeling them in every time I got into a crowd. It's no wonder I have two tears in my shoulder, but it's what I had to do to catch super-spooky steelies and kings!

The vertical and horizontal parameters will change from day to day and, at times, hourly. Successful anglers tweak these vertical and horizontal relationships to keep fish biting throughout the day. Once productive relationships are determined, you want to maintain them. In other words, reset lines exactly as they were. Remember this: repeatability is often the key to success with salmon and trout. Keep track of what patterns work for you. While every day presents a new set of challenges on the water, you can duplicate general patterns when you encounter similar conditions. If you understand the horizontal and vertical dimensions created by controlled depth fishing, you will have fewer tangles and set irresistible spreads that catch more fish.

As you insert lures and gear into your group dynamic, a macro pattern will emerge. The four most popular patterns are the V, inverted V, the M and the W pattern. (These are discussed in *Keating on Kings, Great Lakes*

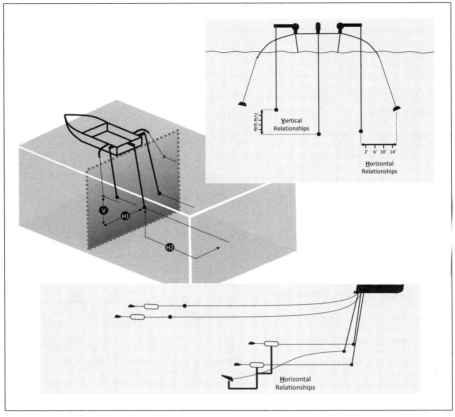

When adjusting lines, keep in mind the many vertical and horizontal relationships between lures.

Chinook Tactics Way Beyond the Basics). The V pattern places our deepest lines directly beneath the boat. As we move away from the center, the vertical depth of lures rises up in the water column. The M pattern is day in and day out my most productive. It takes the V concept and forms two outside legs by dropping one directional diver on each side to the deepest corners of the strike box. If we run coppers and Torpedo SWR's off side planers, we can create multiple Ms. The inverted V calls for running your boom riggers deep and a center rigger or two corner riggers higher in the water column. The W has your corner riggers deep, a higher line (un-weighted flat line, small Torpedo, or segmented lead or copper up the middle) and a diver on each side probing higher levels.

Minor Adjustments Lead to Big Fish

When changing lures, lead lengths, depths, speeds, angles, and delivery devices, the combined effect of our choices will determine what our group dynamic looks like over the course of the day. After determining the vertical and horizontal dimensions of our spread, we want to think about the relationships within the group. The distance between the individual lures and delivery devices is as important as the lures themselves. Every line, delivery device, attractor, and lure is impacting other elements within the spread. The right bait run in the wrong location on the wrong delivery device will not catch fish.

When we change a lure or delivery rig, we must consider how that change will impact the other lures in the water. Within each group dynamic, smaller dynamics or combinations might be relating to one another. For example, a pair of divers running side by side will almost function like a halfback following a fullback down the field. One of those divers might be smoking hot while the other one goes untouched. If we change the unproductive diver, the productive one might go stone cold. Or, let's say we're running three downriggers with a flasher on the middle one and spoons on the corners. The spoons catch fish after fish, while the flasher rod never rattles. We might be tempted to change the middle flasher to a spoon, but we're likely better off to leave the flasher in, as it might be the key, attractive ingredient to making the spoons work.

Remember, listen to the fish and the environment. Adjust your spread to capitalize on the mood of the fish and what the lake gives you.

If you have a plan before you start setting lines, you will more effectively target fish. Experience teaches you to isolate productive combinations of lures. Some anglers randomly troll along, thinking everything is neat and orderly beneath the waves, but the ugly reality of multiple line tangles is a clear reminder that lines are not always where we think they are! Trust me, I've probably untangled more miles of fishing line than you can imagine.

There is a learning curve to trolling. The more time you spend trolling, the more proficient you become. Building a productive trolling spread (group dynamic) is truly part science, part art (gut instinct), and a healthy dose of experience. Strategic trollers learn to weave productive trolling spreads and have far fewer tangles. Sure, it is much easier to just randomly drop lines in the water, but when the drag starts to sing . . . the sandwich hits the floor and Fish On turns into Game On!

Kings and steelhead are frequently found schooling in the same areas during the summer and fall.

CHAPTER 2

Downrigger Techniques That Will Shake the Depths

Who wants to catch more fish on downriggers? Who *doesn't*? Few delivery devices give big water trollers as much of a sporting fight as downriggers do—the fish gets on, and you're not dealing with extra weights, diving planers, boards, or a length of copper line that stretches to the horizon. It's just you and the fish. Ever since Zebra and Quagga Mussels have cleared up the Great Lakes, many struggle to catch fish off riggers like they did in the good old days, and if they continue to run their downriggers like it was 1989, then they can pretty much expect downriggers to produce sporadically.

Over the course of a typical charter season my downriggers produce as many fish, if not more, than any other presentation. Would you like to resurrect your downriggers? Opening your mind to lightening things up as well as adding a Secret Weapon Rig (basically, three colors of lead core off a downrigger) can help your riggers catch fish all day.

Let's keep it simple. Downrigger tactics can be divided into two categories: aggressive and stealth. Trollers must understand the difference between *aggressive* and *stealth* rigger treatments and how to implement them. Beyond that, the key to catching fish off downriggers throughout the day is simply learning when to fish them aggressively and when to go to stealth mode.

Some general factors can help us identify when to run aggressive riggers and when to stealth things up. Time of day, water clarity, weather, light penetration, sea conditions, and how deep fish are suspending will give us general guidelines, but the fish will *speak* the loudest.

Aggressive rigger presentations *kick butt* at first light! The big ol' cannonball goes down almost directly below the rumbling boat, with the lure, be it spoon, plug, meat rig, or flasher-fly, not far behind. Salmon have a huge advantage over their prey and feed actively during low light. They often use their lateral line to hunt, while not being able to see that your fly behind a flasher isn't something good to eat. At times, this set-up can be on fire, but to get the most out of these downriggers, we must understand how to heighten their aggressive appeal and tweak the rest of the spread to appeal to the mood of the fish. Other times to run riggers aggressively include sunrise and sunset, overcast days, or way deep in the abyss. They also work when seas are choppy or when a storm or front is approaching.

Most anglers, without even realizing it, use their riggers as an aggressive presentation all day. As the sun climbs higher in the sky, aggressive rigger presentations often produce less fish and may even go completely dead. Why? The attitude of the fish is changing. Mr. Salmon's world is being transformed as light brightens the waterscape beneath the waves. He may have a full stomach after the morning buffet, or I believe some fish are just more cautious, can see better and want nothing to do with the cannonball blasting through their realm with the boat up above. Regardless of the reason, we need to listen to the fish—they no longer want a *loud* presentation anywhere near our boats signatures!

Many anglers fail to realize that they easily can transition downriggers to a stealth presentation with long stretches of light line or by running a Secret Weapon Rig (SWR). Also, running less attractors and fewer lines directly below and behind a boat can make your presentation more appealing to negative fish.

So when do you want to stealth up and move the lures on the riggers way back behind the boat? Try stealthing up during the mid-day hours or on calm, sunny days. Stealth also works when fighting a strong current or fishing gin-clear water. When the fish are just plain fussy, stealth presentations can bring your riggers to life. Whenever you encounter a challenging current, and the speed just doesn't *feel* right, an SWR can be the best rod on your boat.

I often begin the day at or before first light with aggressive lures on my riggers. When the fish shut off, it is time to pull some of the louder baits and insert stealth into the mix. How many riggers should you change? Do we pull all our aggressive presentations off the riggers as the day advances? The answer to this question depends on how many downriggers you have available and what other presentations you already have in the water. A good method is to pull one aggressive presentation at a time. Insert a stealth set-up in its place and see if it catches fish. If this new presentation gets hit right away, I usually leave the other downriggers as they are for a while—the aggressive riggers might have drawn the fish in, but cause it to disengage. The lonely spoon bringing up the rear triggered the fish to bite. If the first stealth rigger doesn't work or if it is really calm and bright, pull a second aggressive rigger out of the water and add another stealth rod. Once the morning feed is over, I look for a balanced blend of stealth and aggressive presentations.

For example, you start out the morning running four riggers aggressively. The bite slows, so you replace a flasher with either a light-lined spoon or an SWR. As you reduce the ratio of aggressive riggers you can make your subsequent adjustments based on each change. If you have three riggers on

This catch of summer coho was taken by running an aggressive spread of dodgers, flashers, and flies.

your boat, change the center rigger to a stealth spoon and keep the booms hot. If running two riggers, change one. If the one stealth rig gets two or three quick hits, change the other rigger. Even when stealth riggers start to fire, it's often wise to keep one rigger choked with an aggressive flasher/fly combo set within 20 feet of the ball, just to keep the fish honest and hopefully coming into the spread.

Intuitive anglers use other presentations to help interpret the mood of the fish. If side planers with coppers or lead cores start getting hit, that is a clue that we need stealth on downriggers. Riggers too often slow down after the morning massacre when the side planers start popping. When this happens, convert riggers to stealth mode. If the water is clear or the sun bright, chances are good that stealth will be the order of the day. Every day is different, and we need to be creative, observant, and willing to adjust to keep riggers popping throughout the day.

DOWNRIGGER BASICS

Choosing downrigger weights is not rocket science! Pick the heaviest, most streamlined weight your rigger motor (or your own muscles) and boom can handle. Heavier weights (12-pounds or heavier) minimize blowback, which translates into more strikes boated and fewer tangles. Opinions differ as to the best shape of the weight. When running four riggers, I run two 12-pound balls off the back corners and two 10-pound pancakes off the side (boom riggers). If I am targeting deeper layers in the water column (below 80 feet), I use 15-pound balls on the corners and 12-pound pancakes on the booms. Torpedo makes hydrodynamic rigger weights, and many anglers swear by the multi-faceted Shark Weights that also cut cleanly through the water.

I like pancake weights on the booms because when you bend the fin slightly, they impart additional side-to-side action to trailing lures and, planning away from the boat, open the inner group dynamic by a few feet at depth. The more you bend the fin, the greater the angle to the side. Be careful, though; if you bend the fin too much, the weight will spin and cause tangles. Therefore, you only want a slight angle on the fin, about 10 degrees at the most. Properly adjusted, the weight will run a foot or two to the side of the corner riggers. This creates several additional feet of horizontal separation between the boom and corner weights. This slight horizontal separation opens up your group dynamic and reduces tangles on turns and when fish strike. Staggering the weight size will also minimize tangles on turns and when fishing strong currents. When you run a flasher tight off a pancake weight, you get a very aggressive action. As the boat surges through the water, the pancake will oscillate in the water, making the trailing bait dart more.

If you run two or three riggers, the same sized weight can be used on all. If fishing in a strong current, pancakes are tough to use—I recommend you switch them out for cannonballs.

At seminars, anglers are always asking, "what color weights work best?" I have used a variety of colors, and honestly, I never thought the color of the weight made much difference, other than for spring coho fishing. Coho love baits run off orange or red weights! Other than spring coho fishing, my preference was for simple, non-coated, lead-colored weights. That all changed one day.

The Gaudy Yellow Downrigger Weight

It's only human to have opinions. One opinion I've always felt strongly about is the color of downrigger weights doesn't make any difference. After close to 30 years experience chartering, I was certain a plain, lead-colored weight could not be beaten by anything fancier, but one year something happened. I snapped off my last pancake weight in the middle of a charter! No one wants to catch fish more than I do, and the thought of fishing with one less line in the water was sorta like playing football barefoot!

As already mentioned, I prefer to run four Big Jon riggers with 12-pound balls on the corners and two booms (out downs) with 10-pound pancake weights. The different weight sizes minimize tangles on turns and in currents.

That said, the thought of running with one less rod in the water was not acceptable, but I didn't have any extra weights . . . or so I thought. I began rummaging around on my boat hoping a weight might materialize when I came across a relic one of my crewmembers picked up during the popular (and regrettably defunct) Eucker Tournament out of Racine, Wisconsin. It was a chartreuse-yellow Stinger pancake weight. I remember the day, years ago, Steve showed up at the boat with this *weight*. I was appalled at the thought of using it. After lecturing Steve on color, the weight was stowed away in the bowels of the boat, never touching the water.

Well, today was the day the bright yellow Stinger would splash into the world below the *Blue Horizon*, and what a splash it made! After tying on a new snap, I attached the opulent-looking weight. I couldn't believe I was putting it in the water. Since I was putting such a strange looking weight into my spread, I figured I might as well go all out, so I paired it with an old-fashioned yellow Luhr Jensen 0 dodger and a Howie Snowflake fly. The entire rig was set 42 feet below the surface.

That rig wasn't down but a few minutes when a large king grabbed the Snowflake and was off to the races. After netting the fish, the dodger/fly was quickly reset, and a frisky coho smacked the fly almost immediately after it had reached its cruising depth. The rig trailing 10 feet off the chartreuse weight was the hottest rig on the boat for the remainder of the morning. Well, not being one who likes to let small details slip by without scrutiny, I spent my free moments that day pondering—was it the dodger fly . . . or was it the bright yellow Stinger weight that drew those fish in?

The only way to answer a question like that was to go back out fishing, and on the next day, the bright Stinger was in the starting line up. Guess what happened? That rod dominated my rigger action again! Being prone to over thinking any situation, I again looked at that *bright* rigger weight above the surface and asked, "is it the weight or is it the fly?" One way to answer that question was to put the same rig on the opposite boom rigger and run it exactly alike! No one ever said you had to be smart to be a charter captain.

Well, to my surprise, the duplicate rig on a plain, lead-colored pancake had far fewer bites! I tested the yellow weight the rest of that season against a plain, lead-colored weight on the opposite boom rigger. Conclusion: on many days, the color of the rigger weight made a difference, and my catch was greatly improved by the yellow weight in the spread. Interestingly enough, it was often on bright sunny days when it dominated the action from 30 to 60 feet down.

Downrigger Techniques That Will Shake the Depths

A strategic approach to setting downriggers will keep them popping all day!

We all know we can improve our catch by paying attention to small details and tweaking our spreads in response to new data and environmental changes.

Want to Boat More Fish? Read This!

At this point, I need to mention downrigger releases. Releases do more than just hold your line to the weight. The purpose of the release is to keep the line solidly connected until a fish hits and then to help hook the fish. It should not damage the line in any way. Many rigger releases are available, and a complete discussion on this topic can be found in Chapter 4 of *Great Lakes Salmon & Trout Fishing*. My favorite is a #12 rubber band half-hitched to the fishing line and clipped into a Blacks Release. You can view a visual demonstration of this in the *Keating on Kings* DVD Part 1. My second favorite release is the Otter Release. This pinch-pad release is attached to the weight with an 8-inch cord. You can adjust the tension by how deep into the jaws you place your line, and the tether gives you some sensitivity to see when a small fish is on the line.

Whatever release you settle on, if you use a special technique to set your riggers, your hook up ratio will greatly improve. Whenever you set riggers, you want to *load the rod*. This greatly minimizes blowback, reduces tangles, makes it easier to net fish coming in on other lines, and—most importantly—leads to solid hookups. The loaded rod tells you what's happening at the ball and prevents you from dragging small fish. *Loading the rod* helps you boat the fish that strike.

To understand the principle of loading the rod, let's look at what happens when we improperly set a downrigger. Many anglers hook the line into the release, free spool the reel, and then drop the weight. After stopping the weight at the target depth, they engage the reel and try to tighten up the line and bend the rod over. This method does not maintain tight pressure on the rod as the weight descends. Water pressure on the line between the rod tip and the weight creates a belly in the line. This *blowback belly* results in an extra 2 to 10 feet of line between the rod tip and the release. When a fish strikes, the release lets loose, and you reel against slack line. This is what

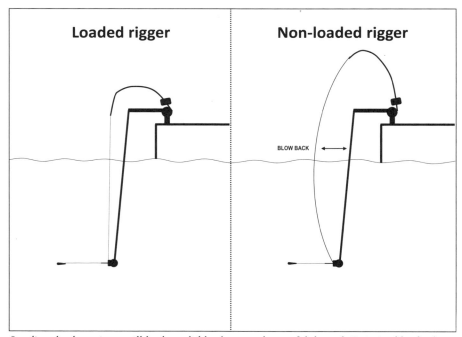

Loading the downrigger will lead to solid hook ups and more fish boated. Excessive blowback will make it hard to tell when small fish strike and will give fish momentary slack line when the line releases from the weight.

happens when a rod goes off, and you pull it from the rod holder and reel frantically but don't feel any resistance.

A poor hook set often results in a lost fish. What do you think is going on at the point where the fish and the hook make contact and the release opens? After striking the lure, the release opens, and the fish has a moment where there is no tension on the hook in their mouth (when the rod is not *loaded*). A poor hook set makes it easier for the fish to escape during the remainder of the fight. When the rod is loaded, solid pressure is on the hook the moment the release opens up. When the angler starts cranking, the fish is already tightly connected!

So, how do we *load the rod?* After hooking the line into the release, engage the reel's drag and place the rod in the rod holder. Drop the weight so it is just below the surface and tighten up the line on the reel. The rod is doubled over at this point and looks like it will break! Next, begin dropping the weight against the drag. *Do not free spool the reel!* Adjust the drag as the weight drops, always keeping a deep bend in the rod. Maximum pressure on the descending weight eliminates blow back. Warning: the first few times you try this, you may get premature releases during the descent. Keep adjusting your release and the reel's drag until you find the sweet spot. I typically set my releases fairly tight. If the fish cannot break the release open, then I loosen up.

Have you ever had a day where you miss a lot of strikes? When every fish that hits your rigger lines pulls hard for a few seconds and then just falls off? When I encounter this scenario, I will use two or three rubber bands and crank the Black's release super tight. When the fish strikes, he is pulling against the downrigger weight, and it requires a great deal of force to pop the release (extra bands don't break easily)! Often you will see the rod bouncing and have to break the release open with a quick upward snap. This method helps set the hook, and you will catch more fish!

AGGRESSIVE DOWNRIGGER TACTICS

When driving down the highway, large, brightly colored, flashing neon signs quickly get our attention. If we are hungry or just ornery after spending the day cooped up in a car, we bite! We pull off the road and order a Big Mac and a large fry. It's no different with the fish. Sometimes, all we need to do is get their attention! Once we do that, it's game on.

Just like a burger-chomping road warrior, hungry fish are attracted to flashy objects, noise, and commotion. Most days present windows of opportunity where fish aggressively feed. The best way to get a bite from these fish is to get their attention. Downriggers can easily be set to function like a bright, neon sign on the watery highway in the depths by following a few proven strategies.

An aggressive downrigger presentation incorporates a variety of elements including the turbulence (*noise*) and visual nuances of the rigger weight, the hum of the cable, and our boats trolling signature. The turbulence created by a sea anchor also adds to the presentation when lines are set just below the wash. The sight, sound, and action of the lure further magnifies the intensity of the presentation. The entire presentation becomes even more aggressive when we set the lures back on short 5 to 20 foot leads off the weights.

What makes a lure aggressive? Generally, any lure that vibrates, rattles, or gives off an extra dose of pizazz that goes beyond a mere flash or wiggle. The most aggressive lure presentations, however, incorporate the use of an attractor. A variety of attractors are on the market, ranging from cowbell spinners to umbrella rigs, but the time proven favorites are flashers and dodgers. Basically, flashers are plastic and revolve in a wider circle, and dodgers are metal and designed to swing side to side (although they also work when you troll faster and make them spin). (See *Great Lakes Salmon and Trout Fishing* Chapter 3 for a basic discussion on attractors.)

Dodgers and flashers have three characteristics that impact our spread: sight, action, and sound. Obviously, fish can see them! They impart action to the trailing fly or natural bait. Audibly, they create a signature as they spin, rotate, and swoosh behind our boats. The impact of each individual flasher transcends the entire inner group dynamic.

Not only can fish see and hear attractors, but also they can *feel* them through their lateral line. The lateral line is made up of thousands of tiny, specially-designed, jelly-filled cells. This feature enables a fish to *hear* vibrations in the environment. While salmon and trout are predominantly sight feeders, they still use this highly-developed *distant touch* sensing system to help them locate and consume their next meal, especially in low-light conditions. Any time darkness or murky water compromises their environment the lateral line plays a greater role in helping fish locate prey.

Are all dodgers and flashers alike? No. Individual flasher brands give off slightly different vibration patterns. As discussed at length in *Keating on Kings* (Chapter 7 of the book and DVD Part 2), the weight of the flasher and its shape impact the vibration pattern it creates. Flashers with fins will have a different action as well. I have found that heavier flashers (such as Hot Spots) work better on rough days and lighter flashers (such as Luhr Jensen Coyote's) work better on calm days. Trolling speed also impacts the vibrational frequency of an attractor's signature. Is the flasher making wide, swinging arcs? Or is it making fast, tight pulsating rotations? Is a dodger *swishing* or *spinning*?

The entire presentation can be made even more aggressive by adjusting the leader length between the flasher and fly. The shorter the leader, the more motion that the flasher imparts to the fly. Longer leads result in less motion and effectively slow down the motion of the fly. If fish are juiced up, chances are a fast-moving, erratic fly will trigger more strikes.

While we could spend an afternoon discussing favorite flashers, space only permits us to list a few favorites such as Spin Doctors, Hot Spots, Coyotes, and Pro Trolls. Both the 8 and 10-inch flashers are used in a host of colors. The base colors include white, pearl, yellow, green, blue, and chrome. Prism tapes, glow tapes, and UV tapes and paint are all used to enhance their appearance. Patterns that incorporate or mix these colors, such as the Green Frog and Nuclear Spin Doctors, are popular. Ultimately, color should be selected based on target depth, water texture, light penetration, and target species. Productive color patterns vary by region. Start with the basics and identify which colors work on your boat based on target depth, species, and current conditions.

Many anglers use 8-inch flashers exclusively. Captain Carl Stopczynski of Fuzzy Bear Charters taught me that adding one larger, 10-inch flasher to a group of smaller flashers can get the entire spread popping. The larger flasher is set 10 to 15 feet behind a group of 8-inch flashers. Most days, the large *skateboard* will be deeper than the smaller paddles.

As far as metal dodgers goes, it is tough to beat the 0 size Luhr Jensen dodger in silver glow, silver, or chartreuse. The Opti dodger is another popular brand. Cameras mounted on downrigger weights reveal that the silver glow finish gives off the most flash. Many days, just adding one silver glow Jensen dodger to a rigger spread draws fish into all the lines.

How to Set an Aggressive Downrigger Spread

The relationships created when you set your lines are as important as the lures and delivery devices. With an aggressive spread, success often depends on *how* and *where* you place individual baits. As you set lines, you must keep site of the big picture an aggressive spread collectively creates. When your inner group dynamic attracts fish, lures set 5 to 20 feet back will attract more fish than longer leads will. Longer leads diminish the total, big-picture impact of the spread for several reasons. First, a flasher or dodger set 10 feet off the weight has a very different action than an attractor set on a longer lead. Metal dodgers have more snap on a short lead. Plastic flashers have a bigger swing or rotation when run on longer leads.

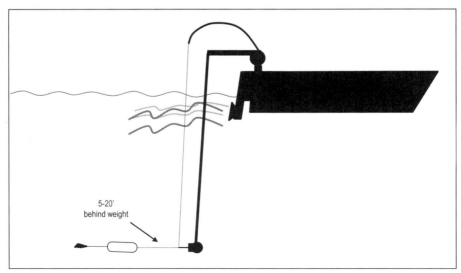

An aggressive downrigger incorporates elements of sight, sound, signature and action to appeal to feeding fish.

Remember, it's the big picture that is drawing feeding fish in and getting them excited and striking!

Running multiple baits in close proximity can further enhance an aggressive presentation. Two to six flashers run in a tight pattern create a tremendous amount of vibration, flash, pop, and sizzle as they move through Mr. Salmon's neighborhood. When running multiple flashers off riggers, pay attention to how far off the weight each one is set. Like a group of offensive linemen, each of the individual flashers is playing off one another. To make a spread of flashers super aggressive, set them with 5 to 20 feet of vertical separation between the riggers. Horizontally, the rigs are all set from 5 to 20 feet back. For whatever reason, this spread really works under low light conditions when fish are actively feeding. If you spread the flashers out, you create a scattered or *open* inner group dynamic. This diminishes the schooling impact of a tightly spaced inner dynamic.

You can add another element to the commotion by setting a braid or wire diver on each side of the boat, just outside a downrigger. If you only have two riggers on a boat, this is a must-use strategy for early morning success! To maximize the impact, set the diver so it is running just outside and slightly above the outside rigger bait. From the fish's perspective, they see a larger school of potential baitfish to attack. The added commotion of the diver and flasher, with the rigger weights and flashers also generates a louder signature, which will attract more fish to the spread.

When I began chartering in the early 1980's, Captain Mike Smith was well known and respected for the huge catches of big kings the *Co Chi I* brought back to port. As impressed as we all were with Mike's fishing abilities, it was his dance move that earned him his nickname, the *Minnow*. A properly-tuned, aggressive spread can greatly improve our catch. When salmon and trout are feeding, they often get excited when they see one of their buddies get hooked up and start doing the *fly dance*. When fish are aggressive, a sense of competition seems to come over them. Last one to the table gets the left overs so to speak. When a school of fish comes upon a group of targets (our trolling spread!), one fish darts in and nails a lure! Instantly, a competitive trigger is switched on, and the other fish become more aggressive. We can see this when casting surface lures to saltwater pelagics such as tuna or mahi-mahi. The colors in the fish literally brighten or "light up" as they strike lures. Whenever we can stimulate competitive senses within fish, doubles and triples can reward us. Many top charter captains catch big numbers of kings and coho early in the morning by running slashing spreads of flashers and flies.

Can we mix aggressive rigger patterns with stealth riggers? Absolutely. I often use a combination of both. For example, if I run four riggers early in the day, I set three of them aggressively and one in stealth mode with a clean spoon or plug. This rig runs immediately behind and below the flashers where it triggers strikes from curious fish that are drawn into the aggressive spread but don't want a fly.

More importantly, this rod helps me interpret the mood of the fish. Once the early bite is over, fish often transition to a negative mood. Many fishermen give up at this point and start thinking about the *Honey Do* list waiting for them at home. But, this is when we need to pick up our game and pay close attention to the subtle clues the fish and environment give us. Many days all the fish are caught on flies for the first hour or two. Suddenly, the flies go dead, but the lone spoon starts to fire. This sends a signal that it is time to remove some attractors and transition our riggers to stealth mode.

Having at least one spoon in the water will help us adjust our rigger presentations to the temperament of the fish. If you run four riggers, put one spoon below the flashers. If you only have two riggers, set both with flashers first thing in the morning. Once the world brightens, replace one with a spoon and let the fish tell you which they prefer. Some days the fish stop striking flies and don't hit the lone spoon set back 50 feet. Try dropping the spoon back 100 feet or more. Or run an SWR.

Copper and lead core side planers also give us valuable info that we can use to adjust our riggers from aggressive to stealth mode. It's not a bad idea to have at least one lead or copper out on each side. These rods help us dial into the fish and tell us when to start transitioning our downrigger presentations. I am always surprised by how many anglers can catch fish on boards but just drag their riggers around with the same lures and lead lengths they've used all morning.

Our sonar can give us clues when to switch, too. If aggressive riggers are working and suddenly go dead, are we still marking fish? If the marks disappeared and the riggers died, we must ask if the fish left the area, or did they spook out from the boat's path and not show up on the sonar? In this case, stealth riggers will likely catch fish.

Once the early bite ends, we need to start thinking about the overall pattern of our downrigger lines. Early, running a lot of flashers is good. Later in the day, just pulling one or two flashers out of a spread often makes the remaining lines productive. Other days, going completely to spoons or body baits can bring our riggers to life.

STEALTH DOWNRIGGER TACTICS

Over the past few years, stealth riggers have been some of the most productive rods on the *Blue Horizon*. Spring, summer, and fall, they produce fish. Anytime I encounter clear water, negative fish, or strong currents, adjusting riggers to stealth mode will produce fish. One other note: clean spoons run on stealth riggers catch huge fish during the middle of the day. If you don't currently incorporate stealth riggers into your spread, you will want to pay close attention.

Secret Weapon Rigs (SWR)

Ever been skunked? It is painful! From one fisherman to another, there is a greater distance between zero fish and one fish, than there is between one and one hundred fish! Charter captains on western Lake Michigan have found the antidote that prevents that smelly critter from sneaking on board—the *Skunk Buster*! These deadly rigs have saved many outings. So, what exactly, is the Skunk Buster? It is a Secret Weapon Rig combined with a Super Slim, Stinger, or Moonshine spoon. Many other spoons work exceptionally well on this rig, and you may develop your own Skunk Buster! Bottom line, SWRs usually catch fish when all other presentations come up short, especially when you encounter heavy currents or just can't seem to isolate productive trolling speeds, these rigs produce.

Why is the SWR so deadly? Can't we just run a clean spoon on light line back 100 feet and achieve the same presentation? We can mimic the lead length, but we cannot duplicate the hypnotic action that is imparted to the spoon by lead core. Sit back, pour a cup of coffee, and let me explain.

First, let's examine the mechanics of an SWR. To set up the rig, spool a downrigger reel, such as we would use with dodgers or flashers with 15- to 20-pound backing monofilament. Then tie three colors (30 yards) of lead core onto the backing. I have used as few as two colors and as many as four colors of lead. On the business end, add a 10 to 20 foot, 20-pound fluorocarbon leader and a small, quality ball bearing swivel.

When setting the rig, let out the leader and the entire lead core, and then put the mono backing into the release. Never put the lead core in the release because it will break. When the rig is in the water, 120 feet of lead line and a 20-foot fluorocarbon leader trail the downrigger weight. We are now fishing in the twenty-first century! These can be set at any depth and with a light action rod, provide a great fight.

What makes this rig different from just setting a spoon way back on mono is the hypnotic action the lead core imparts to the trailing lure. Remember, lead line is thick and interacts with currents and our boats trolling

A Secret Weapon Rig is easy to set up and catches beasts like this when other presentations don't.

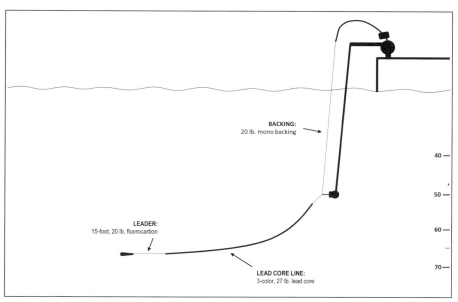

The SRW combines lead core with downriggers.

motion. As we troll along, our lure dances around way behind the rigger in clean water. The lead core line itself imparts additional action to the spoon beyond its normal wobble. It never follows us in a straight line. So while the spoon wiggles or wobbles, it also floats side to side and, at times, rises and falls. It's the most uneven way to put a lure in the strike zone!

While flashers work on SWRs, clean spoons run on 20-pound fluorocarbon leaders with small, ball bearing swivels work best. Shorter leaders of 10 to 20 feet transfer even more action to the spoon than long leaders do. A friend of mine we call *Rockstar* (because of his night job!) runs the *Calumet City Chicken rig* on his SWR. This is a herring strip and bait head, anointed with *secret sauce*, run clean without a flasher. I wouldn't believe it works, but I've seen Bob's fish, and the dude catches some monsters!

A word of caution: SWR's *snake* around behind the boat and can easily tangle other lines off to the side. On turns, they can wipe out a wire diver rig when the two are at the same level. I've also had them tangle with Torpedo SWRs on side planers.

An October outing to deep water illustrates this point. We were making a long southeast pass from 190 feet of water out to 240 feet of water. The

SWR: THE SECRET WEAPON RIG

If you don't already use a Secret Weapon rig in pursuit of salmon and trout—king salmon in particular—it's well worth adding to your arsenal. The Secret Weapon Rig, often shortened to "SWR," combines lead core line and downriggers to create a terrific, reliable, stealth presentation.

Craig McPhee of Badaxe, Michigan is an avid salmon troller who has spent a lot of time on Lake Huron out of Port Austin, Michigan and gets credit for coming up with the concept. Captain Skip Berry, who runs Terminator Charters out of Pentwater, Michigan on Lake Michigan, had a hand in developing the rig, too.

Berry tells the tale: "it was the spring of 200, and Craig was down in Grand Haven, which used to be my home port, and I was showing him the fundamentals of using lead core, which he wasn't familiar with. We went out and spanked the fish pretty good," Berry recalled. "Later on, Craig and I are talking on the phone, and he says, 'why couldn't you add lead core to a downrigger and get some of the benefits?' The more we talked, the better the idea seemed to be. I was already running long leads off downriggers—100 feet and more, so adding three colors of lead and having the lure a good ways behind the downrigger ball seemed to make sense. Not only would it get into clean water below the disturbance the ball caused, but it would be rising and falling on turns a bit, like lead core does when it's out behind planer boards."

"So Craig started doing it on Lake Huron, and I started doing it on Lake Michigan, and we found out that it really did have its times when it caught most of the fish. I ended up going up to Port Austin and fishing a tournament with Craig, and we finished second—most of the fish came on the lead core behind the downrigger. That's when we started calling it the 'Secret Weapon Rig.'"

I fished with Skip sometime soon after he and Craig developed the set-up, and we caught several fish on it. The one time we cashed a check (albeit 12th place, the last check paid) at the big tournament in Ludington, I fished with Skip and some other friends, and most of our fish came on the SWR. —*Dave Mull* lake was beautiful, and a large school of kings, steelhead, and lake trout provided great action. The two hottest rods on this day were a pair of SWRs set at 90 and 110 feet respectively. Both rigs were sporting Moonshine Flounder Pounders. One had a green nose, the other red.

Now, the lake was calm, and we were trolling a straight line on a 100-degree heading over ground. The Flounders were getting hit every five minutes or less. Really! The fish were coming fast, and in the normal chaos that accompanies a charter trip one of our hot rods died. I was a little distracted by my client's antics and maintaining the other eleven lines that were in the water. Fortunately, one of my observant passengers said, "Hey Cap, 'Lucky' hasn't been hit in a while." I promptly brought "Lucky the SWR" up, and sure enough, the rig was firmly tangled with a deep-set wire diver. My autopilot was holding our course and we had not made any turns. The lesson: if an SWR isn't hit, check it for tangles. If it's not tangled, change the lure.

To minimize tangles, speed up on turns and don't turn too sharply. Lead core sinks. Even when trolling in a straight line an SWR runs 6 to 12 feet below the weight. If you are fishing in 50 feet of water and running a SWR down 30 feet, raise the rigger up to 20 feet before making a 180-degree turn. A general rule is to keep the SWR at least 30 feet off the bottom when turning. Otherwise, the lure may sink to the bottom and pick up mussels. Never fish an SWR tight to the bottom in the way you can fish a light line rig. Since the rig is set so far back, it can pick up mussels or weeds off the bottom, not trip the downrigger release, and you'll never know it.

At seminars, I am frequently asked if you can run more than one SWR. Yes, but when running two, set them with at least 10 feet of vertical separation. In other words, don't run two SWRs at the same level. Some anglers will run a three-color SWR on the deeper rigger and a two-color above it. When fishing in the trough (with the waves hitting the boat from the side), the deeper SWR should be set upwind of the shallower SWR. This will minimize tangles when a fish strikes. When fishing deep and in a strong current, you may want to reset your SWRs when you turn around, always keeping the deeper rig upwind.

It's not a bad idea to keep one SWR in the water at all times. Normally, this is my deepest rod in the spread. If it is really hot, I deploy a second one.

You can run them off any rigger on the boat; however, I like running them off the corner riggers. If you run them on a boom rigger, they tend to tangle with diver rods.

The exception to running the SWR as the deepest line is when steelhead and kings suspended higher in the water column. When fish are 20 to 50 feet down, I often run an SWR off a corner rigger set at 20 to 40 feet. The other riggers can be set deep in the water column for kings, coho, or lakers. This one line running above and behind the spread can be a killer. While it can occasionally tangle with fish hitting deeper rigger lines, it catches many large fish.

Light Line Tactics

If shear excitement and sport is your goal on a trolling adventure, then light line rigs run off downriggers offer the best fight in town. Over the years, I've had countless emails from readers and seminar attendees who have achieved great results when they tried the light-line methods. Many said their biggest fish of the season came on light rigs! Others said that a spread of light-lined spoons salvaged many slow days. If you've never used light line, start with one rig. Learn how to weave it into your other presentations.

Before getting too far into this discussion, we need to define "light line." With way too many hours on the water, I have found that 12-pound test line is ideal. It is light, but, it has enough strength that it does not break easily. Some may drop down to 10-, 8- or even 6-pound test. These lighter lines are stealthier, but they break much more easily.

Light line offers more than just great sport; it is one of the best methods to finesse negative kings, browns, steelhead, and lakers into striking. Salmon and trout can be very moody, and spoons run on light line often trigger dormant fish into striking. During the bright, mid-day hours, fish are tough to catch. This is the period that light-line tactics really shine. Also, when trophy-sized fish sink down and hug the lake bottom, a properly selected spoon on light line is often the only rig that will pry these monsters off the bottom.

Why go to all the trouble of trolling light? When combined with a small, quality ball bearing swivel (30-pound Sampo Coastlock) and 12-pound test line, a spoon will achieve maximum action, even at slow speeds. The small swivel is important. A heavy swivel adds additional weight on the nose of the spoon and reduces its action. The combination of a small silver swivel and light line reduces visibility.

I've heard it a hundred times already, "but the kings we catch are way too big to capture on such little rods and reels." Take a moment and Google the IGFA line class record books, and you will discover that anglers around the world are catching ginormous fish on some very thin lines. You may lose a few fish in the beginning, but as you learn how to fight fish on skinny line, you will find that in the long run, you will catch more trophy fish. So, shut up and learn to fish light!

Let me throw in a quick word of caution: the key to winning the battle with *Moby Salmon* on the little rod is, as Kenny Rogers sang, "you have to *know when to hold 'em, know when to fold 'em.*" At the outset of the fight, set the drag light. A freshly-hooked fish is full of fight. Let him run. When setting the drag, the fish should be able to pull line off the reel easily, but there should be enough tension to make the fish fight against the rod. In other words, he should have to work to pull line off the reel. If you are not sure how to set the drag, it is better to set it loosely and tighten up as the fight advances.

Light line exerts less drag as the fish runs. When a big fish runs 100 yards or more line off the reel, light line exerts less drag in the water. As the fish changes course, you can maintain more direct contact with the fish. This results in direct, steady pressure on the hook.

Long runs tire a big fish out. A fish prematurely dragged to the transom is a dangerous creature. A hot fish can easily break off or tangle other lines. As the fish tires, gradually turn up the heat. Boat side, you may have to back off on the drag a bit if the fish is spunky. If the water is cold from the surface down, salmon and trout will fight hard all the way to the net. If you are dragging fish out of deep cold water up through warmer surface layers, the warm water will slow big fish down, and the fight will not last as long.

After every bite, feel the last three or four feet of line in front of a spoon for nicks. Fish often spin during the fight and can nick light line on their gill plates. The abrasion may not break on the fish that caused the nick, but the next fish to strike easily could snap the weakened line. As you gain experience with light line, you will learn when to tighten the drag and when to lighten up. Most trophy fish are lost in the first 30 seconds of striking—or at boat side.

Selecting the right rods and reels for light line will ensure success. If your budget is limited, spend your money on a quality reel. The main attributes are a super smooth drag, a line capacity of at least 300 yards, a large,

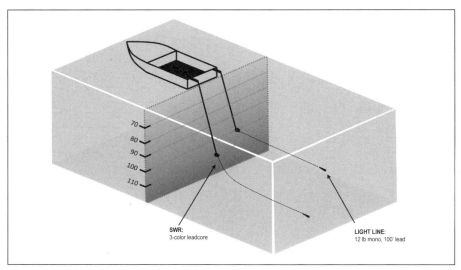

Light line and SWR's off downriggers catch negative fish all day long!

easy-to-grip handle and a high-speed pick-up. I make my living watching people catch fish and find that lighter reels are always a plus. A number of good level wind and bait casting reels are on the market to choose from.

Anglers use a variety of short and long rods for light line applications. In my early salmon fishing days Dad and I used 9-foot rods that were super whippy. We caught a ton of fish on those rods but one fish of immense proportions haunts my memory.

We had trailered our 17-foot Whaler, the *Frick N' Frack*, to one of our favorite weekend fishing destinations—Sheboygan, Wisconsin. I have many fond memories from this town. Like the 25-pound beast we caught on a fly rod in thick fog so thick we didn't think we could make it back to port. We had no Loran C, and GPS was not available back then. We navigated on pure instinct. Or the evening we dined on juicy burgers and beer-battered onion rings. We were camping out in the back of our station wagon, but I spent the night in a porta potty, sick to my stomach. Or the day a ferocious thunderstorm drove us off the lake. We ran back to shore during a downpour of Biblical proportions and hid beneath the 8th Street Bridge on the Sheboygan River. The thunder that storm generated still echoes through my mind.

But, it was the fish that we didn't catch that is foremost in my memories. I will never forget it. Back then, we ran 9-foot fly rods with large, single-action fly reels loaded with 6-to 12-pound line. One particular weekend was plagued with fog, wind, and waves. The last day of our adventure, the wind was ripping out of the northeast, and the waves were crashing over the sea wall. It was too rough for us to venture past the lighthouse. We had driven a long way to fish and were not easily beaten. We decided to troll inside Sheboygan harbor for summer brown trout.

We caught a few browns, but suddenly something—something big—grabbed a lure on one of our light downrigger rods and took off for the open lake at a high speed! This was not a brown trout! The fish made several long runs that we feared would empty our reel, but each time, we managed to halt his progress before running out of line. We thought the creature was playing with us, as if our boat was a toy that he could manipulate at will. After pumping the fish back to the boat, he effortlessly would run back out to the outer limits of our gear, and we'd have to start the tug of war all over. Because of the fog and murky river water pouring into the harbor, we never got a clear view of the fish. But after what seemed an eternity, we got the beast boat-side and his tail broke the surface of the dark water . . . and I will never forget that tail! It was like a whale's tail . . . and that was the last we saw of that beast!

Thirty years ago we had great success running long rods with light line. They still work, but today, I prefer short, one-piece rods of 6- to 7-foot lengths. These are medium light action rods with a soft tip but plenty of backbone in the lower third. They bend over into a tight arc on the downrigger, but there is ample meat in the backbone to *lift* big kings and trout from the depths. Saltwater anglers have developed short rods that are very efficient for capturing large fish.

Short rods have many rigging, fish-fighting, and storing advantages. They are light and easy to hold, which helps inexperienced anglers fight large fish during longer battles. Short rods are easier to set which is a big plus in rough water and from the deck of smaller boats. When big fish dive deep, short rods give you great leverage and enable you to pump large fish to the boat more easily than long rods do—we want to fight the fish, not the rod. They give you far more control of a hooked fish at the back of the boat, too. If a trophy makes an unexpected wrong turn at boat side, it is easy to follow the hooked fish with the short rod. I have often had to free spool a reel (thumb on the spool!) and take the rod and follow the line around a downrigger cable in the water. Once the maneuver is complete, I engage the reel and continue the fight!

Short rods are easy to store. I can drive to a seminar during the winter with my wife and four kids and stick a bunch of rods into my Sienna mini van. Try that with a bunch of long rods! Seriously, if your boat has a small cabin or if you transport rods in your car, short rods are the way to go!

When selecting a downrigger release for light-line applications, you want one that will not crimp the line. A No. 12-rubber band half-hitched to your line and hooked into a Black's Release is ideal. This system will not damage light line. It takes a little practice to set this release, but with experience, it gets to be as natural as breathing. To set, simply moisten the elastic band and half hitch it around your fishing line three to four times. After each half hitch, pull the band tight. The band should not slip down the line after several hitches are applied. If the band slips, loop it around the line one more time.

Next, place the loop into the Black's Release. Tighten the release enough that it doesn't open when trolling. Ideally, the release will open upon the strike, and the rubber band does not break. When resetting the line, you can simply put the same rubber band back into the release. I often use two rubber bands at a time to increase hook ups. This is very helpful when targeting staging kings. Their jaw becomes bony and hard, and they often strike short. If you are fishing in a strong current or trolling deep, you will want to use two or three bands on the line as water pressure often can break a single band prematurely.

True or false: any spoon will work better on light line? TRUE. With a lifetime of salmon fishing experience, I have come to realize that light line makes us better anglers. No matter the brand, size, or color of spoon or plug, light line enhances a lure's action and helps it to blend in with its environment.

Light-lined spoons and body baits can be run throughout the water column. They can be run in a patterned spread of all spoons, or they can be integrated into an aggressive spread of flashers and flies. If you've never tried light-lining spoons, set up one rig with light line and mix this rod into your other patterns. I think that you will be pleasantly surprised!

What makes light line so stealthy? Both the presentation itself, lure selection, and *how* we set the rig come into play. Light line is thin. Fish can't see it well, and because of its diameter, lures can achieve maximum action. Spoons and body baits are stealthier than flashers and flies. Their action is subtler and puts off less vibration. The further back we set the lure, the stealthier the rig.

Productive lead lengths vary from day to day and really depend on environmental conditions and the fish. The general rule is that if shorter leads of 20 to 50 feet don't produce, keep setting spoons farther and farther back. It is not a bad idea to set one spoon back 30 feet and another at least 100 feet. Let the fish tell you their preference.

Spoons set on light line are particularly effective for kings, lake trout, and browns that have taken a negative posture and hold tight to the bottom. Many days, we don't mark these fish because they are so tight to the bottom. In this situation, a lone spoon run 10 to 50 feet behind the weight and set from 1 to 10 feet off the bottom catches fish. The weight is not bouncing the bottom. The idea is to run the spoon just above the bottom.

To effectively *trace the bottom* with a spoon, we want to set the rigger from the bottom up. To do this, drop your rigger weight till it hits the bottom. Trolling motion will pull the weight up off the bottom. Drop the weight a second and third time or more, until you know it is on the bottom, then, raise it from one to ten feet. If the bottom contour is uneven, you will have to adjust this rigger every few minutes to avoid snags and mussels.

When tracing the bottom in deep water, heavier weights minimize blowback and make it easier to stay in contact with the bottom. Don't worry what the downrigger counter registers. Trolling motion creates blowback in the cable. The counter only tells us how many feet of cable are off the reel. It does not tell the precise depth at which the weight is running. For example, let's say we want to fish the bottom in 100 feet. The counter may register 112 feet when the weight is running one foot off the bottom. When I get a rigger super dialed into a bottom bite, I will loop a rubber band on the cable, so I can set the rig back at the exact level.

A two-boat charter I once had with my buddy Captain Jerry Williams helps illustrate this point. On this particular trip, we were targeting kings on the bottom in 200 to 230 feet of water. The fish were on the bottom! My heaviest weight on the boat was only 12 pounds. Jerry was running 16-pound Shark weights. To effectively hit the bottom in 205 feet, I had to let out over 245 feet of cable. Jerry's heavier Sharks hit the bottom with only 215 feet of cable off the rigger.

When you target bottom-hugging fish, take an aggressive approach to lure selection. Change color, size, and brand of spoons until you dial into their preference. Fish sitting on the bottom, especially kings, are moody and selective. Some days it's just a matter of having the right lure in their face.

Light-line rigs can be run exclusively or integrated into an aggressive spread of rigger baits. One of the oldest tricks in the book is the spoon and dodger "tag team." Call it *"Tag Team 101."* This strategy requires you to fish two riggers as a team—one clean spoon on light line and one dodger or flasher. A dodger or flasher on one rod will attract fish to the clean spoon set on an adjacent rod. Set the spoon to run 5 to 15 feet below and 10 to 30 feet behind the attractor. The spoon is set deeper because the flasher often draws fish up in the water column. As they rise up, they may see the spoon and strike it, or they may move in on the dodger, lose interest, drop down, and encounter the more subtle action of a clean spoon. Often, it is just enough to trigger a strike.

No precise formula exists to the tag team, so experiment with exact depth and lead variations. Once you come upon a productive set, duplicate the horizontal and vertical relationships as you reset the lines. Also, experiment with lure selection. Certain teams of lures will consistently work to attract fish and trigger strikes.

If light line is new to you, give it a try! It is easy to incorporate one or two light-line rigs into a standard spread of lines. Light line often catches fish when other methods come up short.

CHAPTER 3

Diving Planers—Down and Out on the Great Lakes

I love watching football on a dreary fall afternoon, especially when the Pittsburgh Steelers are playing. The Steelers have a long history of great quarterbacks and receivers. When it is third and long, the offensive unit huddles. Those not familiar with how the game is played might think the players are praying over the quarterback. While the fans may be praying, it is in the huddle where the QB tells the offensive unit what play they will run.

A well-designed play requires each player to perform a specific role. The receiver doesn't bolt from the line of scrimmage, running willy-nilly down the field, waving his arms, hoping he shakes the 275-pound linebacker breathing down his neck, further hoping that the quarterback, who is scrambling between 350-pound linemen, spots his waiving hands, somehow launching the ball to where the receiver can miraculously leap into the air and catch it.

While NFL players are loaded with talent, success is achieved when the talent is combined with a well-executed plan. When the center snaps the ball, a well-practiced play begins to unfold. Linemen have blocking assignments, and their massive bodies and quick movements are solely focused on protecting the quarterback. Running backs fake the run and throw a forearm at anyone approaching the QB. Receivers head down field, following a well-designed route. They make cuts at specific points on the field. The quarterback knows exactly where to look for each receiver, and when all goes as planned, the ball spirals across the field for a big gain!

A diver, Spin Doctor, and Howie Fly was just too much for this late summer coho to pass up.

Fishing directional diving planers, such as Luhr Jensen Dipsy Divers and Lurk Disco Divers, is similar to the preceding football scenario. To consistently catch fish with divers, you must do more than just throw the divers in the water and randomly let line out, without considering where the divers go in relationship to the rest of the lures in your spread. Maximizing divers into your trolling spread requires strategy. When divers into your spread, think of them as players on a football team. Think about the big picture: the vertical and horizontal relationships created by all trolling devices and lures in your spread. To catch more fish on diving planers, you must weave them into your spread of riggers and planer boards.

Diving planers can be run aggressively or, with a few adjustments, they can be a stealthy presentation. When run with a flasher in close proximity to downrigger lines, they are the loudest, most obnoxious presentation in the water. Adjust the dial to scoot further away from the inner group dynamic, add a spoon on a long leader, and you now have added an element of stealth. They can be even stealthier when you use a Slide Diver.

Bottom line: divers are great tools to help you explore multiple depth zones. When strategically used in combination with your other presentations, they will help you interpret the mood of the fish and put more fish in the cooler.

THE BASICS

In their purest form, divers are an aggressive presentation. They impact their immediate environment visually, audibly, and physically. The degree of impact they have on the fish and your group dynamic depends on a variety of factors that we'll address below.

Vision is a primary sense salmon and trout use to locate their next meal. Fishermen have their favorite diver colors. Do you think the fish have their favorite colors? Whether they see exact colors or *shades* of colors, divers are a visual stimulant that can attract fish or spook them. The side bar has specific color recommendations. As you develop a game plan for running divers, identify which divers colors work for you, based on species, target depth, and environment.

Diving planers have an audible impact because fish can "hear" them. As a diver moves through the water, it creates a great deal of turbulence and noise. This unique *turbulence* pattern comes about because the diver moves through the water at an awkward angle in relation to your forward trolling motion. Think of it this way: rather than being streamlined and slicing the water like the dorsal fin of a shark, the diver is *grabbing water and interacting with it.* Divers displace large amounts of water. On a rough day, as the diver moves up and down and side to side, think of how much water slurps around the diver. Fish are keenly aware of this odd interference in their environment.

Fish can *feel* or *hear* this turbulence with their lateral line. The larger the diver, the more turbulence created. In addition, the lure runs in the wake of the turbulence field. As a diver oscillates back and forth, its signature changes again. (And I bet you never thought you would use your high school physics class!) When selecting lures to run with divers, remember that certain lures will have more appeal than others as they run in the turbulence field the diver creates.

There is a second degree of turbulence created that enhances the *signature* of a diver—the fishing line. When run on wire line, and to a lesser degree, braided super line such as Power Pro, the signature of a diver is enhanced by the hum or frequency of the line. The line stretching between the diver and the rod tip is being pulled tight in two directions. The diver is *pulling away* from the boat, and the rod tip is constantly pulling on the diver as the boat trolls along. This keeps tension on the line. The faster you troll and the larger the diver, the greater the tension. The more line in the water, the more guitar string to work with.

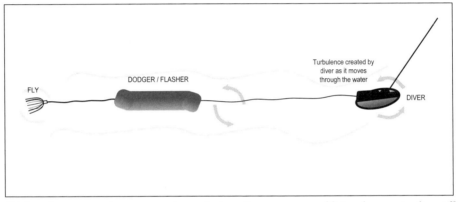

Diving planers are unique presentation tools that allow you to run additional, aggressive lines off to the side.

Do all lines *hum* at the same frequency? No. Wire has the loudest signature. Many days, fish will slam wire divers all day long but ignore a braid diver, run at the exact same depth and position. Is signature the reason? Is the wire creating more harmonics? Wire is stiff, has no stretch and no blowback, and therefore, the line is stretched tighter between the diver and the boat. Mono and braided lines have more resistance, so they develop a belly. Monofilament has the greatest resistance and is extremely stretchy. Because of the stretch and the resulting blowback belly extending between the rod tip and the diver, much of the harmonics and *jigging* action is lost; the force is partially absorbed by the belly in the line. The result: wire line runs more directly to the diver, resulting in more tension and a louder signature.

Divers also impart additional action to lures. As the boat surges through the waves, the rod, which is angled out over the water at a 90-degree angle, pulls against the line and diver. This imparts an additional *jigging* action to the diver and trailing lure. Wire line imparts more jigging action than braid or mono because of the mechanics discussed above.

You can run divers on mono, braid, or wire. Line choice has a big impact on depth penetration for divers. If you are restricted by budget, rod selection, or space, go with braided set-ups for divers. These give you the greatest flexibility. Braid divers can be used to target the top 30 feet, mid levels from 30 to 70 feet, and if you let out enough line, you can reach depths in excess of 100 feet.

Mono divers are great for targeting the top 30 feet. The nature of monofilament line, however, has a few drawbacks that minimize its impact for greater depths. Monofilament is stretchy and, because of its thickness, exerts more drag on the entire line which results in a looping belly between the rod tip and the diver. Fishing a mono diver past 40 feet requires you to let out more than 200 feet of line. Because of the stretch factor, mono acts like a giant rubber band between the boat and diver. Hook up ratios with mono divers set out past 100 feet are lower than divers set on braid or wire lines. Mono divers run out on longer lengths beyond 100 feet have less action and easily tangle with other lines on turns and in strong currents.

Wire line is the best line choice when targeting depths in excess of 70 feet or when targeting kings at any depth. Wire divers are fun and exciting tools. Maybe it's the bone-jarring strike, the rod bucking wildly in the holder, and the sound of the reel screaming as a large king runs for the horizon, or maybe it is the look of panic and excitement in the eyes of the angler trying to wrestle the rod from the holder when a king strikes. Kings don't merely hit wire divers—they crush them! It is the most exciting strike on fresh water. Plus, once you're hooked up, you feel every head shake of a big king on a wire diver.

Many days, large kings will strike a wire diver while ignoring all other presentations, including braided-line divers. While we can only speculate why, some believe it is the signature created by wire. Others think the stiff line and lack of a blowback belly create additional jigging action that is too much for kings to ignore. A little mystery in life is good for the soul.

No matter why, if you target kings on any large body of water, wire divers should be a part of your game plan.

For years, most anglers used the 0 size divers for most applications. Today, many will reach for the larger No. 1 diver when targeting depths beyond 70 feet. One of the best Captains on the Great Lakes, Arnie Arredondo of the charter boat *Phoenix*, believes the larger No. 1 divers are more effective for all levels of the water column. Arnie thinks the larger divers are more stable and will minimize tangles when fishing strong currents.

What's So Special About Divers?
1. Takes lures to a specific target depth.
2. Expands the group dynamic creating horizontal distance at depth by taking baits to the side of the inner group dynamic.
3. Divers add horizontal distance at depth by trailing the inner group dynamic.
4. Divers impart additional lure action through their erratic movement.
5. Fish can see them, which triggers strikes from aggressive fish.
6. Signature. Unique turbulence signature attracts fish that *hear* them through their lateral line. Different line types produce a different signature or *hum*.

If diving planers are new tools for you, begin with one diver per side. As you gain experience, you can add a second (or third!) diver to each side. When running multiple divers, a few tricks will make life easier. Strategic rod holder placement and rod length will minimize tangles. Most anglers will run the deeper diver toward the stern on a shorter rod. The forward diver, which is running higher in the water column, is easier to keep separated from the rear diver if you run it on a longer rod. At times, it will help to angle the rod tip on the forward rod holder up slightly to minimize tangles.

When setting two divers per side, run the deeper diver on a lower setting. For example, set the deep diver on a number 1 setting. The shallower diver will be set from 2.5 to 3.5. When running multiple divers, you might adjust the exact dial settings as you develop a program. Some anglers run two wire divers a side. Others will run one wire and one braid diver on the same side—the braid on the forward diver and usually run shallower. At times, two different line types will place the divers in different segments of water, which can help reduce tangles. If you can't eliminate the tangles, try running a flasher on your deeper diver, and a spoon on the higher diver. This setup will reduce tangles as a diver with a spoon runs much straighter and won't grab the other diver line on turns. If and when you encounter tangles, adjust the dial settings, rod positions on the gunnels, and the amount of line let out off the reel. Once you establish patterns that are tangle free, remember the formula!

LINE CHOICES IMPACT DIVER DEPTH

Mono	0 to 40 feet.
Braid	20 to 70 feet.
Wire	70 to 150 feet.

Here is a typical set up aboard my Pursuit 3000, the *Blue Horizon*, when targeting fish 40 to 80 feet down. I run two divers per side: a magnum wire diver on the sternward rod and a No. 1 diver on wire or braid on the forward diver. The mag diver would be out 230 feet on a 1.5 setting. The higher diver would be set on 2.5 and out 180 feet.

When targeting fish holding in the top 50 feet, I would set a No. 1 wire diver on 1.5 in the sternward position. This diver would be out 150 feet. The forward diver would be set on a 2.5 setting and out 100 feet. When running two or more divers a side, you want to think about, and vary, the vertical separation between the divers. This will help reduce tangles and may impact whether fish strike either diver. When fishing in shallow water or murky water, you can often run two divers close, vertically. This technique is examined later in the book.

THINK ABOUT THE *WHERE* FACTOR

How lures enter the strike zone is hugely important. When setting divers into your spread, think about *where* they are running. Divers give you great

Wire divers are one of the most exciting presentations to catch kings on!

flexibility to establish the horizontal and vertical relationships within your inner group dynamic. While it is easy to understand the vertical relationships created by divers, the horizontal dimensions often make the biggest difference, and many anglers don't consider them.

Divers operate on two horizontal planes. First is the horizontal angle created as the diver pulls off to the side—the distance it travels to the side of the boat. The second horizontal dimension is how far water resistance pulls the diver astern. As you set a diver into your spread, these two horizontal dimensions have a huge impact on the diver baits and nearby rigger lines. Ultimately, downriggers and diving planers can compliment each other—or work against each other and reduce how many fish you catch.

Line choice, diver setting, amount of line off the reel, trolling speed, lure selection, and sea conditions all influence the horizontal placement of diver discs. Generally, the greater the diver setting (1, 2, 3), the further astern the diver will trail. Divers set on higher settings, running further out to the side, are less stable and move around more on turns and as the boat interacts with currents. Trolling rings stabilize divers, to a point.

When launching a diver, think about where the diver will run in relation to your downrigger lines with their lures—the inner group dynamic. By running a diver on a 0 setting, you can run it directly behind the boat, smack in the middle of your spread, in between your downriggers. As you adjust the diver's dial to the side (port or starboard), the diver will pull out at progressively wider angles as it continues to dive. From a subsurface perspective, dive planers can be run close to the downriggers (horizontally) or fanned out to the side.

Set the diver on a steep angle of descent by adjusting the dial to the 1 position, and it will run (horizontally) closer to your downriggers. Adjust the dial to a 2 or 3 setting (or greater), and it will pull further to the side. This may not seem like much but it does open up your inner group dynamic. Some days, you might catch fish first thing in the morning with divers set on a 1.5 setting. By mid morning, you may need to run divers on a 3 setting—taking it farther to the side and farther behind the boat—to get strikes.

Often, divers are most effective tight to your riggers. On other days, a wider spread will be more effective. How do you determine this? Are there set rules? Ultimately, a bit of trial and error is required—you have to let the

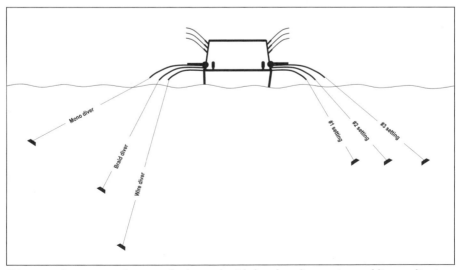

Divers can be set to run deeper, or further to the side based on diver setting and line application. Wire divers achieve the greatest depth and braid divers offer the most versatility. The right side illustrates the position of a wire diver based on setting.

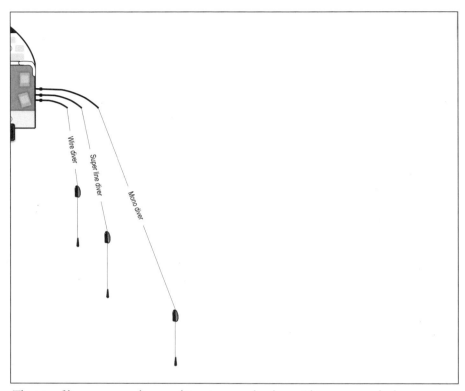

The type of line you run a diver on determines exactly where within your spread a lure runs. Monofilament and braid have more resistance and trail further behind the boat.

fish tell you what they want. Variables to consider include sea conditions, water clarity, current, time of day, fish temperament, and target depth. Lure selection is another variable that greatly impacts how much angle needs to be applied to setting divers. For coho and low-light kings, a group of flashers tightly spaced is better than one or two single flashers. In this scenario, it would be wise to set the diver to run close to downrigger lures.

Keep in mind that when you set the dial on a higher setting (2 to 3.5), you need to let out more line to reach the same depth as you would on a lower setting. For example, 150 feet of braid on a number 1 setting will run roughly 50 feet down. On a number 3 setting, you need to let out roughly 200 to 225 feet of line to reach the same depth. In the preceding two examples, the lures are 50 feet down, but they are in very different positions in relation to the boat. Actual running depth depends on a variety of factors

DIVER BASICS

- Match diver size to target depth. Larger divers will reach greater depths.
- Larger divers have more stability and less motion. They will also hold a depth more consistently than smaller divers, which tend to move around.
- Rings minimize motion and allow divers to reach greater depths. Some days, rings or super rings will produce more fish.
- Snubbers. You don't need them on smaller divers, but if you use them, go with the small, clear, stealth snubber to minimize drag. Mag divers need a snubber to help keep fish on the line.
- Leader material—for flashers, 40-pound test mono and for spoons and cranks, 10- to 20-pound test fluorocarbon.
- Leader length. Flashers work best on long leads of 8 to12 feet. Small 00 coho dodgers four to six feet. Spoons and plugs usually call for leaders 6 to 10 feet long.
- Monster leads of up to 30 feet have been used to win tournaments when targeting kings.
- Divers will reach greater depths with a clean spoon or plug. Flashers and dodgers add water resistance to the back of a diver, causing the planer to move up and back in the water column.
- Does color matter? Everyone has favorite diver colors but here are a few suggestions. Kings: glow, green, and clear. Coho: orange. Steelhead: chartreuse, green, glow, and orange. Lake trout: chartreuse and glow. Brown trout: glow, clear, and green.
- Multiple divers per side. If two divers are tangling, put a ring on the deeper diver and change rod locations along the gunnel. You can run two divers a side on the same line type, or you can mix and match line families.
- If your divers are tripping prematurely, tighten the release. If a fish cannot trip a diver, place your thumb on the spool and quickly give the rod a short, powerful snap to disengage the release.

including trolling speed, lure selection, line choice, and current. When my friend and colleague, Dave Mull, used a smart troll attached to a Dipsy, beaming back depth information in real time, the effect of lure selection was mind boggling. The Smart Troll showed a spoon behind a Dipsy let out 100 feet ran 26 feet deeper than a flasher/fly combo behind the same Dipsy.

There is no other presentation like divers! Running them is not complicated, and when you set them, a little common sense and a well thought out strategy goes a long way toward success. When trying to achieve maxi-

DIVER LOCATION WITHIN THE GROUP DYNAMIC

- Horizontal distance is based on diver setting, line choice, trolling speed, current, wave texture, light penetration, lure selection, and fish temperament. Mono creates additional blowback, which minimizes the horizontal distance to the side, but places the diver further behind your inner group dynamic.
- Wire dives deeper with less line out. Braid requires additional line to reach greater depths. Mono divers require massive amounts of line to reach depths beyond 40 feet.
- At times, fish want divers stretched out to the side.
- At times, especially in low light, divers running just outside downriggers will trigger maximum strikes. Set the diver on a 1 or 1.5 setting to keep it close to the inner group dynamic.
- If limited on rod count, try running your riggers deep and fanning your divers out to the side to probe higher layers of the water column. Once you determine the active fish levels, you can adjust the lines accordingly.
- When fish are way deep or *ghosting* away from the boat, a wire diver set on a number 1 or 1.5 and run below all other lines often draws strikes. A flasher and fly are the ideal lures for this situation. You only want to run one deep diver a side and one rigger down in this deep strike zone. How deep is deep? If you let enough line out, a wire diver can reach 200 feet down!

mum depth, you want to set the diver on a lower number, so the diver cuts a tighter angle of descent. If you target fish higher up in the water column, you often want to run your diver further out to the side.

For a complete discussion on some of the strategies used for running divers, see Chapter 11 of *Keating On Kings*. The methods discussed in KOK are applicable to all species.

Questions Commonly Asked About Fishing Divers

1. If I am limited on rod selection, which line choice is most versatile? Braid divers give you the most options. They are effective for targeting shallow and mid-depth ranges. For levels beyond 70 feet, they can get the job done if you let out enough line.

2. What if I am fishing in an area infested with sea fleas? Wire divers will minimize the battle with fleas. The diameter of wire reduces the amount of fleas that will collect on your line.

3. I seem to lose a lot of fish on wire divers? If the fish are falling off, set your drag just tight enough, so line does not creep off the reel when trolling. After the fish is hooked and has made his first run, you can begin to apply more pressure, and tighten the drag. A clear, stealth snubber may help.

4. When setting divers, I get a lot of tangles? Increase your trolling speed and let line out more slowly. At times, when setting deep divers, I begin letting the diver out in the stern. Once water pressure pulls the diver back and away from downrigger lines, I move the rod out to the side, keeping pressure on the diver as it continues descending. Never *power drop* (free spool) a diver straight down as it will spin! You can, however, with the clicker on, set the diver a few feet under the surface, engage the reel, place the rod in the holder, and loosen the drag to allow the forward trolling motion to pull the diver out. Divers *creeping* down to depth frequently get hit!

5. Is there a presentation difference between wire, braid and mono? Absolutely. Wire imparts a stiffer, jigging action to the diver and trailing lure. There is minimal blowback between the wire rod tip and the diver. As the boat surges with waves, this results in the rod tip *jigging* the diver up and down. Wire also gives you greater control over *where* your diver is within your group dynamic. Wire divers do not move up and down or side to side as much as the other lines. Braid and mono have progressively greater degrees of blowback as water pressure pulls on the line. Therefore, if settings are the same, mono divers will drag further behind the boat than braid, then wire.

STEALTH DIVERS—SLIDE DIVERS AND TORPEDOES

As productive as divers are, some days the fish won't touch them. Whether it's the noise generated by the boat or the loud, obnoxious way a diver enters the strike zone, they don't always work. In these situations, diver rods can be turned into a stealth presentation by using either a Slide Diver or a Torpedo.

Slide Divers are directional divers that have a line release mechanism. This mechanism allows you to set your lure back on longer leads behind the diving planer. When the fish strikes, the release is tripped, and the diver slides down the line. Running a lure 15 to 100 feet behind the diver totally changes the presentation. Rather than having your lure follow directly in the turbulence field created by traditional diving planers, the lure is back in cleaner water. It also minimizes the jigging motion of the diver.

Slide Divers add stealth, but you give up control. Let me explain. On a traditional diver your lure is on a 6- to 10-foot lead, so it always travels immediately in the wake or turbulence field of the diver. Horizontally, it can only get so far astern from the boat. Slide Divers add stealth to the presentation because your lure is now separated horizontally from the boat and your inner group dynamic by the longer lead off the diver.

You give up control of where the rig is running because the long lead behind the diver places additional drag on the diver. This reduces how far to the side the diver can pull. The additional drag also requires you to let out more line to achieve the same depths as the traditional diving planers. Slide Diver has added after-market, heavier weights that can be inserted into the diver that will counter the drag. This is a great asset when targeting deeper layers below 50 feet.

To set a slide diver, you will pull line through the slide diver to the desired lead length. Next, engage the release on the diver, make sure the lure is clear, and begin dropping the entire rig off the side. It's that easy!

Some days, stealthy Slide Divers out-produces standard divers. Many days boat noise and the inner group dynamic spook the fish and getting the lure back an extra 20 to 50 feet will trigger strikes. Slide Divers allow you to run an additional rod on stealth mode off the side. If you run slide divers, you may encounter additional tangles when fish hooked on downriggers run into the longer leads behind Slide Divers. Most of us, however, don't mind untangling a few lines if it puts more fish in the boat!

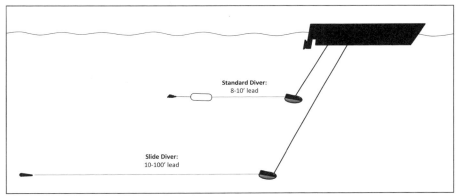

Slide Divers have a release mechanism that allow you to set lures further behind the diver. This is a very stealthy presentation and a favorite of many anglers!

Torpedo Divers offer a second alternative to running a diver rod on stealth mode. These are not actually "divers," but super efficient weights shaped like torpedoes. By adjusting the fin on the Torpedo, it goes out to the side, port or starboard. Like a Slide Diver, they allow you to run your lure as far back as you want, creating a stealth presentation. While Torpedoes will not pull as far to the side as Slide Divers, they do clear your rigger lines. When run in this manner, they are dynamite for all species suspended 20 to 40 feet down.

They are simple to use and are great tools for small boat anglers. I use my braid diver rods for running Torpedoes off the side when traditional diving planers don't work. First, take off the diver and simply attach an 8- to 10-foot, 20-pound test fluorocarbon leader to the braid. (I tie the leader to a swivel on the braid). To set the Torpedo rig, in place of a diver, first drop the spoon or crank back 30 to 100 feet and clip on a Torpedo (the larger Musky and Cuda work best for this method). A variety of release clips work for attaching the Torpedo to your line including the Church Clip, and the OR-16 Release from Off Shore Tackle. Just tie a short length of heavy line between the Torpedo's eyelet and the release clip.

Instead of a release clip, I like to attach the Torpedo to the line with a snap swivel and use a #12 rubber band to keep the swivel and Torpedo in place. A simple half hitch on the braid will keep it from moving. When reeling in a fish, simply open the snap, pull the Torpedo off the line, and boat the fish. The rubber band reels onto the spool.

Okay, your lure is in the water, and you have your Torpedo attached to the line. Now angle the adjustable fin on the Torpedo to port or starboard and let the rig out. This will easily drop down and pull to the side of your rigger. End result: in place of an *aggressive* diver in the water, you now have a *stealthy* bait, slightly out to the side of your rigger baits and trailing the boat at a greater distance.

Another advantage to Torpedoes is that they have minimal impact on a hooked fish. Catch rates on fish that strike Torpedoes are high. We'll discuss another great Torpedo rig in Chapter 6.

CHAPTER 4

Wire Line Strategies— The Old and the New

When I first started trolling in the 1970s, few anglers bothered to use wire line. Wire of yesteryear was a pain. It kinked if you looked at it sideways and it broke easily. Anglers viewed wire as a tool of last resort to dredge lake trout off the bottom. We used to snap a one-to two-pound lead ball ahead of a metal dodger or cowbells and bounce the entire rig along the bottom at ultra-slow speeds. Dredging lakers off the bottom with this rig was not the most exciting way to spend the morning. But, every once in a while, a giant king would smash one of these bottom bouncing rigs, and then it was a fight like no other, with the taut wire transmitting every head shake right to the angler's forearms and heart!

When I was young, I thought it was nothing to pull a mess of trout off the bottom. That myth was shattered one day as I learned a painful lesson. It was a summer day in the early 1980s and fishing was tough. For the past several days, wire, fished on the bottom, hooking up with sluggardly lake trout, had provided the only action. On this particular day, I ran my 23-foot Mako out to a popular drop off known as The Hill. This drop off falls from 55 feet down to about 100 feet, and it had been a reliable lake trout area.

One of the top charter boats of the day, the *Linda Sue* had left port at the same time, so I conveniently set lines a respectful distance behind Captain Jeff Heintz. If the *Linda Sue* was in the neighborhood, the fish must be, too. I was still young when this occurred, and like many youths, I was rather impressed with my own abilities. I figured it wouldn't take much to catch a quick limit of lake trout, which we also called "Spotted Sportsters." (When you're a charter captain faced with an absence of salmon, you learn quickly how to convince your clients that catching lake trout is a spectacular sport).

Why do some of us have to learn about humility the hard way? I thought I knew every thing—fishing wire on the bottom was like falling off a log. Four hours of trolling resulting in a handful of lakers showed me I didn't know quite as much as I thought I did.

Remember, I was shadowing Capt. Jeff's boat. When we got back to port, I learned that Jeff had more than 30 lakers and kings stuffed in his cooler! I was beyond mad at myself. That day I realized two things: first, I knew the fish were on the bottom, and second, I realized I didn't have a clue how to catch them.

I vowed that never again would I let another angler out-fish me by such a wide margin! After the beating I took in 70 feet of water, I became much more interested in wire-line tactics. Through experience, I learned the art of bouncing bottom. I perfected my bottom game and even won a number of major tournaments by catching bottom-hugging brutes.

The more experience I gained with wire, the more I began to ask myself, "Why are we only using wire for bottom oriented fish?" Why not use it for suspended fish? As a charter captain, I had plenty of opportunities to try new wire techniques. I began mixing wire in with traditional spreads.

I'll never forget the first time I randomly dropped a suspended wire with a 20-ounce sinker in the middle of a May steelhead spread in the 1980s. We were somewhere *beyond the middle of nowhere,* way out deep, with a full spread of planers and divers focused on the top 20 feet of water. Like many days out there, we were catching plenty of steelhead, but a little voice inside my head kept asking: "What might be down deep?" Back in the early days of the Great Lakes salmon fishery, we always caught loads of kings in the late summer and fall. Where were the schools of kings in May?

You never know till you try, so on a whim, I launched a size 0 silver Luhr Jensen dodger—the large size—with a small West River Sutton spoon trailing it down the chute. We didn't have line counters back then, so I just kept letting it out further and further. Suddenly something slammed that little spoon and sizzled line off the reel at a blinding speed. The customer had a hard time prying the rod from the old spring rod holder on the tran-

The author and his dad enjoying a day on the water.

som. This was no lake trout! It could only be a king because we thought the fish was going to spool all the line off the reel. Fortunately, the fish ran out of gas, and we eventually boated the beast.

On this day, I learned that big kings that traditional presentations missed could be caught with suspended wires. After that first fish, I began setting wires out 200 to 500 feet when targeting steelhead in the spring and late fall. Soon, large spring kings became regular parts of the catch along with steelhead, and we extended our fall season by targeting immature kings way deep, as well.

Soon, 7-strand, stainless steel wire line became a regular part of our spreads. These days, we still use wire to fish low and slow for lake trout, but we also pull it at higher speeds to effectively target suspended fish. Adversity often forces us to move to the next level and that's what happened in the world of wire line fishing.

WIRE LINE PROPERTIES—TRADITIONAL WIRE VS. COPPER

Today, wire line is a standard part of the modern Great Lakes trolling arsenal. In the past, wire was difficult to use and broke easily. Today's wire lines, both 7-strand as well as 19-strand, are user friendly. Tangles, kinks, and break offs are infrequent compared to the days of old. Wire line rods and reels are also much lighter and user friendly. Manufacturers have also added a second type of wire to the arsenal—copper wire. While the intricacies of how, when, and why to run copper are discussed in the following chapter, it is important to highlight the differences between traditional and copper wire first.

The two line types differ greatly and offer anglers unique presentation possibilities. Pick up a spool of wire and a similar size spool of copper, and you will quickly realize that copper is much heavier. Copper line, like lead core line, is basically the weight that helps take a lure down to the fish. Multi-strand stainless steel wire line adds a bit of weight to get a lure into the depths but usually works in conjunction with a diving sinker (Dipsy Diver, Luk Disco Diver, etc.) or a lead weight to get deep.

Copper has a thicker diameter, is harder to work with, and tangles are a nightmare, but you don't have to fear copper! The following chapter examines ways to simplify some of these headaches and make copper user friendly. As we forge ahead with this discussion of wire line, we'll refer to traditional, stainless steel wire as "wire." Copper wire will simply be called "copper."

Most anglers prefer 30-pound wire in a variety of blends from single strand to Torpedo Wires Nineteen Strand wire. Torpedo brand wire is so supple that you can even tie knots with it and splice it to other types of line. Wire is still wire, so you still have to be careful and watch for kinks. Twenty-pound wire is also available. Its thinner diameter minimizes water resistance and allows greater depth penetration with less line off the reel. The lighter wire, however, kinks more easily, and break offs can be a problem.

Copper line comes in 30- and 45-pound test lines. Copper is much heavier than wire or lead core. The heavy weight of the copper line is what allows copper to sink and reach greater depths than other line types. In other words, no divers or sinkers are attached to copper lines. Just the pure weight of the line will take the rig deep.

Wire, on the other hand, needs help in the form of a diver or weights in order to achieve significant depth. Wire is deployed in three unique presentations: directional divers, sinkers, or just run clean or "flat" off the stern. Wire divers are an aggressive presentation. Weighted wires and wire flat lines are a bit stealthier.

Wire creates a *hum* or signature as you troll it though the water. In *Great Lakes Salmon and Trout Fishing,* wire lines are compared to guitar strings. An acoustic guitar with metal strings has a very different *pitch* than the nylon strings of a classical guitar. Wire has a unique vibration pattern. This signature is further influenced by the angle at which the line is cutting through the water and how much weight, or tension, is pulling it taut. A wire diver, pulling to the side, will cut the water at a different angle than a wire down the chute with a one-pound ball. Likewise, large divers cut the water sharper than the standard number one size and have less side-to-side motion (more stable), which could also alter the frequency of wire. There are days that large divers out-fish standard divers and visa-versa. Some anglers feel that 20-pound wire creates a higher hum and out fishes 30-pound wire. Do fish pick up on this signal through their highly sensitive lateral line? That's a question to ponder over a beer at the end of the day, isn't it?

The main reason to use wire is that it can make you a better angler. It expands your reach on the water (vertically and horizontally) and gives you more presentation options. Because wire doesn't stretch, it imparts an additional *jigging* action to lures compared to mono, and some braided lines. Wire and copper are both important components to open up your group dynamic and allow you to run additional lines. Both catch tons of fish!

WIRE LINE TACTICS

Great Lakes anglers are some of the most ingenious anglers in the world. Through countless hours of experimentation, anglers have developed a variety of wire presentations for catching fish throughout the water column.

No matter how you deploy wire, the terminal set up is similar: simply attach a swivel to the end of the wire with a loop knot. The swivel can be attached to a diving planer or leader. If running weights on wire, simply attach a 6- to 10-foot fluorocarbon leader to the swivel. For running dodgers, use 40-pound mono, for spoons 20-pound fluorocarbon. The weight can be clipped to the first swivel. When running wire as a flat line, I like to attach a two- to four-ounce keel sinker to the swivel and add a 10-foot leader of 20-pound fluorocarbon.

Warning: When working with wire, a little slack line between the rod tip and terminal gear can lead to loops and kinks which lead to breakoffs with fish on the end. I advise clients to reel the first swivel into the rod tip. No kinking! No breakoffs!

Modern anglers pair wire with diving planers, suspended ball weights, bottom bouncing weights, Torpedo Divers, Offshore Tadpoles, snap weights from Offshore and Church Tackle, and on flat lines with keel sinkers. Some trollers have been experimenting with stainless steel wire in place of copper and lead core.

Wire divers are the most popular wire presentation and easy to use. The standard size diver is the most popular, but magnum wire divers can easily reach depths of 150 feet and beyond. Torpedo diver has recently introduced their Deep Sea Diver that can reach depths of 400 feet! The Deep Sea Diver changes the pitch and force of the diver. When this diver is combined with a 12 oz. Cuda Torpedo, the rig gets deep, really deep!

Some anglers only run wire divers when targeting depths beyond 70 feet, but many days, a wire diver will out produce braid and mono divers at higher levels of the water column, especially for Chinook salmon. We tend to get stuck on thinking certain presentations are only good for certain levels of the water column, but if the way that wire can enhance lure action and add to the signature down deep, why wouldn't it make shallower lures more productive at times?

How shallow can you run a wire diver? We recently had some tough July fishing—fishing just plain stunk! One particular day, I had a mid-morning charter—not exactly prime time to fish. I spent four hours trolling in 50 to110 feet of water, and with time running out, the cooler was empty. Not ready to accept defeat, I contemplated my options. Just then, Capt. Brian of the *Confusion Too* called to tell me he had set up in 30 feet of water with his 11 a.m. charter, and *he had a triple*! After hearing this, I had my group reel in lines, and we sprinted towards the beach. With less than an hour left in the trip, I just started putting out the lines that were already set up.

One of these lines was a wire diver with gold Starburst Super Slim. I set this rig—heretofore considered a "deep water only" setup—out 45 feet. Remember, the water was slightly murky, and we were in 30-foot depths. This wire diver took our only fish that trip. If you've spent any amount of time on the water, you know there is a greater difference between zero and one fish, than between one and a hundred!

You can run wire divers just about anywhere. When fishing for browns in murky water, I've caught fish on wire divers in water as shallow as 15 feet. The key was the water was murky. The wire diver was on a 1.5 setting and was 15 feet off the rod tip. I ran a small diver on mono outside the wire diver that was 28 feet off the rod tip.

Why are wire divers so effective? Wire line places a diver and lure into the water column differently than braid. Wire line is stiff and has no stretch. The line between rod tip and the diver is direct, no blowback loop. As a boat surges through waves, the rod tip pulls on the diver directly. This imparts a unique *jigging* motion to the rig. On braid or mono, water resistance creates a belly in the line between the rod tip and the diver. With these presentations, the rod is pulling against the belly in the line, which results in less jigging action imparted to the diver and lure.

Wire also places the diver into a different location within the group dynamic than braid or mono. Some days, it's all about the relationships

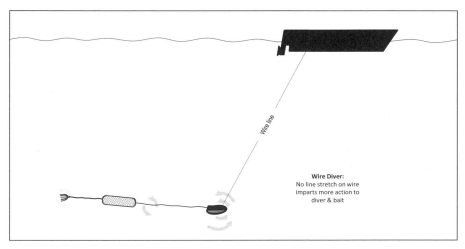

Wire divers catch fish!

between rigs that make the difference between success and a boat ride. If you want to run a diver a few feet outside a boom rigger, wire will cut the water and hold a steady position immediately outside of a downrigger bait. Some days, just having an extra flasher and fly outside the same rig on a downrigger makes a difference.

Wire divers will dive deeper than braid divers and give you more control over *where* a wire diver runs within the group dynamic. Since wire does not hang as far behind the boat, wire divers can be set on a 1 to 1.5 setting and run just outside short downrigger baits. Early in the morning and when fish are aggressive, this is a dynamite strategy. When fish are spooky, you can run wire divers further out to the side by adjusting the dial to a 3 or greater setting. This really opens up the inner group dynamic.

Does diver setting really make a difference? Recently, my long time friend, Brad Gregorio, took some of his work clients out on a charter. Fishing is a lot like riding a bicycle. Brad may no longer fish for a living, but the man can still fish! When Brad is on the boat, I can step back and relax a little as he is more than capable of running the deck.

On this recent afternoon, our divers were dead. We were catching plenty of kings, steelhead, and large coho on riggers and lead core lines, but Brad, who worked as a first mate with me for many years, loved the savage strike of a wire diver. Without my knowing, Brad took one of our wire divers, turned the dial to a 3 ½ setting, and let it back out. The rod was slammed almost immediately. I was surprised, and after boating the large king, the rod was reset. I then noticed that the angle of the line was different than it had been all day! Brad told me he changed the setting. That minor adjustment, altering the dial setting from a 1.5 to a 3.5, made all the difference in the world. For the rest of the afternoon, that wire was as productive as any other a rod on the boat.

Wires are typically run with the standard size number one diver and the larger 0 size diver. The larger divers are more stable (less side-to-side motion) and allow you to reach greater depths with less line in the water. If you are fishing a strong current or trolling at speeds above 2.4 knots (2.8 mph), this can be a huge advantage. The larger divers also tangle less. Because they have less blowback, they rarely tangle with fish that strike off the

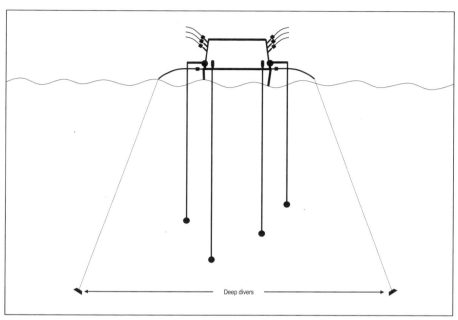

Dropping a wire diver to the lower corner of the strike box is deadly for catching negative fish down deep.

downriggers. On the flip side, some days the additional motion of smaller divers will trigger strikes.

When running two divers a side, tangles can be a problem. Running a large diver on the inside (deeper) line and a smaller (shallower) diver on the outside rod will reduce tangles. As you seek a two-diver program on your boat, experiment with rod position, dial setting, and placement.

When fish are deep, many charter captains will drop at least one wire diver a side deep. As the boat passes over fish, they are often driven down and off to the side. A wire diver running out on 250 to 400 feet of line will catch many of these *ghost* fish.

While many anglers only run one wire a side, others have great success with a four-diver spread. My good friend Capt. Arnie Arredondo of Phoenix Charters has dialed into a four-magnum diver spread. Arnie catches huge numbers of big kings and consistently out fishes other captains. When Arnie talks, we listen! Arnie believes that the larger divers track truer and tangle less than the standard diver. The smaller the diver, the more it oscillates and wanders up and down and side-to-side when trolled. On turns or when the boat sideslips left or right, this wandering motion is magnified. The mag divers track straight, so Arnie runs two a side, usually one on a 1.5 setting and the other angled out on a 2.5 setting. Arnie usually sets the divers with 50 to 75 feet (measured on the line counter) of separation between the two divers.

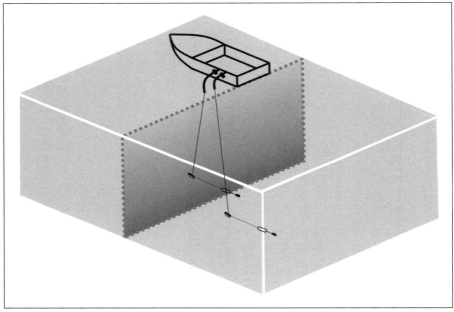

Running two wire divers a side is a favorite technique for catching fish on the Great Lakes. At times having the divers close together will be best. Other times, you want to add more vertical separation between the divers.

When running mag divers, it is advisable to use a small, clear "stealth" snubber (sold by Dreamweaver and Wolverine Tackle among others) to avoid tearing lips and busting leaders. Larger divers exert more drag, so to keep the diver from creeping line off the reel when trolling, you often have to crank the drag tighter than you want it. When a large fish hits, be ready to loosen the drag—really fast! The snubber will buy you a few seconds of time.

Running wire on long flat lines with 2- to 4-ounce keel sinkers is discussed at length in Chapter 10 of *Keating on Kings*, so we won't go into great detail here. Essentially, when a wire is dropped back 200 to 500 feet astern with a keel sinker, it becomes a stealthy presentation that reaches fish in clean water. These lines will rise and fall in the water column as you turn and adjust your speed. For anglers who do not have copper or lead core, this is a low cost way to add some stealth to the spread and target the upper 50 feet of the water column.

You can also add smaller Torpedoes to wire and run them down the chute. Essentially, you will attach a 6- to 10-foot, 20-pound test fluorocarbon leader to the wire. The Torpedo is attached to the leader. This rod can easily be set down the chute and run 100 to 300 feet astern. It is easy to run and takes many fish missed by traditional presentations.

Running sinkers or ball weights on wire is another animal altogether. Years ago, this was a favorite tactic of lake trout and salmon anglers alike. With the advent of lead core, copper, and divers, many anglers have gotten away from this presentation. Does this method still work? The answer is a resounding yes! In some ports, anglers continue to troll these *thumper rods* with great success. Many anglers have learned to read the action on the tip of a thumper rod to dial into productive trolling speeds. A metal dodger adds a great deal of action, and the wire line telegraphs that action to the rod tip.

To set up a thumper rod, simply attach a swivel to the end of your wire line. Next, add a 6- to 10-foot leader of 40-pound mono and attach a dodger or flasher/fly, and you're ready to start *thumping*. Target depth will determine weight size, but most anglers will use 6- to 24-ounce sinkers. These rigs are generally run straight off the stern; however, some anglers run them off large mast and ski type side planers. *Segmented thumpers,* referred to as "hybrid wires" below, can be run off the larger Church TX-44 and Big Bird in-line planers.

Because of the properties of wire and the physics of motion, thumpers offer a unique way to enter the strike zone. Wire is stiff, heavy, and cuts the water. When you attach a 1-pound sinker or heavier, the weights motion swings like a pendulum through the water. This imparts a unique *dancing* motion to the trailing lure as your boat interacts with the waves and current.

Keep in mind the mechanics of this presentation to avoid tangles. Heavier weights achieve greater depth penetration with less line off the reel.

Heavier weights descend at a sharper angle and will trail closer to your inner group dynamic. Lighter weights will require more line off the reel to reach the depths of heavy weights, and the entire rig will trail further behind the boat. Higher trolling speeds and strong currents will increase blowback and may require you to let additional line off the reel. If you slow down, the entire rig will drop deeper. Always keep in mind *where* this rig is relative to your riggers and divers. If you run long leads, such as a Secret Weapon Rig, off your rigger, thumpers will tangle. Long thumper lines can also tangle with deep wire divers off the side, so turns need to be gradual.

A wire hybrid is created when you join a segment of wire line, say 100 feet, and splice it onto a line counter reel spooled with braid. This rig can be used with a flasher and run with 6- to 16-ounce sinkers or Torpedoes. Attach the weight in front of the flasher's 10-foot leader of 30- or 40-pound monofilament and then drop the wire into the water. After letting all the wire out off the reel, hook the braid backing into a release on a side planer and send the rig out to the side. (The reason for the braid is it will hold in the planer board clip and not abrade the clip as wire can. Braid also has a thinner diameter, so it takes up less space on a reel spool and runs planers nicely out to the side). These rigs are devastating to early morning kings.

Wire line combined with 1-pound, or heavier, ball weights become a dynamite technique for prying lakers, and even kings, off the bottom. Catching fish off the bottom is hard work! It requires a great deal of vigilance as you constantly adjust your line to *feel* the bottom. Grilling is an art form, and we season the meat with a super-heavy rub of spices or lightly season it with a sprinkle. When targeting fish on the bottom, you can rub the bottom with several different techniques. You can set those wires so the weight just taps the bottom occasionally, or you can plow the bottom—kick the sand or clay in their face approach to catching trout.

When tapping the bottom, let out the wire until the weight contacts the bottom. After hitting bottom, water resistance will pull the sinker up and off the bottom, so you must drop the rig a second, third, and possibly a fourth time until you feel steady contact with the bottom. Once you've determined you're on the bottom, reel up just enough line, so the weight is just *ticking* the bottom occasionally. Experienced bottom bouncers will constantly tweak the line as they adjust how frequently the weight comes in contact with the bottom. Some days, a tap every few seconds is needed. Other days touching bottom every 10 seconds will draw strikes; other days a tap every 30 seconds.

As you adjust bottom-bouncing lines, think about what is happening along the bottom layer of the lake. How close to the bottom are fish sitting? Are they feeding on the bottom or just above the bottom? Speed is critical to success. You know you are going too slow if you are grabbing mussels, weeds, clay, or any other debris. Another clue you need to speed up is when your lines *stick* in the bottom for a moment then pull free. There is an experiential learning curve to fishing the bottom. When you do catch fish, remember what the *rub* looked like.

To pound the bottom—really plow it—we must fish in an area that has no mussels. The slight tapping approach outlined above can be used in some areas with some mussel colonies as long as you check hooks regularly for hitchhikers. In the Lake Trout chapter we discuss lures that float your hook off the bottom and minimize mussel snags.

The smiles say it all, good job dad! Any chance you get, take your kids out on the water and get them involved, whether it's setting lines, choosing lures, or explaining what you are doing.

Consistently catching fish off the bottom is an art form. Experienced bottom bouncers have learned how to read the rod tip to determine how hard they are rubbing the bottom. When you are really plowing bottom, the rod tip will constantly be jumping and vibrating as the sinker *rolls* and *taps* its way along the bottom. In this scenario, the weight is in almost constant contact with the bottom. Just how frequently you need to make contact with the bottom really varies from day to day. Experiment! You might be surprised at how many strikes you get while you're adjusting these lines.

For a complete discussion on the basics of rigging and running wire, see Chapter 4 of *Great Lakes Salmon and Trout Fishing, The Complete Troller's Guide.* A discussion on advanced wire line techniques and strategies can be found in Chapter 10 of *Keating on Kings, Great Lakes Chinook Tactics Way Beyond the Basics.*

CHAPTER 5

Copper Line Tactics—Stealth, Versatility, and More

Copper line provides a highly versatile stealth presentation that can catch aggressive and negative fish in a variety of situations. If copper is new to you, think of lead core—heavy lead core. Even though the properties of copper are very different from lead core, the techniques used to fish the two lines are similar.

Both are stealth presentations used to reach suspended fish off to the side of the boat. The major presentation difference between the two is that copper achieves greater depths with less line off the reel. Unlike lead core, the weight of copper far exceeds the resistance factor, so copper descends at a much sharper angle than lead core or wire. It also sinks much faster than lead core. Its fast sink rate is one reason copper line makes a unique impact on presentation and lure action. Because of copper's weight, no divers or sinkers are attached to the line. Just the pure weight of the line will take the rig deep. For anglers looking to get every edge on the fish, copper will expand your stealth reach deeper into the water column.

In its infancy, copper was used exclusively to target deeper layers of the water column in excess of 50 feet. The problem was copper caught so many fish that anglers wanted to use it to target the upper layers of the water column. Thanks to ingenuity, today, many anglers use segments of copper line in place of lead core to target fish in the top 40 feet. As we'll see below, segmented coppers can effectively target all layers of the water column.

THE MECHANICS OF FISHING COPPER

To better understand how copper works, let's compare it with lead core. The principle of fishing the two lines is simple: the more line you let out, the deeper they run. Now, pick up a spool of copper, and you will quickly realize it is much heavier than lead core. Because of its weight, copper sinks at a steeper angle than lead core (or traditional wire). Both types of line require you to let significant amounts of line off the reel, but copper requires significantly less line off the reel to reach similar depths. Lead core reaches a maximum depth of 50 feet because the bulky resistance created by the Dacron eventually overpowers the sink rate of the lead. No matter how much line you let out, lead core doesn't go much below 50 feet. Copper, on the other hand, will continue to sink and achieve greater depths as more line is let out.

How deep does copper run? Before entering this debate, you need to understand that trolling speed, lure selection, waves, and currents influence actual running depth. In other words, your 300-foot copper won't run at exactly the same level all the time. If you are trolling into 4-foot swells at

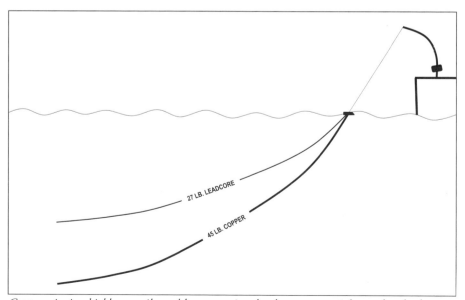

Copper wire is a highly versatile stealth presentation that has a greater sink rate than lead core, enabling you to reach greater depths with less line out.

2.6 kts. (3 mph), your copper will run shallower than the same rig trolled at 2.0 kts. (2.3 mph) on calm days without any currents.

While we can debate the actual running depth of copper, what is clear is that the more copper in the water, the deeper it goes. For example, it takes 300 feet of copper to make it down 50 to 65 feet, but an additional 150 feet of copper will take a lure down to the 70- to 80-foot range. Lead core's sink rate drastically decreases once you get past 10 colors (100 yards) of line.

When copper first hit the scene, anglers ran 300-, 450- and 600-foot segments. Wow, that's a lot of cranking! When trolled at 2.2 kts. (2.5 mph), these segments were going down around 55 feet, 70 feet, and 90 to 110 feet. A flasher/fly rig adds significant drag, which planes the line up 5 to 10 feet when compared to a clean spoon on the same length rig.

Today, anglers use segments of copper to target the top 50 feet of the water column off of side planers. Some of the best tournament fishermen on the Great Lakes regularly pull 50- to 250-foot segments of copper to surgically target specific levels of the water column. Generally speaking, a 50-foot copper is about 10 to 15 feet down. A 100-foot copper will reach 20 feet, a 150 copper reaches 25 to 30 feet, and a 200 copper is roughly at the same level as 10 colors of lead core, which is 35 to 45 feet.

Copper line impacts lure action differently than lead core does. Lead core drifts around, pushed by currents, during the troll and imparts what seems to be a hypnotic, dancing motion to lures. Copper is heavier and stiffer, so it maintains a direct tension on the trailing lure. Rather than adding a dancing action to lures, copper tends to impart a jigging action, especially when run on trolling boards. Every time your boat surges on waves or turns, copper immediately rises or sinks. This is often all it takes to trigger strikes. Anglers who don't want to lose the hypnotic effect of lead have created hybrid coppers by attaching two to three colors of lead to the end of copper. This gives them depth penetration, jigging action, and the hypnotic side-to-side drift.

Like many things in the modern world, anglers have a choice when it comes to stealth tactics. For levels 50 feet and deeper, copper or Torpedoes are the only game in town. When targeting the upper 40 to 50 feet of the water column, you have a choice between two different, but productive, techniques—copper or lead core. What is the essential difference between copper and lead? Copper takes roughly a third less line in the water to reach the same depth as lead. One hundred feet of copper is at about the same depth as 150 feet of lead core, and 200 feet of copper is close to the same depth as 300 feet of lead. Lead and copper each impart a very different action to trailing lures. Copper is stiff, so it adds a jigging motion, especially in rough water. Lead adds its signature hypnotic motion.

Is copper more productive than lead core? Both catch fish, but copper reaches greater depths. Copper requires you to crank less to boat fish, is harder to work with, and requires larger rods and reels to run. If you travel from port to port, you will find great tournament anglers and charter captains who fish lead or copper exclusively. Others, like myself, use both presentations.

Copper Basics

Copper is a bulky, heavy line that comes in 30 and 45-pound tests. The heavier line achieves greater depth and is harder to break. Copper requires large reels that have great line capacity. If you are setting up multiple reels for copper, the longer segments will need to go on the biggest reels. High-speed reels will also minimize shoulder damage when reeling long coppers attached to big fish (and boredom when you need to reel in to change a lure). A variety of rods can be used with copper. The key property to look for is sufficient backbone for hauling the line through the water. I have used short 7-foot rods and longer 9-foot rods. Rods for copper don't need special guides or tips in my opinion, although some captains disagree and feel that hard guides can wear down the copper line. So far, I've not seen any evidence of this and have had zero issues. No roller guide rods have been necessary for copper so far on the *Blue Horizon*.

To set up a copper rig, begin by spooling 30- to 50-pound braid or 30- to 50-pound mono backing onto the reel. I prefer 40-pound braid, such as Power Pro. Make sure you have enough backing to run a planer out to the side and withstand the run of a hooked fish. You don't need as much backing as you might think. Fish that strike copper rigs usually don't make long runs, compared to the same fish on mono, braid, or traditional

Copper wire and spoons are a dynamite stealth presentation for all levels of the water column.

wire. This is because the copper line is so heavy. Just pulling against the copper line quickly tires a large king. I like to keep at least 150 yards of backing on the spool. After spooling on the backing, attach the copper to the braid with either a tiny 50-pound test Spro swivel or the "haywire twist" described under *Navigating Tangles*. When using the Spro, attach the braid with a Polamer knot. Mono can be attached with an improved clinch knot. To attach the copper, use a haywire twist. To tie it, simply pass the end of the copper through the swivel and tightly twist about a two-inch tag end around the copper line. This entire connection easily passes through guides and the level wind.

Once the reel is spooled, attach a Spro swivel to the end of the copper with the same knot. For running spoons, attach a 10- to 30-foot leader of 20-pound test fluorocarbon leader. For flashers or dodgers, upgrade to 30-pound test fluorocarbon. A quality ball bearing swivel, small for spoons and larger for flashers, completes the rig.

NAVIGATING TANGLES

For those of you who have used copper, do you remember your first multi-copper tangle? If it was like my experience, it was monumental! I was ready to give up running copper forever. Who needs to catch all those extra fish, right? Before you get discouraged, let me offer you some hope. There is a learning curve to running copper. With experience and a little coaching, you will soon realize that running copper is not that difficult. I'm going to repeat the important part of the last sentence: running copper is not that difficult. After my first copper disaster, Capt. Arnie told me a few tricks that made life easier. Let me share his tips and a few more details.

First, let's talk about detangling a mess. Do you remember those lectures your parents gave you about patience? You will make a few mistakes but learn to move *slowly* through tangles and be patient with yourself. There are two types of tangles—those that you just cut and start over and those that can be untangled. Believe it or not, when copper is moderately *kinked* and *squiggled*, you can gently smooth out the line between your fingers and it's good to go. If a kink has seriously weakened the line, cut the line, but you don't have to throw the entire spool away and start over! Some brands, such as Blood Run Copper, are easier to untangle.

If you have a tangle in your copper but still have more than 100 feet of line out in the water, you can salvage the good line still in the water and keep fishing. Without reeling or pulling in the line, first cut out the tangled or weakened portion. Have someone hold onto the end of the line trailing the boat or wind it onto a cleat. My buddy Dave Mull has a Church Clip tied with a loop of heavy mono to a cleat at the corner of his boat just for holding copper and lead core. Next, take one end of the copper, make a small loop, and twist the tag end tightly. Now, take the other tag end, pass it through the loop, and twist the line back on itself. This will form a very small knot that can pass through the guides and will not break. You can also use a Spro swivel here and twist the two copper ends to the swivel. With a little practice, it takes only a minute to splice copper and will save you time and money. You'll be back fishing in no time!

Another hint that will help avoid tangles is to set your inside planer boards a good distance from the boat. When a fish hits a downrigger, it may run to the side and tangle with planer board lines. If it tangles copper, things will get ugly. For this reason, I put all the copper in the water, then let out an additional 20 to 30 feet of backing before putting the Church

Board on. If a fish runs toward the planer and tangles, it usually tangles with the braid backing. It is much easier to untangle the fish from the braid. I also keep a spare spool of copper on board so reels can be topped off after a serious tangle.

RUNNING COPPER ON SIDE PLANERS

Copper lines can be run down the chute but they reach their full stealth potential when you send them out to the side on side planers such as the Church Walleye Board or the larger Church TX-44 Planer. The Off Shore Tackle OR12 Side Planer works well, too.

Planer boards give you great vertical and horizontal stealth to the stern and the side. When running multiple coppers off the side, run the shorter, shallower coppers on the outside. These lines are running higher in the water column and will pass over the inside coppers when you hook up with a fish.

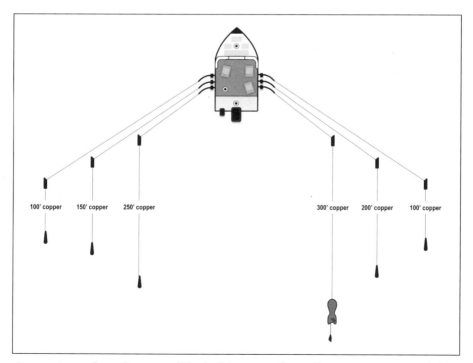

Copper wire can be used to target all levels of the water column. Shorter segments can easily be run on side planers outside of longer coppers.

The smaller Walleye Boards and Off Shore Side Planers work great for 50- to 250-foot copper segments. The larger Church TX-44 should be used for 300 foot or longer coppers. This big board does not exert that much pressure on the rod, but it effectively pulls the longer, heavier coppers forward in your spread, making it easier to reel in fish that hit outside planers. The big boards running farther forward make it easier to reset those rods with shorter lengths of copper back on the outside, too.

When attaching copper to planers, never place the copper into the release. Let all the copper off the reel and then hook the braid or mono backing into the release. A variety of releases are on the market, and different brands of planer boards use different releases. I have found that the Church Vise Grip works best when you turn the release backward.

Copper has less horizontal movement compared with lead core, but it has a much greater vertical range of motion than lead core. When you turn, copper sinks really fast! Keep this in mind when trolling a zigzag course. If you slow down or take your boat out of gear, copper sinks really fast! If running coppers in shallow water, you cannot slow down, or you will catch the bottom. When letting copper out in shallower water, you may have to let the line out slowly to avoid sinking into the bottom.

When you turn, copper sinks much faster and deeper than lead core. If you are trolling in 80 feet of water and have a 300 copper set far out to the side, how deep will the line sink on a sharp turn placing the planer on the inside of the turn? My guess is it will stick the bottom. You get the idea. When running longer coppers in less than 120 feet of water, you need to watch your turns and at times, shorten lines as you turn. Also, it helps to kick up your speed on turns when running copper. Like lead core, I sometimes reel my boards in closer to the boat on the inside of a turn. Once the boat straightens out and I think the lines are pulling straight, I let them back out to their original positions off the side.

Some anglers have made some great catches by *mooching* their coppers. They run 50- to 200-foot segments of copper on boards. They mooch their lines by dropping the boat into neutral and allowing the spoons to sink. After the neutral drop, they engage the engine and pull

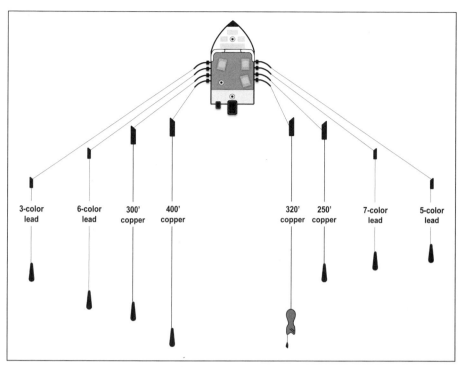

Copper and lead core can be run together. Run lead core lines on the outside planers. In this diagram lead core is used to target the top 30 feet and copper is targeting the 30- to 70-foot-level.

the lines back up. Obviously, they dial into a precise rhythm of rising and falling, but the mechanics of this presentation are pretty clear. At slow speeds, heavy objects sink. Apply speed, and the same object will rise up in the water column.

Can you run a mixed stealth spread of lead core and copper? Absolutely, coppers and leads work great when run together. The rule that minimizes disaster is to keep the deeper lines on the inside planers. For example, let's say you are targeting kings suspended between 60 and 90 feet down. The top of the thermocline is 40 feet down, and steelhead and coho are cruising the 20- to 50-foot level. You can target the kings with a 300 copper on the port inside planer and a 350 to 450 copper on the starboard inside planer. You can run segmented lead cores of 5 to 10 colors on the outside planers. If you're a *Copper Head,* you can run shorter segmented coppers on the outside of your deep coppers. You can be as creative as you want with this, and if you have enough anglers on board, you can turn your boat into a minesweeper.

Spoons, flashers and flies, natural bait, and body baits can all produce fish on copper. Remember to select lure colors based on how far down in the water column you target. Remember, any attractor adds additional drag, which causes the line to ride a bit higher in the water column than a clean spoon does. On your boat, determine which lures work best and go from there.

The Copper Hybrid

If you can't make up your mind whether to run copper or lead, you can do what my buddy Jim Klausing does. He runs a hybrid copper-lead core stealth rig. Jim has great success when he attaches three colors of lead to his 150 and 300 copper lines. He uses a tiny 50-pound Spro swivel to attach the different lines. This is a high-end swivel that fits through the rod guides.

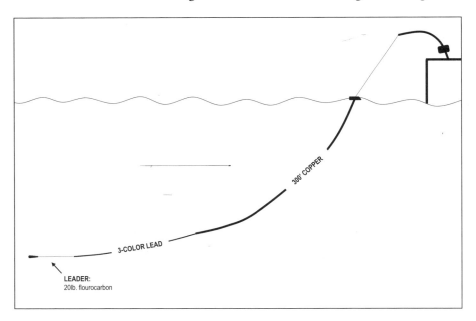

The Copper hybrid combines the best of copper and lead core. The copper gives depth penetration and 3 colors of lead core add the signature hypnotic action to a trailing lure.

Copper line produces big fish!

Jim loves the depth the copper gives him, but he believes the lead gives his spoons a little more *dancing* action. Jim is a tremendously accomplished recreational tournament angler, and this rig combines the best qualities of both presentations.

Here's how he sets up the rig: Jim uses the Spro swivel to attach his braid backing to the copper. After spooling on the copper, he uses another Spro to join three colors of lead to the copper line. Simply twist the copper onto the Spro. For the lead core, break off the lead from inside the last six inches of the sheath. Simply tie an improved clinch knot with the Dacron into the Spro. On the business end of the rig, Jim attaches a 20-foot leader of 20-pound fluorocarbon. His favorite lure on the 150 hybrids is a green frog Spin Doctor with a green Howie Fly. On the 300 coppers, he prefers to run spoons, such as Super Slims, Stingers, Moonshines, and Silver Streaks.

Some of the best charter captains and tournament anglers on the Great Lakes feel copper line is the best stealth presentation available. If you are not running copper, give it a try. It catches fish.

COPPER BASICS

- 30- and 45-pound copper are standard (Blood Run recently introduced 65-pound copper).
- Reels with fast retrieves and large line capacity.
- Backing is 30- to 50-pound braid or 30-pound mono.
- Place enough backing on the reel to send a planer to the side and withstand the run of a large king. Fish do not run as far on copper because dragging all that heavy line tires fish (and anglers!) out.
- Leaders for spoons are 20-pound fluorocarbon, 30-pound fluorocarbon for flashers.
- You can attach copper to the backing and leader with Spro swivels or knots.

Dave Mull with a late fall king taken on a Yakima Mag Lip run on a 450 copper line off a Church TX-44 planer.

CHAPTER 6

Lead Core Madness

Nothing but bright sunshine, calm seas and crystal clear, icy cold water greeted us as the *Blue Horizon* cleared the pier heads at the crack of 10:00 a.m. It was mid July, yet the water in front of the harbor was almost cold enough to make icebergs. I scanned the horizon for signs of life—clouds, wind, boats, birds, anything . . . but all I could see was the shimmering reflection of the sun off the water. Where does one begin fishing on a day such as this?

The previous day, the surface temp along the shore was warm, and we fished four miles offshore. We were targeting kings and coho 60 to 90 feet down in about 100 feet of water, but on this day when I saw how cold the surface temp was, my game plan changed before we were more than 100 yards from the pier heads.

For the past several days, a strong offshore wind had blown the warm, near-shore water out and *rolled* the lake creating an upwelling. This had brought the cold water in and scattered the bait and game fish from the shore to Timbuktu. I instinctively knew yesterday's strategy wouldn't work and went into the cabin and pulled out my segmented lead core rods. My plan was to run out about five miles and set out a spread of segmented leads and light line riggers to target the top 50 feet.

We had two options. The upwelling might have brought the fish into the shoreline, or the fish could have been blown out to deeper waters. This particular day, my gut feeling was telling me to go deep, but before committing to the deeps, I needed some peace of mind. After clearing the pier heads, I turned the boat to port and ran a zigzag course from the beach out to 45 feet. I was looking for bait balls on my sonar or seagulls sitting on the water. After 15 minutes of looking, it was apparent that the water was void of life.

Upwellings on the Great Lakes frequently *roll* cold water, bait, and game fish into the shallows. But not always! Sometimes, an upwelling will create a warm water wedge. While cold water will creep in at an angle along the bottom, the warm wedge forces the bait and game fish offshore to deeper water, rather than moving them into the shallows.

On this day, this appeared to be the case. Time to go deep. Not knowing where to set up, we ran out about five miles and began setting a full spread of lines in 160 feet. The surface temp was warm, but cold water started about 30 feet down and ran all the way down to the bottom. After setting lines, we trolled a course out to deeper water with very little action. Okay we did have one strike from a mighty 14-inch king salmon. After about two hours, I was out of stories and my group was getting restless. You can only take the "Hey Cap, can you divide this lone fish, so it feeds our six families," so many times.

As we continued our steady path deeper and deeper, I began to wonder, *should we have set up on the beach?* Did I miss something? As I contemplated throwing myself over the side, a 5-color lead on a Church Board was ripped,

Lead core on side planers is one of the best presentations to catch big kings suspended in the top 40 feet of the water column.

and a chrome missile exploded from the water far astern. Fish on! iPhones and beer cans went flying as our crew stumbled into action! With a spunky 8-pound steelhead doing his best to throw the Stinger spoon from his jaw, a high diver and an 8-color lead went off in stereo. Now, this was fishing!

We spent the rest of the trip catching a mixed bag of kings, coho, steelhead, and lake trout. While a few kings were taken below 100 feet, the vast majority of our action came on segmented leads targeting the top 40 feet. The leads all had small to medium spoons, both Dreamweaver Super Slims and Michigan Stingers. On this day, a wedge of water had set up; the bait and game fish moved higher up in the water column, but the current blew them out over deeper water. They were sitting so close to the surface that only stealth tactics would draw strikes during the middle of the day.

WHY FISH LEAD CORE?

Bright sunshine above . . . icy cold, clear water below . . . and fish suspended in the top 40 feet equal one of the toughest fishing conditions any salmon and trout angler ever will confront. Lesser anglers will quickly give up and head to the golf course, but those with an understanding of lead core will catch fish all day long. Summer upwellings move large volumes of cold, clear water in from the depths and dump it along the shoreline and into the upper reaches of the water column. When combined with bright sunshine, cold water high in the water column presents anglers with tough fishing conditions.

While the fishing conditions may be tough, the weather is usually great with this pattern, so I think it is safe to say that we all want to be out on the water harvesting fish!

Lead core lines off side planers are one of the most effective techniques to catch suspended fish in these conditions. Some of you may be hitting the protest button right now and saying, "But catching fish on lead core is no fun!" True, lead core may not be as sporting as other tactics, but don't you think catching fish is more fun than taking a nap on a slow moving boat? Lead core also allows you to run extra lines, which translates into more fish!

Lead core presentations are useful for targeting any negative fish. No matter where you fish, some days, biological factors, full stomachs, local weather, and adverse water conditions can make any fish tough to catch. Lead core is often the best presentation to get these negative fish to bite.

The modern Great Lakes are super clear giving fish great vision. These fish not only can see well, but they also hear the vibration signature of boats as they approach. This drives fish down and off to the side. These fish may remain spooked for a period of time, making them tough to catch.

TAKING LEAD CORE DEEPER

Many anglers make a 10-color lead their deepest lead. When a 10-color is not getting deep enough, try splicing two to three more colors onto the full core. This slight adjustment will often put you back in the strike zone. A 12-color lead core has been a dynamite rod during the late summer and fall on the *Blue Horizon*.

But thankfully, fish have a small brain and soon forget! (Wouldn't it be nice if our wives forgot so easily?) That's the beauty of lead core. Lead core adds three elements of stealth to your presentation. Horizontally, lead core lines put lures well behind the boat. When you send the line out to the side on a planer, such as a Church Walleye Board, you add a second degree of horizontal separation. Between lead cores hypnotic action and the surging of a planer on the waves, this presentation often drives fish crazy.

Lead core and side planers have another big advantage over other tactics. When salmon and trout school in the top 40 feet of the water column, they tend to spread out and scatter. A spread of segmented leads off planers allows you to cover a wider path as you search for these high-riding fish. Planers allow you to load a shallow strike zone off each side of the boat with far more lures than you can set off the transom of any boat.

Today, lead core strategies are multi-dimensional and far-reaching. Let me explain. Many of us don't give much thought to how to catch fish in the top 40 feet of the water column. When the fish are deep, we all want to be very precise about *where* our presentations are running. Yet, when the fish are suspended in the top 30 or 40 feet, we often just drop some lines back on the surface or on a full core and hope the fish find it. *A full core equals 10 colors or 100 yards of lead core line.

When the fish are so close to the surface, we often just think that they will find our lures, and we don't have to hit them on the nose to draw a strike, so to speak. We tend to think that fish sitting higher in the water column are easier to catch.

This is a big mistake! A salmon or trout that is suspended within 40 feet of the surface is much harder to catch than a fish sitting in deeper, darker water. For this reason, we need to have highly-focused stealth tactics. Segmented leads allow us to target these fish with great accuracy. When combined with a side planer, lead is a dynamite tactic to present our lures to fish in clean water completely undisturbed by boat noise or the intrusion and water displacement from downrigger balls or divers. Segmented lead core may be the best tactic for negative fish suspended from 10 to 30 feet down.

Why Does Lead Core Catch so Many Fish?

Why is lead core so productive? Is it the line? The presentation? Both! Lead core line does more than sink; it actually adds a unique, almost *hypnotic motion* to lures. Lead core is a unique line made up of two very different materials. An inner filament of lead is encased in a bulky, buoyant Dacron sheath. Lead and Dacron exert two very different forces on the line when trolling. The weight of the lead causes the line to sink. The bulky Dacron casing exerts drag on the line and *floats* the line upward in the water column. This combination of sinking, buoyancy, and drag gives lead its unique, hypnotic presentation.

Some of the newer lead cores, such as Tuf-Line Micro Lead and Sufix 832 Advanced Lead Core, use Spectra fiber and Micro Dyneema fiber sheaths, achieving strong line with thinner sheaths. Initial tests show these lines can get to depths similar to copper because of their decreased water resistance.

As the boat trolls through the water, the line is constantly interacting with the boat's motion, the water, and currents. In other words, lead core lines don't trail straight behind the boat . . . they move back and forth, up and down. This gives the lure an added touch of appeal. Not only does a lure display its own action, but the lure *dances* around as it wobbles.

Additionally, any trolling speed adjustments or course alterations change the location of lead core lures in the water column. Speed up, Dacron-coated lead rises up in the water a few feet. Slow down, it sinks. When run off the side on planers, this rising and sinking motion is greatly enhanced—think of a water skier zipping outside the wake of the towboat. Lead core moves around more than any other presentation. This imparts a very different action to the line and lure than any other presentation. Some days, presentation is the key to success. Frequently, the added *dance* of lead core triggers hesitant fish into striking.

Presentation also plays a part in lead's effectiveness. First, you have to let a great deal of line out to reach target depths. As the line trails a trolling boat, it enters the water with a very gradual angle of descent. This places the lure well behind the boat in clean water, undisturbed by the boat. This reaches fish that the boat didn't spook or that have forgotten about the boat. When you run lead core off side planers, you add a second degree of horizontal separation.

LEAD CORE BASICS

Lead core is available in 10 color, 100-yard spools. The lead core line changes color every 10 yards. By counting colors, anglers know how far astern their lure is and can make an educated guess as to what depth it is running. A full core (10 colors) of lead in the water, with a spoon, runs roughly 30 to 45 feet down, depending on trolling speed. The slower you go, the deeper it runs.

Historically, many anglers only ran a single 10-color lead off the stern, then fishermen started running one 10-color lead a side on trolling boards. This is a great strategy for targeting fish holding 30 to 45 feet down, but when fish are above this range, a full core isn't effective since the trailing lure runs below the fish. As we know, fish tend to look up in the water column when feeding.

Today, enterprising anglers have started running segmented leads to target fish in the upper layers of the water column. Segmented leads from 2 to 8 colors long (20 to 80 yards) work great when targeting suspended fish over deep water, or when targeting fish in shallower depths of 20 to 50 feet.

LEAD CORE BASICS

- 27-pound test lead core is standard for Big Water applications.
- Fluorocarbon leaders will catch more fish than monofilament.
- 20-pound fluorocarbon leaders from 10 to 20 feet long will produce more fish than longer leaders. Shorter leaders translate more of the *hypnotic* action to the lure.
- Backing is 20-to 50-pound braid or 30-pound (or heavier) mono. Make sure you have enough backing to run a planer to the side and line to spare when a large fish runs.
- A variety of knots attach lead to the backing and leader. The simple method is to pull the Dacron sheath back and break off about 6 inches of lead. Straighten out the Dacron and tie an overhand loop in the sheath. Tie the braid backing to the lead core loop with a polamar knot. At the other end of the lead core, attach the fluorocarbon leader to the Dacron loop with an improved clinch knot.
- When running segmented leads or full cores on boards, never put the lead core into the release. Attach the board to the backing.
- How deep is lead? Three to five colors run 9 to 20 feet down. Six to eight colors run 20 to 30 feet. Ten colors run 30 to 40 feet. Actual running depth depends on the amount of line deployed, lure selection, line diameter, trolling speed, current and sea conditions.
- When running multiple lead cores, run the shorter segments on the outside planers.
- When mixing leads and coppers in a spread, run leads outside coppers.
- When running a Torpedo SWR, keep it inside other coppers and lead cores.
- When fighting large fish on lead core and boards, as the fish gets close to the boat, the board has a tendency to dive down in the water. To avoid this, place the rod tip by the water's surface as you crank in the last 50 feet of line. Once the board is within reach, raise the rod, unclip the board, and it's game on!

You may be wondering how deep segmented leads run. Check out the general depth chart in the side bar. Use this to determine what segment lengths you want to run.

If you are limited on rod selection and can't carry a wide variety of segmented leads, you can dial a 3-color lead core into any depth by adding a Torpedo. Three colors of lead core in the water is enough line to give you the *hypnotic* presentation, but three colors on its own runs only about 12 to 18 feet down. When the fish are deeper, you can add a Cuda Torpedo to reach deeper depths. Simply let out your three colors of lead, attach the Cuda to the braid backing, and send the entire rig down. This rig can be used to target multiple levels of the water column, depending on how much line you let out. This will take some experimentation to determine the actual running depth, but it is a way to make one or two rods do double duty.

When fish descend beyond the reach of a 10-color lead, some anglers resort to longer lead core rigs with up to 20 colors of lead. You would think that doubling the amount of lead core in the water would double the depth, but the added drag of water pressure against the Dacron over powers the sink rate. Even though you have 200 yards of line in the water, the lure only gets about 50 feet deep. Reeling in 200 yards of line to catch a single fish is brutal on the arms!

Thankfully, we have much simpler ways to catch fish! When fish go deeper, it is easier to run copper or to use a Dive Bomb or Torpedo to take a segmented lead deeper. The Torpedo SWR is discussed at the end of this chapter. Some anglers clip sinkers onto the leader of a lead core. This adds depth penetration; however, the weight on the business end of things minimizes the *hypnotic* impact of the lead core. If greater depth is the end goal, you are better off running copper or using Torpedoes or Dive Bombs ahead of the lead core. A shorter segment of lead, say three to four colors, is easier to get deep with a weight on braid backing than with miles of lead core.

RUNNING LEAD CORE ON SIDE PLANERS

Lead core is far more productive when combined with side planers. The boards expand your reach and allow you to run extra rods, and when you zigzag through the water, the boards greatly magnify the leads natural rising-and-falling action. Every time you turn, leads on the outside of the turn rise up and leads on the inside of the turn sink down. When fish are off, this jigging action can trigger many strikes.

My favorite board for lead core is the Church Walleye Board. It runs well in all sea conditions and is easy to rig. Never clip the lead core line into a release! The release will pinch the lead, and broken lead weakens the Dacron from the inside out. The line eventually breaks. Before attaching the board, let out all the lead on the reel and then attach the board to the braid or mono backing at least five feet from the knot.

Kings that hit downrigger lines often run out and tangle with side planers. To help avoid horrendous tangles and lost gear, I keep about 20 to 30 feet of backing between the board and the lead core. It seems that when kings run to the side they aim for the planer and run a few feet behind it. If you have a longer length of braid between the board and the lead core, the king will tangle up with the braid. It is much easier to untangle the fish from braid than from lead core, which gets damaged much more easily than braid does.

Captain Dan fishing with two of his daughters. Dads, take your children fishing!

Always attach a board to your backing, not the lead core. Church has a great adjustable release on their board. It is easy to use, and when it wears out, you can attach a new release in seconds. To keep the board from falling off the line, the Church Board has a pin on its stern. Most anglers simply open the pin and place their line behind the pin. This keeps the board on the line, but if the release on the front of the board opens on a short strike or from a big wave, the board will slide all the way down to the lure . . . and you get to reel in a long, empty line to reset. Greg MgGee of *Blue Fairway's* taught me a simple trick to keep the board from sliding down the line. The trick also has helped recover boards when a large fish broke off!

A #16 rubber band is all you need. To pin the board to the line, simply half hitch the rubber band to your backing. When you pull the pin out on the stern of the Walleye Board, you will drop the pin into the loop on the rubber band. Don't forget to place your line behind the pin as well. Now, even if the release opens up, the board will not slide down the line. The Church Walleye Board is easy to use, and the *Keating on Kings* DVD *Part I* has a great visual demonstration showing how to run lead on boards.

Integrating Lead Core with Other Presentations and Other Interesting Facts

Lead core is easy to run and can be intermixed with all other presentations. One popular strategy is to use segmented leads to target the top 40 feet and use riggers and divers to target deeper layers. Another strategy involves setting coppers into your spread inside of lead cores. This method gives you maximum stealth over a broad segment of the water column.

Even if your riggers are catching fish, you still might want to place a lead core or two off the side to help you interpret the mood of the fish. Often the fish will stop biting more aggressive presentations behind riggers, but they start hitting stealthier leads or coppers. When this happens, change your riggers over to stealth mode.

If you take to the water with little information about the fishing, it can pay to start with several different presentations. For example, two riggers,

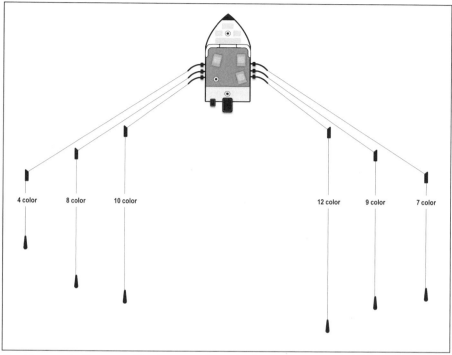

Stealthy spreads of segmented lead cores are dynamite for catching suspended fish in clear water.

two divers, and two lead cores gives you three widely different presentations to help you dial into the fish. Once you determine a pattern, you can add more of the productive set-ups.

Running multiple leads per side is easy—if you follow a few rules. Always run the shorter segments on the outside. For example, if you run 10 and a 5 color off the same side of the boat, run the 5 color on the outside planer. When an outside lead core planer gets hit, the fish pulls the board back, and easily clears the inside planer lines. When resetting the line, simply attach the board, float the rig back, engage the reel, and let it pull itself back into formation where it was. If running coppers and leads together, run the coppers inside and deeper than the leads.

A word of caution! Lead core sinks on turns. When trolling a full spread of leads, speed up when turning. Also, a gradual turn prevents tangles. When fishing in shallow or at middle depths, consider how deep your leads are running before you make a 180-degree turn. For example, if you are running a 10-color lead in 55 feet of water, on a side planer, where do you think the lure will go when it's on the inside of the turn? Turn too sharp, and it will snag mussels. Many times, a spoon on a lead will pick up a mussel, and you won't know it. When turning in shallower water, I speed up and crank the boards in closer to the boat. If I think I am too shallow to avoid mussels, I will reel in the longer leads, take off the board, and reel in some of the lead line. I reset the rod when the turn is complete. If you take your kids fishing, let them help with reeling in the lines and resetting. This is a great way to keep them involved with the action.

FISH SEE *UP*! TRICKS FOR OUT OF TEMP FISH

While fishing my way through a slow charter, I had one of those rare *light-bulb* moments and, I would have missed it if one of my clients hadn't pointed it out. On this particular July morning we were targeting a mixed bag of salmon and trout in 70 to 120 feet of water. The early bite was mostly riggers and divers set 50 to 80 feet down.

My clients didn't want to catch the easy fish that bite at sunrise, so we missed much of the early bite. Action was fair up until about 9 a.m. and then it came to a grinding halt. We felt like we were trolling the Dead Sea. I was dumbfounded. Conditions were perfect: a slight chop and a cloudy sky. Suddenly, the sun popped out, and the world brightened, as did our action! Our 6-, 8- and 10-color leads started popping, but the action was on and off. We would get two or three quick bites, then nothing, then one of my customers noticed that our lead core bites only happened when the sun was out. Every time the clouds rolled in, we had no bites on the leads.

Since that day, I've noticed this pattern when fish are holding in the thermocline from 40 to 60 feet down. The leads, which ride higher in the water column in the upper layers of the thermocline, or just above it, often get very few strikes early in the morning. Once the sun is higher in the sky, the lead cores often come to life.

My theory is that fish hold in cold water just below the thermocline. As we know, fish look up in the water column when feeding. When the lighting is poor, these fish cannot see lures that are 10 to 20 feet above them. Once the sun brightens the water, the fish easily can see the baits above them. Since the lines are out to the side of the boat and far back, the fish frequently rise up for what appears to be an easy snack.

Since then, I've tweaked my lure selection to capitalize on these *out of temp* opportunities. I run baits that have maximum *flash* appeal on bright days to draw these bonus fish up from deeper levels. Some of my favorite lures for this scenario include the magnum Moonshine RV Wonderbread, the magnum Blue Thunder Stinger and Silver Streak, the magnum Reverse Puke Silver Steak, and the standard size Ludington Special Stinger.

Sometimes it pays to run a lead high, off to the side, and out of temp on bright days. They produce bonus fish that would be missed by your deeper rigs.

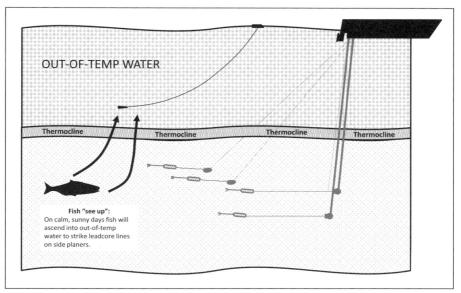

Fish see up! On calm sunny days fish will ascend up, into warmer water, to strike highly visible lures on lead core run on trolling boards off to the side.

Before you run out and spool up with lead, you need to consider the ratio of weight (lead) to resistance (Dacron). The breaking strength of lead core is based on the Dacron sheath. The weight of the lead is pretty standard. Traditional lead core has a thick, bulky casing. Today, there are several new varieties of lead on the market that have thinner super-fiber sheaths. These new lines have a thinner diameter, take up less room on a spool, and can be run on smaller, lighter reels. The thinner lines have the same weight as comparable standard lead core, but they are sleeker and lack the bulky drag that imparts more *dancing* motion to lures. Since they have less drag, they achieve slightly greater depths with less line in the water. Less drag also means that they impart less hypnotic motion to trailing lures than traditional leads.

Both new and old versions of lead give you great stealth off side planers. You just need to know where in the water column your leads are running. Some days, more motion will trigger strikes; other days it won't make a difference.

THE TORPEDO SWR—ULTIMATE STEALTH, MAXIMUM VERSATILITY

It was just one of those days. A few random bites first thing in the morning and then . . . it was as is we were fishing on the Dead Sea. Radios and cell phones were singing the same, tired tune. There was no wind, no marks, no fish and even my clients were lifeless.

I must have had a little extra coffee that morning because I decided to step out and try something new. The few hits we were getting were coming on SWR *Skunkbusters* set 90 to 120 feet down. Wouldn't it be nice if I could run a few more of those rigs? Wouldn't it be nice if I could send some of those SWRs out to the side, into the clean, undisturbed water just beyond my boats reach?

I am a big fan of Torpedo weights. I had never combined one with three colors of lead core and a Church Walleye Board, but today was the day! I figured if I could clear my rigger and wire divers, just maybe, one of these sleek weights could help me run an SWR out away from the boat. I took a

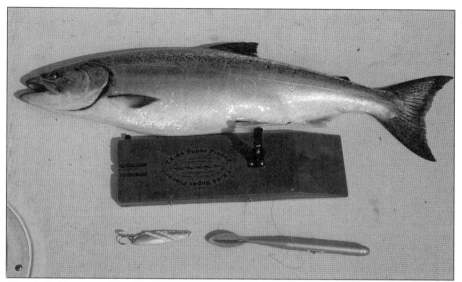

The Cuda Torpedo, a TX-44 Church side planer, and a Dreamweaver Super Slim are a highly versatile presentation that allows you to fish deep in the water column.

line counter reel spooled with 30 lb. Power Pro and added three colors of lead and a 20 lb. fluorocarbon leader. I then attached a small, 30 lb. Sampo coastlock ball bearing swivel and Ludington Special Stinger. I then let out the three colors and clipped a 12 oz. Torpedo Cuda to the braid backing 2 feet in front of the lead. This entire rig was then let out, slowly down the middle, about 250 feet.

So far so good, but now came the moment of truth. Could the Walleye Board pull the entire rig out to the side and not tangle my riggers or divers? I clipped the Walleye Board onto the braid backing, and with great anticipation, the red planer floated back. I engaged the reel, and it was a beautiful sight! That red planer gracefully pulled the Torpedo and all that line out to the side without a hitch, and it rode in place inside my other planers!

What happened next on this late summer morning really caught me by surprise. The board was out only a few minutes before it started surging backward with a big king clamped down on the spoon. After boating the fish and resetting the line, I quickly phoned one of my fellow captains and let him know that I was not the brightest guy on the lake. I've been using Torpedoes for several applications, but it took me several years to finally work up the courage to attach that unique weight to three colors of lead and run it on a board off the side.

After boating that king, the rod was deployed, and the results were the same—Fish On! While the other rods on the boat merely did the backstroke, the Torpedo SWR took fish after fish for the remainder of that morning. What could have been a very slow charter turned into a great success because of one, innovative rig. Yes, when I returned to the dock, I quickly spooled up another rig to run off the opposite side of the boat.

Since running that first Torpedo SWR, I began running one a side, on the inside of my planer spread, on a regular basis when targeting fish below 70-feet. You know what? Most days, once the sun was well up, those rods out produced every other rig. On flat calm days, they were equivalent to throwing a stick of dynamite off the side of the boat.

At this point, you probably have a number of questions about how to run this rig. How deep can they go? I think time will tell, but I can tell you I've caught Zebra Mussels off the bottom in 150-feet of water. I've also pulled many large kings from the depths! Their actual running depth depends on trolling speed, current velocity, lure selection, and wave texture. Basically, I found that three colors of lead, a spoon such as a Super Slim, Stinger or Moonshine, a Cuda Torpedo, and 250-feet of braid was getting down 90-120 feet, depending on the preceding variables. You can figure depths up and down from that point.

What makes these rigs so effective? Basically, you are taking the hypnotic presentation which three colors of lead gives to a lure, dropping the presentation deep in the water column, and then sending it out to the side of the boat. This rig goes deep, is out to the side of your inner spread (horizontally), and is trailing behind your boat (horizontally). The entire rig is running in clean water that has not been disturbed by the boat, downrigger cables, or sonar beams. As the trolling board surges through waves, it imparts additional jigging motion to the rig. The Torpedo acts like a pendulum, and as you turn, the depth of the lure will change drastically. It very well may be the ultimate stealth weapon. Because of the sleek Torpedo design, there is minimal drag on the tackle, allowing the use of lighter gear when compared to running full cores and copper set ups.

Your first reaction may be that this rig is a disaster waiting to happen, but I have found it relatively easy to deploy. When setting the rig, make sure your rigger lines are deep and out of the way! In other words, don't set a deep Torpedo on top of an SWR running 40 feet down. Secondly, after attaching the weight to the line, drop the rig slowly. If you power drop it, you may snag your riggers or divers. A slow drop will allow the trolling motion to pull the entire rig behind your boat. After attaching the board, let it float straight back for a moment, to clear divers, then engage the reel, and allow the entire rig to pull out gradually to the side. When turning, I found that these rigs move around in the water column, and if you are running it close to the bottom, you must be cautious on sharp turns, as it will sink into the bottom and pick up hitchhikers.

This is a very versatile rig and allows anglers with a limited rod capacity or budget to productively target a large vertical section of the water column. A reel loaded with braid and three colors of lead core combined with a Torpedo Cuda enables you to effectively fish throughout the water column from 15 to 150 feet down based on how much line you let out. If you desire,

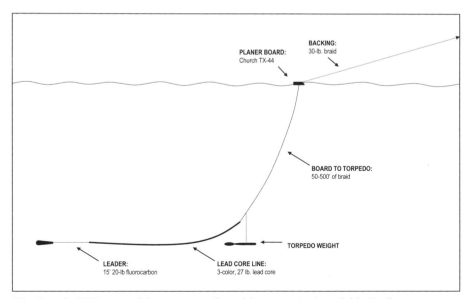

The Torpedo SWR is one of the most versatile stealth presentations available. It allows you to use one rod to fish the entire water column. It allows you to easily target the 70 to 120 foot level off to the side with braided line.

you can run it even deeper. While this presentation is similar to copper, you can run it on much lighter tackle and effectively use smaller reels. Reeling braided line is much easier than dealing with miles of copper, as well.

The Torpedo SWR can be used to target fish at all layers of the water column. Torpedoes come in four sizes, and you can adjust the amount of line you deploy and the size of the Torpedo to target a variety of vertical layers of the water column.

NAVIGATING TANGLES

When you tangle a lead core, don't throw away the entire rig! Cut the line at the tangle and splice in additional colors to restore it to its original length. For example, if you lose four colors of lead, cut off the tangled portion. Next, pull back the Dacron sheaf, exposing the lead. Break off the last six to eight inches of lead. Pull the sheath back out and tie an overhand loop into the Dacron. Next, take a fresh spool, or the remainder of the lead after a tangle has been removed, and break off the lead in the last six inches. Take the Dacron and tie an improved clinch knot into the Dacron loop of the line coming off the reel. You can now reel the line onto the reel, and you are ready to go. This small knot will easily go through the guides. I do this quick repair on charters all the time and have even done it with a fish on the end of the tangled line!

CHAPTER 7

Coho—Silver Fun

Coho salmon. This is the fish that began the coldwater salmon fishing revolution on the Great Lakes. Since the first fish were stocked into Lake Michigan back in the middle 1960s, countless anglers have reaped a huge harvest of these silver fish across the region. While stocking programs continue to keep Lakes Michigan and Ontario filled with these great eating fish, naturally reproducing populations have firmly taken root in Lakes Superior and Huron.

Coho are highly migratory and prefer the upper layers of the water column. Their preferred temperature range is 50 to 56 degrees. A few key details will help anglers dial into Mr. Coho in spring, summer, and fall.

SPRING COHO

As winter releases its grip on the Great Lakes, icy water temps greet anglers eager to fish. Depending on where and when you start fishing, you might face water temperatures of 38 to 45 degrees. Those who have ice in their veins may take to the water amidst ice flows and water temps in the low to mid 30s.

Remember, coho *prefer* 50- to 56-degree water. Early spring water temperatures in the Great Lakes are much colder, so before unpacking a spring fishing plan, let's review a few basics that should influence our strategies. Coho have spent the winter in ice-cold water, and their metabolism, and appetite, has been low. As the waters begin to warm, their metabolism increases, as does their appetite. During late winter and early spring, schools

Coho are a schooling fish, when you find em, action is fast and furious!

of hungry coho move into the shoreline in search of warm water and an easy meal.

The bottom line is that we want to concentrate our fishing efforts on the warmest water we can find. Some areas along the shoreline warm before surrounding waters. Power plant discharges, industrial runoff, and river and stream mouths warm the shallows and create microenvironments within the larger environment. Discharges, rivers, and streams also wash an assortment of nutrients into the water, which attracts bait and predators. Since these microenvironments are part of a larger environment, understanding how local wind patterns impact these areas helps us find fish. Onshore winds keep the warm water trapped against the shoreline. Offshore winds blow warm water out and mix it with cooler lake water. In Indiana and Michigan, some coho move into streams to feed during March. These fish are not up these creeks and rivers to spawn yet and return to the lake.

Other shoreline features that warm surrounding waters are large, concrete break walls. These structures absorb sunlight and radiate the warmth into the surrounding waters. Winds blowing into these break walls hold the warm water close and attract baitfish. Harbors also warm rapidly as the water trapped inside break walls holds heat. This warmer water mixes with lake water and can make the area within a half mile of the harbor mouth productive. Any irregularities in the shoreline such as break walls, jetties, rock riprap, wave troughs, and near-shore drop offs also attract fish.

If larger features are not present, near-shore water that features a gradual drop off—say from the beach out to 20 feet—will warm faster than areas where deep water comes right into the shoreline. Water clarity also influences warming patterns. Dark, murky water absorbs sunlight and warms faster than clear water. When looking for fish along the shoreline, look for areas that are different from the surrounding environment.

Not all coho come into the shoreline. When looking for fish beyond the 30-foot level, the playing field is much larger as coho can be scattered just about anywhere in the cold water. When heading to deeper water, look for surface temp breaks and color lines. How to fish these features are discussed in the Steelhead Chapter. Once the water warms and stratifies, look for coho in and just below the thermocline, the horizontal break line between warm surface water and the colder water beneath it.

Anglers may be surprised at just how close to shore coho feed. One May morning, we had made an excellent catch of coho and steelhead out in 160 to 200 feet of water. On my afternoon charter, I planned to return to the same area. Our plans changed, however, when we cleared the pier heads. I was about to push the throttles forward when I glanced down the beach and noticed flocks of seagulls wheeling and diving into the water. This could mean only one thing: something big was chasing bait right against the beach. I made a hard turn to starboard and ran the boat into about 10 feet of water. Birds squealed and feasted on baitfish all down the shoreline! We quickly deployed mono side planers and instantly hooked up with fish! We soon caught a limit of coho, and we did it in 6 to 15 feet of water. When the coho push the alewives against the beach, action is fast. While kings make movements toward the shoreline early in the day, coho will move into the shoreline at any time, even under a bright sun.

In a typical spring season, coho are caught over a wide variety of areas, both in shallow water and over deep water. Some years, the big schools of fish move right into the shoreline; other years, the majority of fish hold over middle depths or deep water—sometimes way down in the water column if baitfish are deep. In a typical year, a combination of shallow and deep-water fishing scenarios unfold so let's dive into how to find and catch coho!

Lure Selection for Spring Coho

Few things in life remain the same. One thing that has is that in spring, coho love to hit green peanuts flies. Shallow water or out deep, it is hard to beat a 00 red dodger and a peanut fly for catching spring coho. Peanuts are about a half-inch long, made of tinsel or hair, and are tied on a No. 4 treble hook. Some of the time-proven peanut patterns (tinsel) include green, green/gold, green/blue/gold, teal/mirage, and candy apple green. One pattern that has stood the test of time is the Peter fly. This lime green (hair) and gold (tinsel) fly is named in honor of Capt. Peter Nied, one of the greatest coho fishermen on the planet. He is one of the anglers who first started fishing with these small flies. Other colors to try on dark days include pearls and pearl blue patterns. If coho are feeding on flies or bugs on the surface, then purples, purple/black, and green/black peanuts are dynamite. On sunny days, peanuts of black and blue tinsel with a touch of purple are hard to beat.

Peanuts work best with the 00 red Luhr Jensen dodgers. This small, plain red dodger has no tapes or dots. For plastic coho flashers, it is hard to beat the small 00 red or orange plastic Spin Doctors with orange cracked ice tape. The little red dodgers and flashers both work great behind planer boards, divers, riggers, and flat lines. In other words, just put them in the water, and they will catch fish! If you get tired of catching fish on red dodgers, try a clown dodger, which is yellow with red dots on both sides. The 00 red Action Flasher, with its bent ends, is a killer for steelhead and takes plenty of coho, too.

Leader length for spring coho should be roughly 14 to 18 inches from the back of the dodger to the eye of the hook. Peanut flies are small, and the coho hit them throughout the spring; however, as the water warms and coho put on weight, the larger, one-inch *slider* flies start working. Slider flies are tied on a hard plastic tube; the leader runs through the tube and is tied to a small treble hook. Some days, the larger flies work better, but other

Spring coho provide fast action, making them a great fish to introduce children to big water trolling.

days, the peanuts work better. Most days, I run a combination of sliders and peanuts. If a pattern develops, then I adjust accordingly.

For the larger flies, the same color patterns used with peanuts work plus two other colors—*Green Liz* and *Blue Liz*. Green Liz is made of ¾ green tinsel and ¼ yellowish white Mylar. Blue Liz is blue tinsel with bluish-white Mylar tied in. I like to run these two flies on my outside Yellow Birds behind a 00 red or orange Action Flash flasher.

While many great coho fishermen run exclusively small flies and dodgers, plenty of coho get caught on body baits. In fact, when fishing super cold water, 34 to 42 degrees—small cranks on light line often are the best baits. Some of the most popular cranks include Thin Fins, Shad Raps, jointed Rapalas, and jointed Rebels. A variety of plug colors work, but those with reds, orange, chartreuse, green, gold, and black are most productive. If the coho are feeding on gobies, then brown and orange color patterns draw strikes. Spoons are not as productive for spring coho, but any of the standard salmon spoons can produce the occasional coho during the spring.

SPRING TROLLING SECRETS

Many consider coho to be the ideal game fish. If you are new to big water trolling, spring coho are a great target for cutting your teeth. They travel in large schools, have an endless appetite, and strike throughout the day. While larger adult coho can get moody, spring coho are always willing to pick a fight with just about any brightly-colored object. Once you learn to master the basics of coho fishing, the greatest challenge is finding fish.

Let's discuss a foolproof game plan for great coho fishing. Even though these fish are aggressive, determining the right trolling speed will improve your catch. Since the fish usually are concentrated near the surface, you won't struggle with sub-surface currents. Finding the right speed is often a matter of pure experimentation and a healthy dose of watching *how the lines are hanging*. In cold water, slower speeds of 1.5 to 2.0 kts (1.7 to 2.3 mph) usually trigger more strikes. As the water warms into the upper 40s and 50s, speeds of 1.7 to 2.5 kts (2.0 to 3.1 mph) are typical.

Since most fish will be found in the top 20 feet, a mix of divers, mono side planers, and flat lines are all you need. Spring coho are frequently attracted to the turbulence created by a spinning propeller. A diver set just outside the boat's path on 20 to 40 feet of line is hard for a hungry coho to ignore. Dive planers, such as Dipsy Divers and Lurk Disco Divers, are super easy to deploy and work great off any size boat.

Let's begin with the basics—diving planers, aka "directional sinkers." Since we are not trying to get very deep, the smaller divers work as well as the standard size divers. As discussed below, you can mix different size divers together into a spread. The main line can be mono or braid. For mono, I prefer 20-pound Blood Run or 17-pound clear blue Stren. For braids, I've had great results with 30-pound Power Pro; braided line is great when you might run your dive planer farther out—the no-stretch line makes it easy to pop the release with a snap of the rod. When running a plug or spoon off the diver, use a 5-to 7-foot, 20-pound fluorocarbon leader. Dodgers and flies get a 3- to 6-foot, 40-pound mono leader between the diver and the dodger. While any color diver will work, my favorite diver colors for coho are orange, orange with orange cracked ice tape, white, and pearl. No snubber is needed, but if you must use one, go with the smaller, clear stealth snubbers.

It is super easy to run one diver a side, but you can get considerably more action if you run two per side. Spring coho are aggressive and attracted to the commotion that divers create. The more commotion you put in the water, the more fish you will attract. Many captains run a standard size diver on an inside rod and a small diver to the outside. The inside diver is set on a 1 or 1.5 setting and run out just 20 to 30 feet. The second rig, the smaller diver, is set on a 2 or 2.5 setting and run out on 30 to 60 feet of line. As you troll through the water, the smaller diver will run just outside and slightly behind the larger diver. For this double diver set up, I run the inside diver on braid and the outside diver on mono. This double dodger/fly rig coming through the water produces many double hook ups—sometimes in stereo, which means the high diver and low diver fire at once! When all four divers fire, you have what is commonly, if politically incorrectly, called a Chinese Fire Drill.

Some days, the hottest rod is a diver set just out of sight—really! When trolling in 10 to 20 feet of water, I may run the divers out on only 15 to 25 feet of line. Believe it or not, the coho come that close and strike! Setting a diver just beyond your vision is deadly in murky water. If the water is clear,

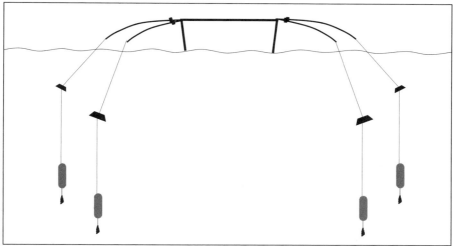

Running two divers with 00 red dodgers and a Peanut fly, side by side, is one of the most productive presentations for catching spring coho.

as it often is in deeper water, you will have to run the divers out on enough line to get them out of sight. In gin clear water, try kicking the divers out on a 3 setting.

While divers target aggressive fish attracted to your boat, side planers take your baits beyond your boat's path and reach fish that have not been spooked by your boat's signature. They also expand your reach and let you run more lures in the surface strike zone. Some of the more popular boards include Yellow Birds, the Church TX-12 and TX-6 Planer Boards, and the Offshores OR-12. The smaller the board, the lighter the line you can use. When using in line planers, remember that your line must be able to hold up in the release clip. I prefer 20-pound test Tournament Blood Run and 17-pound clear blue Stren for planer lines. These two lines are easy to see and minimize tangles.

Since you are targeting the top few feet of the water column, your strategy for implementing planers is quite different from running lead core or copper on planers for a variety of reasons. First, with mono planers, you want the planer to release on the strike and slide down the line. This helps keep the line from tangling with other planers when fighting a fish. A good line release is needed, and if you are using lighter line, you want to make sure the release will not crimp your line. I use the Otter release with Yellow Birds. This release can be adjusted for tension. In heavy seas or when targeting larger fish, the pin can be inserted deeper into the release. On calm days or when targeting small fish, place the pin lightly into the release.

The mechanics for running boards is simple. The rod should have enough backbone to withstand the pull of a planer across the waves. The reel should have enough line capacity to withstand the run of a large king, brown, or steelhead that might strike. I use the same rods, reels, and line I run my flasher/fly rigs with off downriggers to pull planer boards in the spring. On the business end, I employ a ¼- to ½-ounce bead chain keel sinker to keep the planer from sliding down and hitting the fish. The sinker also keeps the lure or dodger from skipping on the surface. The leader off the sinker to the lure or dodger is 4 to 8 feet long. When pulling spoons or cranks, I use a 14-pound or 20-pound fluorocarbon leader. For dodgers or flashers, 20- to 40-pound fluoro or mono will work just fine. Sinker size will vary depending on how deep, or not so deep, you want to go. For spring coho I typically use ¼, ⅜ and ½-ounce sizes.

Lead length off the boards has a huge impact on your catch rate—and your tangle rate. While there is an overall pattern to setting lines, remember that each day the most productive leads are dependent on wave height and fish temperament. The general range is 10 to 100 feet. A well-thought-out system will minimize tangles.

When running two or more planers on a side, the overall pattern will resemble an inverted V as you troll. The longer leads (the legs of the V) will be on the outside planers. As you move into your boat, the leads will get progressively shorter. This principle applies whether you are running two or six boards a side. Since the boards release on a strike, the planer will slide down the line, and as you reel in the fish, the entire rig will move behind the boat, crossing behind the shorter leads off the inside planers. If you set short leads on the outside, you will experience tangles when fighting fish. When resetting a line, let the lure out the appropriate amount, pin the board on the line, float the rig straight back, engage the reel, and let it pull back into its original position.

Both long and short leads will catch fish. A few clues, however, will help you make adjustments. To begin the day, I usually start each trip with at least one of the inside planers set on a 10- to 15-foot lead. Often the boat will spook fish off to the side. The first thing those fish see is your lure, so fish on! Also, fish look up as they feed. On calm days, a lure tight off a planer is close to the surface and may be the best rod. It's easy for fish to see it against the surface background.

Let's look at the typical lead lengths for a six-planer spread: three on each side of the boat. On the starboard side, set the outside planer back 80 feet, the middle board 40 feet, and the inside planer 20 feet. This is a fairly spread out pattern. On the port side, keep them closer together by setting the lures, from the outside to the inside, back 40, 30, and 15 feet.

Some days, spreading the lures apart will trigger strikes. Other days, setting them in a tight group will be more productive. Looking at a tight planer spread from a horizontal perspective, the lures run close together as you move horizontally to the side of your boat and trailing horizontally behind the boards. For example, you may set the boards to run 10 to 15 feet apart. If the leads off the individual boards are set in 5-foot increments, you can create a compact school of baits moving together. A group of 00 red dodgers tightly spaced in murky water can be devastating on coho. Other days, you will need 20 feet or more of horizontal separation between individual boards. On flat, calm days, I put my outside planer in a different hemisphere. Let the fish tell you what they want. Once a pattern is established, you can adjust the lines.

Weather and wave height greatly impact productive lead lengths on boards. On rough days or if your boat is surging, you might have to run your leads a bit longer to draw strikes. I remember a time I was trolling with the wind and waves pushing us from the stern. Trolling with the waves, the down troll was a smooth ride, and the boards with short, 10- to 20- foot leads caught all the fish. When I turned to go back into the waves, the longer leads caught fish. This was due to the fact that as we trolled into the choppy waves, the boards jumped across the surface and pulled the dodgers with them. On this day, the short leads were jumping around and too erratic to entice the fish to strike. The boards where the lures were stretched

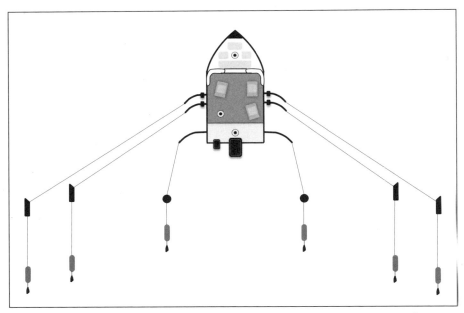

A six-rod spread of dodgers and flies is a proven pattern for catching aggressive spring coho.

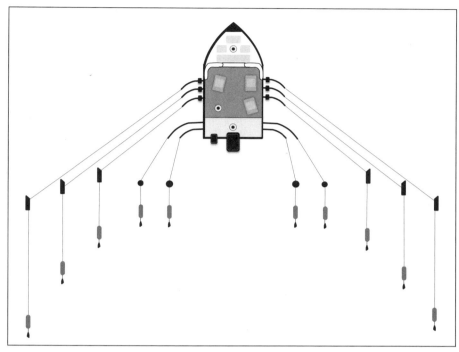

By adding more lines, anglers can create more commotion, which attracts coho.

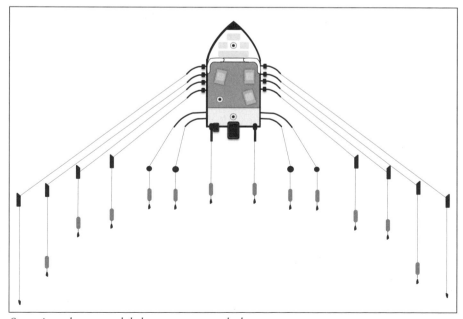

Some times the more red dodgers you put out, the better.

back 30 to 60 feet minimized the impact of the waves and surge and provided just the action that the coho wanted.

You may be wondering about downrigging for spring coho. To be honest, downriggers work great, but the truth is you can catch more coho off divers and boards. With downriggers for coho I prefer orange weights. Remember, coho love red and orange! I usually choose the 00 red dodger and flies set back 5 to 30 feet behind the weight. Some days, however, coho won't hit riggers in shallow water.

Downriggers are more productive over deep water. When fishing in water deeper than 50 feet, the 00 red dodgers set from 10 feet down to 30 feet will produce fish. During the spring, another consistent coho catcher, especially for larger coho, is an 8-inch flasher set for kings. These are run anywhere from 30 to 80 feet deep.

A Few More Tricks for Spring Coho

Integrating planers and divers for coho is easy. When your divers set just out of sight get hammered, try setting a planer 20 feet off the side on a 15-foot lead. In this scenario, coho are attracted to your boat's signature. A board just out to the side puts one more lure into an aggressive strike zone where *lit up fish* are easier to entice into striking.

If divers set to run slightly deeper, say on 50 to 100 feet of line, catch fish but your boards are dead, add more weight to your outside planers. I like to use 5/8-to 1-ounce keel sinkers, run the rig back at least 70 feet, and troll in a lazy, zigzag pattern. This will drop those flashers or dodgers down into the strike zone, and some days, these outside rods will be hot.

As spring transitions into summer, schools of coho scatter. The *June Swoon* can present some challenging fishing conditions. Anglers deploy a mix of spring tactics and summer tactics and lures to keep catching coho during this period. Locating fish is a daily challenge as some fish drop down in the water column and hang out in the zone where 48- to 54-degree water intersects the bottom. A second group of fish moves offshore and roams the vast open stretches. These offshore fish suspend from the surface to 30 feet down. They often mix with steelhead and lakers and surface breaks are your clues leading you to action.

When targeting the near shore fish, large metal dodgers and summer spoons will draw strikes. The offshore coho prefer the spring dodger and fly set ups and small spoons. One of my favorite presentations for transition coho are three-and four-color lead cores with 00 red dodgers and peanut flies or 1 inch flies. Some days, this is the only rod the coho hit! Any time you find summer coho suspending 15 to 30 feet down, this rig will take fish!

SUMMER COHO

Just as the seasons change, so do Mr. Coho's behavior and the watery environment in which he lives. Consequently, your techniques and lure selection need to change with the seasons if you want to keep catching fish.

While spring coho seem unaffected by weather changes, boat pressure, and any form of angler error, Mr. Coho has now entered his adolescence, and while he's not as moody as a king (or adolescent child), he can exhibit moments of lockjaw. In other words, he is not as easy to catch as he was in the spring. Coho are voracious feeders as they pack on weight in preparation for the fall spawning run. Many fish will double in size in just three or four months.

The watery world of Mr. Coho is also changing. In spring, the entire

Dodgers, flashers, and flies are the best lures for coho.

water column was cold. Now, as the lakes warm from the surface down, a thermocline sets up. This drives coho deeper in the water column. It also pushes many of them offshore. With the advent of a thermocline, wind-driven currents become more pronounced. These currents have a big impact on baitfish and predator locations. They also have a huge impact on lure presentation and trolling speeds, as is discussed in the chapter on currents.

Coho are a schooling fish that roam vast expanses of the lakes. You may find them close to shore, if conditions are favorable, or in the middle of the lake, literally. They seek out their ideal comfort zone and food. They are not structure oriented and are far less light sensitive than kings. They also prefer to suspend higher up in the water column than kings and lake trout.

Like all fish, water temperature is a key variable that can lead you to fish. Coho prefer 48- to 54-degree water. If bait is present, they will tolerate water up to 60 degrees for short periods of time. Coho that oriented themselves along the shoreline in spring begin sliding out to deeper water as the water warms.

While kings will drop down in the water column, coho respond to warming water in one of two general ways. Some schools will suspend in the top 20 to 50 feet and move offshore to roam the deeper parts of the lakes. One June, prior to the ridiculously expensive fuel prices, we chased schools of coho 20 miles offshore before we quit following them. Offshore coho are nomadic and strike spring presentations well into summer.

Other schools of coho will migrate parallel to the shoreline and drop deeper in the water column. These fish seek out cold water and may descend down to depths of 100 feet or more. Most of these fish, however, suspend from 30 to 70 feet down. In a typical year, you will find schools that follow both patterns. No matter where you find coho, they prefer to feed in the thermocline and just below it. If bait is present above the thermocline, they will race into the warmer water to feed.

Coho are a nomadic fish that travel great distances within the individual lakes. While they can turn up just about anywhere, it is ultimately the currents, water temperature, and forage that determine their location.

As you build a well-thought out plan to target summer coho, remember the basics:
- Coho are aggressive feeders.
- Nomadic and move great distances.
- Prefer to feed in and just below the thermocline.
- Often found suspending between 30 to 70 feet down.
- Less structure-oriented than kings.
- Downriggers, divers, copper, and lead core are all effective tools to present lures.
- Dodgers and flies are the most effective lures.

Lure Selection for Summer and Fall Coho

As coho descend down in the water column, the lager 0 size metal dodgers in yellow, silver, silver glow, and green work best. Yes, the plastic flashers will take loads of fat summer coho, but truthfully, if you are targeting coho, the metal dodgers are far more productive. Leader lengths from the dodger to the fly vary from 18 to 24 inches. If the fish are aggressive or the water is calm, shorter leaders are best. Negative fish or rough water calls for longer leaders.

Before moving on, let's get one thing straight: many anglers believe that metal dodgers must be *swishing* from side to side in order to catch fish, but to make a dodger *swish,* you have to troll at slower speeds of 1.5 to 2.0 kts. (1.7 to 2.3 mph). Many days, however, you can troll at faster speeds, and a *spinning* dodger is the best presentation. In other words, feel free to spin dodgers at higher speeds. Just make sure you use a quality ball bearing swivel on the nose of the dodger. When I troll at faster speeds with dodgers, I like to run longer leaders of 24 to 28 inches between the dodger and the fly. This slows down the *whip* of the fly.

Metal dodgers work off downriggers, divers, coppers, lead core, and wire lines with ball weights or Torpedoes. When targeting coho with dodgers on downriggers, it is best to run them 5 to 15 feet behind the cannonball—the disturbance of the ball seems to attract these aggressive fish. Leads off divers can be 5 to 12 feet back.

Productive fly size can vary, but the standard size 4-inch flies work well. Shades of greens and aqua are the most productive. Other colors such as pearls, pearl blues, mirage, and the old-fashioned white also take plenty of coho. If action slows, try a well-worn fly that is no more than one or two inches long. When running these old flies, only run one or two beads beneath the fly.

Plastic flashers are also great for summer coho. Spin Doctors in shades of yellow, chartreuse, green (the Green Nuclear), glow, and the assorted frog patterns are some of my favorites. Spinnies can be run anywhere but work best off divers, coppers, and lead core. Other flashers such as Hot Spots, Pro Trolls, and Coyotes also work.

Productive summer coho spoons are as varied as the people who use them. If I had to pick a handful of spoons to run, it would be the number 5 Diamond King, Super Slims, standard-size Stingers, and Silver Streaks, both regular and magnum size. Favorite spoon patterns include the Ludington Special, Carmel and Green Dolphin, Old Yeller, and Orange and Red Gangster. Truth is hot spoon colors change from day to day, so get creative!

Summer Tactics

Whether you run to the deeps or fish closer to shore, you can find coho early in the morning feeding in the upper reaches of the thermocline. Early in the day, coho are aggressive, and your boat attracts fish. A large metal dodger choked 5 to 10 feet off a downrigger is a hot rod at sunrise. Typically, my boom downriggers, rigged with 10-pound pancake weights, are my most productive coho rods at dawn. I believe that a 10-pound pancake moves around more in the water than a heavier weight. This additional motion triggers many strikes. At times, a chartreuse Stinger pancake weight really draws the coho into your spread. If you are targeting summer kings, you will most likely have plastic flashers on the riggers. If you want to catch big coho, add a few metal dodgers to the spread.

Summer coho are aggressive by nature, so running wire or braid divers just outside your riggers will create more commotion and attract feeding coho into your spread. On overcast and choppy days, this loud spread can produce fish all day long. Other days, and especially on bright, calm days and/or when coho are holding in the 20- to 40-foot layer, you must fan your divers off to the side.

If the aggressive spread doesn't work, then mix in some stealthier presentations. Keep the metal dodgers on your downriggers, but kick your divers out to the side. Add lead core and coppers out on boards. Lengths of lead and copper will depend on how far down you are targeting. Spoons and dodgers, flashers, and flies all work off planer lines. While spring coho were not super fussy, lure speed is now a big factor. Just like targeting kings, you will need to experiment with speeds and angles. Coho are a schooling fish. Once you find fish, chances are good that more coho are in the neighborhood.

While enticing summer coho into striking is not difficult, boating coho over 8 pounds is a challenge. Big coho are great fighters that spin and twist. Their twisting and spinning antics easily snap leaders and result in many lost fish and colorful descriptions from the angler left holding the empty line. When fighting coho, never stop reeling, even if you *think* line isn't coming in. This will compensate, sometimes, for the quick bursts coho make toward the boat. Often, it is this momentary slack line that allows the coho to spin and escape. Also, try increasing your trolling speed. This will help get a better hook set. If you speed up and the fish stop striking, slow back down.

If you are missing lots of strikes off your riggers or divers, tighten the release up! Make the fish fight to pull the line off the release. Many days, I will set my Blacks Releases so tight that the angler who picks up the rod has to help pull the line off the weight. Another key factor is to use No. 2 short-shank hooks on flies. You will boat more fish with this hook. Coho are notorious for spinning and escaping. After every strike, inspect the fly. Make sure the leader line is not wrapped in the backside of the hook.

If you have an opportunity to go after coho this season, don't let the chance slip away. They may not be the biggest fish in the pond, but what they lack in size, they more than make up for with their willingness to bite. Their schooling tendencies and aggressive nature lead to fast action and frequent doubles and triples. When it comes to eating, they are hands down the best eating salmonid found in our fishery. Whether grilled, baked, or pan fried in coconut oil, they are dynamite!

CHAPTER 8

All Day Kings

A myth widely circulated among Great Lakes anglers perpetuates the belief that big kings can only be caught at sunrise. But is the early bite the only time you can catch big numbers of kings? Do they really stop biting the remainder of the day? Believe it or not, if you adjust your strategies, pay close attention to the environment, and fine-tune your presentations and fishing location, you can catch these magnificent breasts from sunrise to sunset.

Before diving into the tactics, lures, and thought processes involved in making decisions for all-day Chinook action, let's explore a few of the basic characteristics that influence king salmon behavior. Your strategies will be far more productive if they are specifically engineered to the patterns these great fish follow. Kings like to eat, prefer cold water, and are structure oriented. Their general temperature range is 42 to 54 degrees, but their ideal range is 42 to 48 degrees.

Based on scientific data and countless hours of angler observations from all around the Great Lakes, we now realize that king salmon move around in the water column, and within the individual lakes, much more than we ever realized. King salmon are a pelagic species prone to making long migrations. Many Pacific Ocean kings travel 1,000 miles or more in their lifetimes. Some strains travel across the northern Pacific, and some strains migrate hundreds of miles up coastal rivers to spawn.

The migration patterns of Great Lakes kings can be analyzed from several perspectives. On the macro level, kings make seasonal migrations that may take them across the length and breadth of an individual lake several times during their four-year life spans. Based on fin clip data, we now know that some kings born in Lake Huron tributaries migrate to Lake Michigan for part of their lives and return to Lake Huron to spawn. Other fish stocked at one end of a Great Lake will be caught on the far shore. The migration patterns of Great Lakes kings are closely tied to the seasonal warming and cooling of the lakes, baitfish availability, and the spawning urge. In other words, to find kings we must key on the fish's desire for comfort, food, and sex.

King salmon also make daily horizontal movements parallel and perpendicular to the shoreline: they move down the shoreline, out deep, and back toward shore. Kings frequently move shoreward to feed at night and are sometimes chased out deeper by boat pressure or increasing light levels. Currents, which often parallel the shoreline, also move baitfish along the shoreline, and kings follow the bait.

Additionally, we now realize that kings make vertical movements up and down in the water column throughout the day. These vertical movements are heavily influenced by sunlight and the need to feed. To catch kings throughout the day, you need to adjust your lures up or down, and you might have to change your trolling location relative to the shoreline.

Where you find fish over the course of the day changes because the world beneath the waves looks very different, from Mr. King's perspective,

Big kings are one of the most exciting fish to catch in fresh water! This beast was taken in the middle of the day way deep.

as the amount of sunlight entering the water column transitions from the dark of night to the bright hours of midday, back to darkness. Waves and clouds also affect light intensity below the surface. If the wind kicks up the seas, light penetration below the surface will be different than on a flat, calm day. If clouds increase or decrease, the world beneath the surface will look subtly different, based on how much light is penetrating the water column.

King salmon are highly sensitive to light! Many experienced anglers believe kings do not like an overabundance of light. As light penetration into the water column changes, lures and presentations look different to the fish from one hour to the next. Successful anglers have learned that they might need to change lure colors, sizes, brands, lead lengths, and presentations as they tweak the trolling dynamic of their spread and keep lines popping. If you visit my boat at the dock, you will notice different lures on my rods after an afternoon charter compared to what I started with early on the morning run.

The world of Mr. King Salmon has a rhythm, and we need to adjust our fishing strategies and lure selection to capitalize on that rhythm. Many anglers take to the water, set lines early, catch some fish, then sit back, relax, and don't make any adjustments! Nothing wrong with relaxing on the water, but if you want to keep reels singing, you have to invest a little sweat. You might have to change lures and switch presentations or move to a different location. There is a bit of an *art* to knowing when to change lures and when to let the A-team ride. Let's unpack the fine points of slamming kings throughout the day.

EARLY MORNING KINGS

Early morning is an exciting time to be on the water! As the sun casts its first rays of golden, pink light across the water, kings come to life. Schools of large, feeding fish move up in the water column and often seem to hit just about anything you put in the water. These fish are on the hunt. Like a car full of teenage boys pulling into McDonalds after football practice, these fish are hungry and eagerly scramble to the front of the line. These early morning fish are relatively easy to catch.

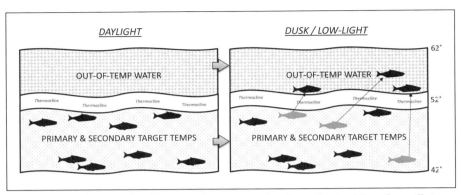

King salmon make vertical and horizontal movements though out the day. They often will rise up into warmer water during low light conditions to feed. At times, they will move shoreward, into warmer water to feed, and retreat back to cooler, deeper water during the day. Anglers who dial their strategies into these movements catch kings all day long.

Kings frequently make vertical movements up in the water column and horizontal movements shoreward during the night. Anglers who take to the water before sunrise often find kings higher in the water column than during midday hours. These early morning fish often feed throughout all the layers of the thermocline, as well as in the colder zone below.

As sunlight invades the day, kings retreat deeper into the water column. Many days, the action comes to a grinding halt, and kings all but vanish from the sonar screen. Fish that made horizontal movements into shallower water frequently retreat back to deeper water and drop down to the bottom.

If kings move up and in during the cover of night, how far in do they move? I used to think I knew everything about this, but my buddy Jim Kauth taught me that I don't know everything and need to leave room to be surprised. Jim and I have a unique relationship. He can help me fix anything in my house and I can dial him into the fish throughout the season.

The story begins with my buddy planning on fishing the full moon night bite from his 20-foot Alumacraft. Before going fishing, Jim called, and I told him exactly where to fish. Fishing was on fire! We were targeting the 70- to 100-foot level early in the morning and then sliding out to deeper water for the remainder of the day. I assumed Jim would do well by fishing in that range.

The following morning, I was driving to my boat around 4 a.m. and I called Jim, who had been fishing all night. From the tone in his voice, it was quite apparent that he was a bit excited. I could hear all kinds of shouting in the background as Jim told me, "we only need one more king for our three-man (15 fish) limit!" Being an astute angler, I immediately asked him if he was in the 70-foot range. To my surprise, Jim told me that they were about 1.5 miles inside of *where all the kings were supposed to be*. They were absolutely pounding the fish in 40 to 55 feet of water.

Since they were nowhere near where the fleet had been fishing all week, I assumed he was catching smaller fish, but Jim let me know that they were catching large, mature kings! What a surprise. Jim, a recreational angler, was absolutely beating on the fish, way inside of where the "experienced" charter fleet had been fishing all week. He made a huge haul of big fish in 45 to 55 feet, in the middle of the night. The lesson we can learn? Those fish were not in that zone during the daylight hours when the fleet was working the waters. They had moved up (vertically) in the water column and moved horizontally toward the shore into warmer, shallower water to feed. While I had assumed the fish had stopped their shoreward feeding movement at 60 feet because the water got too warm, Jim discovered that schools of fish had moved much closer to shore, into warmer water (54 to 60 degrees) to feed under the cover of darkness. Jim capitalized on this and made a big catch!

So, just how far will kings move horizontally in the water column at night or early in the morning? This varies form region to region and ultimately depends on water temps, forage availability, and structure. I don't think they will swim through 3 miles of 70-degree water for a meal, but shorter distances are a real possibility. In the weeks following Jim's big nighttime catch, I started my early morning charters fishing closer to shore (usually 1/2 to 1 mile) and caught fish in areas I had previously driven past. My largest king that year was a beast taken early in the morning following this principle of horizontal movement.

The point I want you to understand is that off your homeport, you might find kings closer to shore than you ever considered fishing during low-light conditions. Keep track of weather conditions and *where* you catch fish. Start identifying patterns and trends off your port.

As discussed in *Keating on Kings,* the ideal temperature range for kings is 42 to 48 degrees. A secondary range extends up to roughly 54 degrees. To catch kings in the middle of the day, you need to fish in cold water. Early in the morning, however, you can often find kings on the warm side of their comfort zone, in water in the 52- to 58-degree range. A good rule to follow is to look for the intersection of 42- to 54-degree water and the bottom. If there is bait in that zone early in the morning, chances are good that some kings will be feeding close by. If a lot of bait is within a mile (to the warm side) of the 54-degree water, kings might move up into this warmer water (55 to 60 degrees) to feed, even when it is a mile or more away from the colder water. In some regions, anglers have documented kings venturing into even warmer water, closer to shore, to feed. In other parts of the Great Lakes, they stay over the deeper, colder water but swim up and feed throughout all layers of the thermocline. Structure, water temperature, the presence of baitfish, and currents all influence fish movements.

Early Morning Tactics

Because the morning bite is short lived, we want to start fishing in an area that has fish! Water temperature and the presence of baitfish are the two variables that will lead you to fish. If I leave the dock before sunrise, I run

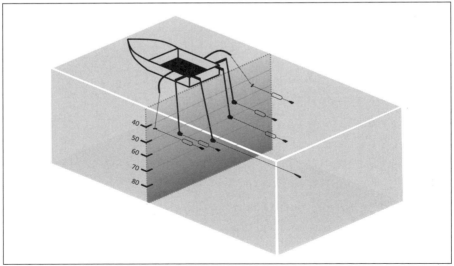

Early in the morning kings are aggressively feeding. An aggressive spread of tightly-spaced flashers and flies will draw more fish into your inner group dynamic, and trigger strikes.

out to the level where cold water intersects the bottom. As I approach this zone, I will slow down, in slightly warmer water, adjust the gain on my sonar, and look for signs of life—bait balls and game fish marks. If I see life, I will set up; if not, I will go out to deeper, colder water and look for life. To capitalize on the early bite, you want to set up as quickly as possible in the pre-dawn darkness. If you struggle with boat control and the wind is up, you may want to set up trolling with the wind.

If you hit the water at first light, an aggressive spread of flashers and flies is devastating on local king populations. The key to catching kings with flashers and flies is *where* and *how* you set them within your spread. At first light (before sunrise to 30 minutes after sunrise) a tight spread of flashers set close to one another will draw more attention and strikes than a spread that has individual flashers spread out.

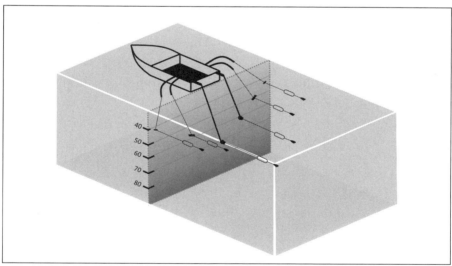

This 4 diver, 2-downrigger spread allows small boat anglers with a limited tackle selection to catch big numbers of kings.

As you think about your spread, visualize what all your lures look like from the fish's perspective. I believe that a group of flashers moving through the water together looks like a school of baitfish to kings on the hunt. Early in the morning alewives and other baitfish *ball* up into compact schools. I am creating a school of bait beneath my boat. Salmon and trout are moving around, hungry, and looking to feed. Tightly-grouped flashers *swimming* through the water will be more visible and audible from a greater distance. The fish will see the overall impact of your spread, move in, and target single lures.

The second reason to run a tight spread is that multiple hook ups are common. When kings feed in low light, they are aggressive and competing with one another. You want to set your lines in such a way that capitalizes on this brief feeding frenzy. When a *lit up* king races in and slams a bait, a second (and at times, a third or fourth fish!) will race in and hit remaining lures.

Let's look at several rod spreads (the inner group dynamic) for boats of all sizes. Early in the morning, my downriggers and divers are usually the most productive rods. You can strategically implement this four to seven rod spread in a variety of sets including two downriggers and two divers, four downriggers and two divers, or three downriggers and two to four divers. Which combination of rods you run depends on your experience level, boat beam, and number of anglers aboard. If you are short on riggers or don't have riggers, deploy multiple divers or Torpedoes. Side planers can be added to this spread at any time. I typically start the day with four downriggers and one diver off each side.

Faster trolling speeds, 2.3 kts. (2.7 mph) or greater, make setting lines easier. I set divers first by placing the diver in the water, letting it out about 20 feet, engaging the reel, and placing the rod in it's holder. I loosen the drag just enough so that the trolling motion pulls the diver out at a steady pace (it is not in a free-fall). It is not unusual for the divers to get smashed as they are creeping out! When this happens, the drag must be set to fighting tension immediately, so the fish doesn't spool the reel.

As the diver creeps out, I set the downriggers. I run 12-pound cannonball weights off the corners and 10-pound pancakes off the booms. If I am fishing a heavy current or targeting way deep kings, I will upgrade to 15-pound cannonballs on the corners and 12-pound pancakes on the booms. The fin on the pancake is slightly bent, maybe 10-degrees, so the weight planes away from the boat a bit. This horizontally opens up the inner group dynamic at depth.

Horizontal stretches from the weight to the lures on the deepest corner rigger running a flasher is 15 to 20 feet. The boom flashers are stretched back 8 to 15 feet. I position a diver off each side, so it runs as a *teammate* with each boom downrigger. The diver rig is set to run about 5 to 10 feet above the downrigger bait and slightly to the side. Once the rods are set, the overall pattern of the inner group dynamic looks like a V moving through the water. The boundaries of the lures in the inner group dynamic extend 10 to 20 feet astern and roughly 5 to 10 feet off to each side. I typically start with five flasher/flies and one spoon. If flies are super hot, all rods get a fly.

If you only have two down riggers, then create two separate teams—a port team and a starboard team. Each team will consist of a rigger and a diver. Run one flasher 10 feet off the weight and the other 15 to 20 feet back. The divers should be set to flank the rigger baits slightly higher in the water column.

Many days, one diver a side will produce more kings than when two or more are in the water per side. You can, however, easily add a second diver to the early morning spread. This will help you maximize the early bite and make your *school of lures* look a little larger and more appealing to Mr. King Salmon. In this scenario, set the divers in a wing pattern. The rigger will be the deepest line, and each diver will be roughly 5 to 10 feet higher in the water column. When running this spread, the magnum divers track straighter, minimize tangles, and hold their position tighter horizontally to your downriggers. If running multiple divers causes tangles, try running a magnum diver on your low diver and a regular diver higher in the water column. Set the deep diver to a 1.5 and the high diver on a 2 or 2.5 setting. This slight variation will reduce tangles. Again, every boat fishes differently, and you may have to adjust diver settings to minimize tangles in your own spread.

When running a three-rigger spread, set the boom riggers and divers as described in the preceding paragraph. You can set the middle rigger in a variety of ways. Try running an 11-inch paddle on a 25-foot lead and run it deepest in the spread. Another tactic is to run a clean spoon below and slightly behind the other riggers—a set sometimes referred to as a "tailgunner." Then some days, just run the middle rigger with an 8-inch flasher fly and adjust it throughout the strike range.

Here's what this all looks like for a scenario where the fish are feeding in the 40- to 60-foot layer. Facing the stern, the four riggers are numbered from one to four (left to right). The number one rigger is set 50 feet down, lure stretched 12 feet back. The number two rigger goes down 60 feet with the flasher 20 feet behind it. The number three rigger keeps the fish honest with a spoon set in one of two ways: a clean spoon run on 12-pound test line set 70 feet down and stretched back 25 feet or a Secret Weapon Rig set at 40 feet. The number four rigger is set 55 feet down with a 10-foot stretch. A diver would be set to run just above and outside the number one and number four riggers in this spread.

The entire group represents a school of baitfish. Within the big picture, you have two smaller dynamics. The three flashers on the one side are a team. On the opposite side, the number four rigger and the diver are a separate team, running together. The lone spoon is either just below and behind the entire group or set on a long lead in it's own world—the injured straggler that's an easy meal.

Knowing how far down and where all your gear is actually running is key to success. If your inner group dynamic doesn't produce at first light, then running glow spoons on coppers and lead cores is well worth trying. Many anglers also like to launch glow Spin Doctors and Pro Trolls on coppers at first light. These lines, usually taken out to the side on inline planer boards, take longer to set than riggers and divers but work extremely well on staging kings.

LISTEN TO THE FISH—MAKE ADJUSTMENTS

The aggressive, tightly-spaced spread discussed above is dynamite, but some days, you might have to make some adjustments. Here is a typical progression and some tricks to tweaking I use on my charter boat to dial in my morning spread. I often start with a same-color, same-size flasher spread at dawn, usually an 8-inch flasher (they may be a different brand). If that doesn't fire up, I'll add a single yellow or green flasher in with the white-based flashers. Other times, inserting one 10- or 11-inch paddle in the spread works. The big paddle should be stretched 20 to 40 feet off a down-

Making adjustments to your spread will keep kings biting all day long.

rigger. Sometimes, a single, chrome Luhr Jensen 0 dodger with a mirage/pearl blue Howie or Super Frog set 8 feet off the weight, and just above the plastic flashers, brings the entire spread to life.

If the tightly-spaced inner group dynamic isn't working, start spreading your riggers and divers out. Drop a corner rigger well below the other rigs. If the fish are cautious, this lone rigger well below the group can trigger strikes. It will also help you determine when fish are dropping down in the water column. I often set a spoon on this deep rigger, but some days, a flasher fly produces more strikes. Divers are set to run further out to the side or go to Slide Divers.

If a clean spoon stretched 10 to 20 behind a group of flashers isn't working, try stretching the spoon on a longer lead off the rigger, anywhere from 50 to 150 feet back. This rod will tell you when it is time to transition your downriggers and divers to stealth mode. Some days, setting an SWR high in the water column, above the other riggers, really hammers big kings. Staging, mature kings sometimes roam the upper layers of the thermocline at first light. I will also reduce the amount of flashers I'm running on riggers in favor of clean spoons.

If the riggers and divers don't catch fish out of the gate, by all means, put your lead cores or copper rigs in the water. Leads and coppers are stealth presentations that appeal to fish that are boat shy or have taken a negative posture. Even if you only run one or two stealth rods off the side, these rods are your barometers. When the fish start striking side planers, it is time to transition most of your aggressive downrigger rods to stealth mode and add more side planers.

Early Morning Lure Selection

Many great lures are on the market today. The point I'm trying to make here is not so much that you have to have one particular lure to catch fish. Rather, combinations of lure types, run properly on the right presentation for the job and in relation to the entire group, will catch more fish.

Early morning kings are aggressive, so it is a good idea to run aggressive lures that appeal to their temperament. Flashers and flies are the ideal lures for these fish. Flashers are a visual stimulant, and they give off vibrations that the fish can *feel* with their lateral line. Faster trolling speeds up to 2.7 kts. (3.1 mph) will trigger strikes and provide better hookups from feeding fish.

Some of the more popular flashers are Spin Doctors, Hot Spots, Coyotes, DW Paddles, and Pro Trolls. Favorite flasher colors and patterns vary from region to region and year to year. Dominant base colors of white, yellow, green, and silver are available plain or woven into a myriad of different patterns, such as Dreamweaver's Chrome Frog Spin Doctor. Glow, UV, and prism tapes can often help trigger strikes. If you don't know which brand of flasher to run, start with several varieties and let the fish tell you their preference. I often start with a mix of Hot Spots, Spin Doctors, and Coyotes. If one brand is hot, change up the slow rods.

Early in the morning and when waves are choppy, I like to run new, full-bodied flies. There are many flies on the market, but two historically productive flies are the Howies and A-Tom-Miks. These 4-inch flies come in a zillion colors, and anglers in each region have their favorites. Select fly color based on target depth and sky conditions. Typically, shades of green and mirage work best in the top 70 feet, and pearl-blues, pearls, whites, and glows work in the zones below 70 feet. The one fly color that transcends all depths is aqua. In recent years, flies that incorporate several different colors, such as the Howie *Bull Frog, Super Frog,* and *57 Special Flat,* have been stud baits at all levels.

How long should the fly leader be? The quick answer is that shorter leads result in more action being imparted to a fly. Longer leads slow the action of the fly. A general rule is to start with your leaders three vertical wraps from the back of the flasher to the hook. For an 8-inch flasher, this is 21 to 24 inches. If I am trolling at faster speeds during the middle of the day, sometimes, longer leads, 24 to 28 inches, will slow the action on the fly and trigger strikes. A comprehensive discussion on lure selection can be found in the DVD, *Keating on Kings Part 2, Lure Selection and Advanced Techniques.* Leader length pros and cons are discussed in the previous DVD and *Keating on Kings, Great Lakes Chinook Tactics Way Beyond the Basics.*

Spoons can also be incorporated into an early morning spread. Among my favorites are the Moonshines. Many glow spoons are on the market, but the finish on the Moons is the best. Both the standard and mag sizes work. Favorite early morning Moonshines include the RV Blue Jackal, RV Dancing Anchovy, the RV Blue Flounder Pounder, Green Flounder Pounder, and the RV Holdout. Other deadly early morning spoons include Dreamweaver Super Slims in Chicken Wing, Orange and Red Gangster, and Carmel Dolphin. Magnum Stingers in Dr. Hook, the regular size Ludington Special, and the Reverse Puke Silver Streak are other reliable fish-catchers.

MID MORNING BLUES

You know the saying, *all good things come to an end . . .* I know that feeling all too well out on the water. After a ferocious start to the day, the sun starts climbing higher into the sky, and everything changes! We've all been there. It's a humbling experience. One minute, you think you're going to run out of room in the cooler and before you know it, you're trying to remember if it's been 30 or 45 minutes since your last strike.

This key transitional period in the day separates the men from the boys. The truth is, many anglers just quit trying after the morning bite ends. My parents didn't raise any quitters, and I've learned that if you pay attention to the clues the environment and the fish give you, make some adjustments, and focus on three key areas, you can catch big kings all day long. The three areas to focus on are location, fine tuning lure selection, and learning how to properly set and adjust our lines.

Let's look at location first. To help explain how I analyze conditions and make decisions to keep catching kings throughout the day, I have developed a three-option approach:

- Option 1—Don't give up! Continue to fish in the area that was hot at dawn and wait for the fish to fire up again. Kings often feed hard at first light, go negative, and then start feeding again mid-morning. Some days, a different group of kings moves in on the bait that held fish at a specific location at first light. If this new school has not fed, the mid morning action can be fast.
- Option 2—Troll out to slightly deeper water (usually a ½ to 2 miles farther out than the early bite) and finesse negative fish from the lower levels of the water column. Kings that moved up and in at first light frequently drop down into cooler, darker water during the day.
- Option 3—"The Hail Mary Pass." Some days, the best plan is to run (or troll) offshore to deeper water and look for a different school of fish. Out there, you can target deep water kings, which tend to be more aggressive than kings holding in shallow and mid levels. You might also find a different species, such as steelhead or lakers.

Each of the three preceding options has merit, and I utilize all three approaches throughout the season. How do you make the best decision each trip? Before discussing the strategies used to catch fish in each scenario, let's examine the variables that can lead you to make the right call on any particular day. The goals of this book are to teach you how to think through various situations, analyze the clues available, and learn to make wise decisions on the water. Sounds a bit like life, eh?

Key variables I analyze to help determine *where* and *how* to fish include water temperature and clarity, sky conditions, surface texture, sonar, boat traffic, radio chatter, yearly patterns, weather, and the presence of baitfish. The right interpretation of these factors will lead you to active fish.

Water temperature is the primary variable that makes the lake smaller and helps you avoid trolling in dead water. Let's assume that you set up in the Option 1 area and caught a bunch of big kings at sunrise. Now, as you analyze the day, ask yourself: was I catching fish in cold water (42 to 50 degrees) at first light? Or was the early bite in warmer water (54 to 60 degrees)? Or did the early morning fish come way out of temp in 60-degree water or warmer? If the water is warmer than 54 degrees, kings will be tough to catch during the day. If the water is 54 degrees or cooler, even tight to the bottom, then some kings may stay in the area. The colder the water, the more likely kings will be around. If the water is warm, then it is usually time to get out of there!

Is the lake flat calm and sky sunny or is there a chop on the water? Is the water gin clear or is there a tint or stain? Kings don't like bright light so super clear water, calm seas, and bright skies tend to drive kings out and deeper. Murky water minimizes light penetration, and kings often stick around in darker water as long as the water is cold.

Did you mark fish at first light and did the marks disappear? Or are you still marking fish? If the marks are still there and the water cold, then I will try and catch them! If the marks disappeared, you have to ask yourself if the fish left. Or if the lake is flat calm and the sky sunny, is it possible the fish are still in the area and being spooked by your boat? If that is the case, then you might be able to catch them with stealth presentations off side planers.

What about bait? Was the graph full of bait at dawn, but the clouds of forage fish disappeared as the day brightened? If the bait is gone, chances are the fish have moved elsewhere. If bait and cold water are present, you might want to think about toughing it out and waiting for the fish to turn on or for another school of kings to move into the bait. Many anglers will adjust their presentations and finesse kings into striking.

Kings do not like pressure, and boat traffic tends to scatter schools of fish. All the cables, lines, lures, engine, and sonar noise spook kings. Fishing boats congregate at first light. As the action tapers off, many anglers follow the crowds. This can be a huge mistake! I do not like getting stuck in the middle of a pack that is drifting off to deeper water. If you were working kings at first light and the other boats leave, but you are still marking bait, and the water is cold, consider staying in the area a little longer. Kings often turn back on again once the traffic thins out.

Experience is a wonderful teacher. One morning, I had an 8 a.m. start time because my clients showed up late. I was pretty sure we would have a so-so day with the late start. As I ran out to the fishing grounds, I could see a large pack of boats drifting toward deeper water. I knew the other boats did well in Zone 1 at first light, so I decided to set up there, even though a friend called and told me the fish had quit biting. The water was cold, so I began setting lines and had the area completely to myself. I quickly discovered that the kings were still hitting! On this day, once all the traffic cleared out, the fish moved back into the bait and continued to feed. Lesson learned: if the pack is drifting off to deeper water, fish that were *spooked* out of the area often return to the structure if cold water and bait are present. Boat traffic really can make or break a location, so don't follow the crowd. Learn to circle back on fish after others have left.

Once you've made a decision on which location to fish, you need to have a plan. Let's look at some of the specific ways to approach each of the preceding three scenarios and the lures to run.

TACTICS AND STRATEGIES OPTION 1

If you find cold water, baitfish, and light boat traffic, then slugging it out with kings after the early bite ends is often an excellent plan. This happened to be the case on one Saturday in July recently. At this time, we had a strong king bite going in 70 to 90 feet of water during the week. Along came Saturday. The weather forecast was stellar, and a number of club tournaments were set for the weekend.

This particular Saturday, my morning charter was scheduled to begin at 6 a.m. No amount of persuasion could convince my group to start earlier. Most of the fleet left port between 3:30 and 5 a.m. Not me! Six o'clock came and went, and my boat was the only boat still tied up at the dock. Late, again! I retied a few leaders and listened to my buddies talk about how good the early bite was and how they were running out of room in their coolers . . . blah, blah, blah. No problem, I love starting a game being

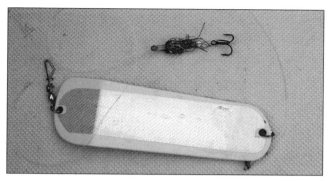

Sometimes running a sparse fly is what big, moody kings want. The fish on the cover of this book fell for the fly and flasher in this picture!

down 21-0! Finally, my guys found the harbor, and after what seemed like an eternity to park their car and walk to the boat, we were off. By the time we were under power, it was 6:45 a.m.! At this time of year, sunrise was shortly after 5:00 a.m., so for all practical purposes, we had missed the early bite.

I must confess something: I was more than a little perturbed with my group. Not only had I tried to talk them into a pre-dawn start to beat the crowds, but they were late! Not only did we miss the easy fishing, but we had lost valuable fishing time. With all the tournaments going on, everyone was going to be fishing their A-game. With our late start, the stage was set for me to look like a real looser! Don't ever let anyone tell you charter captains are not competitive.

As we ran east, the lake looked like the invasion of Normandy. From north to south in 70 to 100 feet of water, a band of boats a mile wide extended from Kenosha, Wisconsin to Winthrop Harbor, Illinois to Waukegan, Illinois. I should add that the lake was flat calm, and there was not a cloud in the sky. It was easy to believe all the reports that said the fish had shut off with a slam.

My plan was to blow through the fleet, run offshore, and find fish that had not been disturbed by the invasion. As I approached the fleet, I realized I would have to slow down and carefully zigzag through all the boats and side planers. Looking at my graph, I saw a thin strip of bait on the bottom and decided I would set up ½ mile inside of the fleet. At the end of my morning charter on the previous day, I had trolled into 50 feet of water and finished with a big flurry at 11 a.m.

I began setting lines in 55 feet and was hit almost immediately! By the time my lines were set, we were 4 for 7. To tighten up a long story, I worked the inside edge of the pack, staying about ½ mile inside the hundreds of boats, and took a 20-fish limit of mostly mature kings and large steelhead in just over three hours of fishing. Yes, Virginia, you can catch big kings on a sunny, flat calm day, even in relatively shallow water.

On this day, the huge pack of boats had spooked the fish. After the early bite, the fish shut down, and the heavy boat traffic pushed them to the inside or shallow side. The surface temp was in the mid 60s, but there was ice-cold water on the bottom (44 degrees) and plenty of bait to keep the fish from going deep. The water had a slightly greenish tint, as well. I was on stealth mode and had the fish to myself! I am convinced that if the fleet had realized the fish were going nuts just inside of the pack, the party would have quickly ended.

This day, the best option was to stay in the area that was producing at first light. As often happens, the fish fed hard at first light and backed off when the flotilla of boats invaded. The edge of a pack of boats is often a good place to fish. If cold water and bait are present, fish will often feed aggressively at first light then back off. As the morning wears on, either the same fish begin to feed again, or different fish that are hungry move into the area to feed.

If you choose Option 1, you may have to adjust your spread to stealth mode once the early bite ends. This is when it helps to have a variety of different presentations in the water. Learn to *listen* to the fish and the clues your lines give you. What in the world is Captain Dan talking about? If you have lead core or copper planers out and they start to get hit but your flashers on the downriggers are dead, change your riggers to stealth. Pull the flashers and put clean spoons on light line or Secret Weapon Rigs on the riggers.

I often keep one flasher or dodger on a boom rigger just to keep the fish honest. If the lone fly is triggering strikes, I will put a second flasher back on a rigger. Now, if adding a second flasher to your inner group dynamic shuts the first flasher down, go back to running only one flasher. Be creative and keep trying different blends of presentations and lead lengths until you connect. While I may start with four downriggers, I often streamline my inner group dynamic to two or three downriggers.

If you are limited on how many rods you can run, try various segments of coppers, lead cores, or Torpedoes off boards. Until I start getting steady bites, I aggressively adjust my lines throughout the potential strike zone as I try to determine where the active kings are holding. Divers may need to be adjusted to run farther out to the side than at first light. If divers are dead, try Slide Divers. Some days, fishing a spoon just off the bottom catches fish that don't show up on your graph. If you know fish are present and they won't bite, then adjust your trolling speed and angle. Often, it is the minor adjustments to these key details that will change the outcome of the day.

When everything comes together, big numbers of kings can be caught all day long!

Part of dialing into the fish involves tweaking your lure spread. Don't change every lure! Keep your dependable lures in the water, but do change some lures. Remember, as the day brightens, everything below the surface looks different. You often have to adjust lure colors once the sun is up. When targeting negative mid day kings with spoons the color, size, and brand of spoons can greatly impact success. Large kings often key off a particular sized spoon. For this reason, I aggressively change spoons. I don't change every rod, but I do systematically change several rods every 10 minutes or so. The goal is to dial into what the fish want. Once you identify a new pattern, you can adjust all the rods accordingly.

My favorite mid morning spoons include the Dr. Hook Stinger and Stingray, the UV Green Dolphin and Blue Dolphin Super Slim, the RV Wonderbread and Green Flounder Pounder Moonshine, the Kevorkian and Green Puke Stinger, and the magnum Reverse Puke Silver Streak, to name a few. Some days, sticking with the basics is best; other days, finding a new pattern steals the show. Experiment with flasher, dodger, and fly colors as sky conditions and light intensity change.

One last word on Option 1 . . . don't panic! On many days, the fish hit in flurries. Just because you had a slow hour, don't quit. I've had many trips where the mid and late morning produced great action.

TACTICS AND STRATEGIES OPTON 2

Option 2 is my favorite strategy. All around the Great Lakes, kings congregate in the 60- to 100-foot range at first light. The glaciation process that carved out the Great Lakes formed many drop offs in this range that tend to run parallel to the shoreline. Some of these drops are steep and others are gradual. These drops deflect and magnify currents and attract baitfish. (*Keating on Kings* examines the impact of structure on kings.)

Big kings feed along these drops in the 60- to 100-foot range at first light and then retreat to slightly deeper water. The actual depth of water varies by region, but 100 to 150 feet of water is a pretty typical range for these fish to set up in midday. In some northern ports, deep water can be found closer to shore, and kings may move out to 200 to 400 feet of water. Once kings leave the ledges, they may suspend outside the breaks, or they may drop down to the lower third of the water column. Some days, they will drop all the way down to the bottom. Kings that retreat to the bottom often evade detection by sonars. Option 2 is a great strategy, but you have to finesse these kings into striking.

The point to remember is that kings drop deeper in the water column

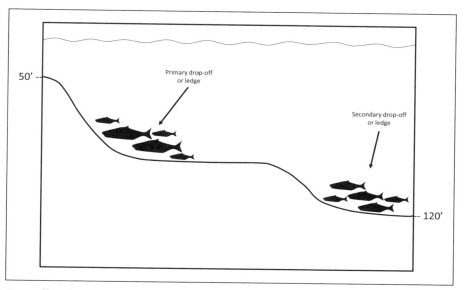

Drop offs and shelves typically run parallel to the shoreline on the Great Lakes. These breaks deflect currents and attract kings. For mid day action, target deeper break lines outside productive early morning drop offs.

during midday hours. If you targeted a drop off at first light, there may be another, more subtle, drop off in deeper water (directly offshore from the inside drop) that the fish will move out to during the day. I have a mark on my GPS that has produced plenty of big, late morning and mid afternoon kings. It is 1 mile outside the major 80 to 100 foot drop off. This particular shelf is about a ¼-mile long, and the bottom falls rapidly from 118 feet down to 130 feet. Also, look for areas where deeper water is closer to shore. For example, when you look at a contour chart, you might notice an area where the 130-foot contour line swings in closer to shore. These fingers or lobes of deep water often hold cold water and kings during the mid day hours. These subtle contour abnormalities alter currents. Any variation in the bottom or currents will attract fish.

What are the clues that suggest you should fish Option 2? Warm water or heavy boat traffic in the area you fished during first light are strong factors suggesting a move from Zone 1 to Zone 2. If you marked fish earlier and the marks disappeared, then sliding out to Zone 2 often puts you back into fish. Did the forage fish disappear from the graph? Clear skies and calm seas are variables that must be considered but are not conclusive in and of themselves. But, add warm water to calm seas, and this slight move is usually a good one. Truth is, some days kings just slide out to deeper water for no apparent reason.

Once I work up the courage to leave an area that was (or wasn't) producing fish (Zone 1), I troll at a perpendicular angle, heading out to deeper water, looking for signs of life. On the troll to deeper water, you should pay close attention to your graph, trolling angle, and speed. Watch your lines, too. If I begin to mark fish or get strikes, I level off and troll parallel to the shoreline. If the graph was empty and you suddenly mark some bait or game fish, you might want to make a pass parallel to the shoreline. Often, you will catch more kings on a troll parallel to the shore versus a perpendicular angle. This has to do with currents and getting your lures at the right speed at depth.

As you troll out into the lake, closely watch your lines. If you were trolling parallel to the shore earlier, you probably had a good angle and speed, and everything looked good. Now that you are trolling a different angle, heading away from the shoreline, your boat and lures will interact with the current differently. Currents often run parallel to the shoreline, so now the current might hit your lures from the side. This will require you to adjust your trolling speed and make course alterations. If your lines don't look right in the water, try making minor course adjustments. For example, instead of trolling on a straight 270 degree heading over ground, try angles of 280, 290, 300 and 260, 250, and 240 degrees. You get the idea. What you are doing as you look for fish is trying to determine the best speed and angle to trigger strikes. Many people just make two straight-line passes: one out to deeper water and one line back to the inside. While you are covering ground, you might troll right through a school of fish and never know it, because your tolling speed or angle was off.

I attack Zone 2 with a mix of aggressive and stealth presentations. If the fish are holding below 60 feet, the early morning flasher and fly program on the riggers and divers might keep producing fish as you slide deeper. You might need to pull a few flies and add some spoons or meat rigs. If the fish are in the top 60 feet, spoons might work better. Wire divers set deep or kicked off to the side are steady producers in Zone 2. Copper and lead core

This chinook hit a flasher and fly on a Dipsy Diver in the middle of the afternoon.

lines are two of the most productive presentations in Zone 2 during mid day hours. Both clean spoons and flashers with flies, such as Spin Doctors, work well on these lines. Often, a combination of tactics produces the best results when woven together.

As you slide out to deeper water, you want to adjust your lines between the thermocline and the bottom. Kings make vertical movements in this zone, so be aggressive as you look for them. Don't just set your lines and wait for them to come to you! Some days, mature kings zoom up to the thermocline when you least expect it. These fish are often feeding up there and strike stealth presentations off planer boards.

One of my favorite strategies for mid day hawgs is to drop one clean spoon down and trace the bottom. The spoon is run on 12-pound test line and set back about 50 feet off the rigger. When setting this line, set it from the bottom up. In other words, drop the rigger weight down to the bottom. After hitting the bottom, trolling pressure will pull the weight up off the bottom. Drop the weight a second time to the bottom. You might need to repeat this process a few times until the weight is right on the bottom. Once you've determined precisely how many feet of cable you need to reach the bottom, bring the rigger up so the weight runs 1 to 5 feet off the bottom.

Ideally, the weight and spoon will run just above the bottom, but not on the bottom. When *tracing* the bottom, you must make frequent rigger adjustments. I reconnect with the bottom every so often to make sure the current didn't alter the cannonball's position, and I check for debris every 15 minutes. If this rod starts to produce, consider dropping a wire diver deep off each side. Putting a second rigger on the bottom often causes enough disturbance to shut kings off, but since the divers are off to the side, all three lines can heat up.

You can, however, put a second spoon down along the bottom without putting another downrigger weight in the bottom zone! To do this, run a 3 or 4-color Secret Weapon Rig off another downrigger. Because of the weight of the lead core line, the spoon will run about 12 to 15 feet below the weight. The downrigger weight runs 15 to 20 feet above the deeper weight on the downrigger that is tracing the bottom. You can further minimize weight disturbance by using different size downrigger weights. I run a 15-pound ball for the bottom rod. The SWR runs off a 12-pound weight. To get the lighter weight down deep, I let out more cable, so this lighter weight runs significantly farther behind the deeper weight.

Big kings that hold just off the bottom are moody during the middle of the day. You might need to aggressively change spoons and flashers and flies on deep rods. Some days, it's just a matter of picking the right spoon or fly. When changing spoons, incorporate size, brand, overall color pattern, and surface patterns into your selection matrix. If spoons don't work, try a lone flasher and fly down by the bottom. Bottom-hugging kings are very fussy about what they will strike.

The beauty of Option 2 is that if the fish don't cooperate, you can easily slide back into Zone 1 where you caught fish earlier in the morning.

TACTICS AND STRATAGIES OPTION 3

If Options 1 and 2 are a bust, then it's time to go deep. While the idea of picking up lines and moving offshore to the middle of nowhere intimidates many anglers, let me assure you—some days this is the best option. Some anglers pull lines and run offshore; others will troll to the deeps. Fish are not evenly distributed everywhere offshore, so even though you might need

LAKE ONTARIO CHINOOK TACTICS FROM CAPTAIN RICHARD HAJECKI

Crazy Yankee Sportfishing www.crazyyankeesportfishing.com 585.704.7996

- Use your graph to locate schools of bait before setting lines.
- Kings favor 42- to 60-degree water, but the largest kings are caught in 41- to 42-degree water.
- When kings are suspending 20 to 40 feet down, spoons work best. For kings below 50 feet, flashers, flies, and meat rigs produce best.
- Target speed on his sub-troll is 2.0 mph.
- Capt. Rich's favorite presentations are wire divers with the white/green dot Spin Doctors and A-Tom-Mik Hammer flies.
- Favorite spoons for all species are the Dreamweaver *Sea Sick Wobbler* pattern in the Dreamweaver (regular and mag.), and Super Slims.
- During July and August, steelhead can be found suspending above kings in the water column. For summer fishing Capt. Rich locates the 60-degree water, and sets his lines from that level down.
- During spring Rich always keeps one rigger set between 125 and 150 feet.
- Lake Ontario currents are strong because the Niagara River is pushing a huge volume of water into the lake, and the St. Lawrence Seaway is pulling water out of the lake. Predominant currents run east and west, and intensify closer to the shore.
- When setting lines, view your spread three-dimensionally. This will minimize tangles and produce more fish. Capt. Rich says the real key to success is paying attention to small details!

to spend a little time hunting, once you find the productive level, numbers can add up fast.

Deep-water kings are easier to catch during the mid day hours than their cousins who haunt the lower layers of the water column closer in. They are more aggressive, less impacted by weather changes, and often feed throughout the day. You can strictly target kings, or you can set a multi-species oriented spread. It is fairly common to find kings, steelhead, lake trout, and coho suspending in the same areas offshore.

The same lures that produced inshore may work, but if you encounter gin clear water, you must tweak the colors. Since water clarity and target depths are often deeper, or shallower, than when you were fishing closer in, you may need to use a totally different spread of lures. But not always! Certain spoons and flies just seem to work wherever you find yourself.

As far as tactics, fish in open water can be caught on a variety of presentations. Fishing out in the "blue zone," as Lake Ontario guys call it, allows you to use a variety of different presentations. Ultimately, productive presentations depend on the depth you target. On any given day, you could find fish anywhere from the thermocline down to the bottom. For this reason, it is often a good idea to run a variety of different presentations to help you dial into the fish. For example, if the thermocline is higher up, then shorter segments of lead core and copper are productive. If the fish are holding deep, then riggers, coppers, and Torpedo SWRs and wire divers get the job done. You often find fish scattered throughout the water column. This is fun fishing and gives you tremendous flexibility. You can target steelhead higher in the water column, and kings, lakers, and coho down deep simultaneously. It's very easy to run a far-reaching spread of lines offshore.

Deep water kings are nomadic. Faster trolling speeds help you locate fish, and believe it or not, trolling fast is extremely productive. For this reason, using heavier downrigger weights of 12 to 15 pounds makes life easier. Another thing to keep in mind when hunting fish in open water is that some days you mark more fish trolling in one direction over another.

Kings are somewhat predictable and patternistic. Each season, they get into patterns. They do the same thing week after week, and there have been seasons when the deep water bite never happened. Many years, however, the deep water bite is dependable, making Option 3 a solid choice.

AFTERNOON AND EVENING STRATEGIES

I love fishing in the afternoon! Some of my best and heaviest career catches of big kings have been made after lunch. If you venture out in search of kings in the afternoon, you quickly learn you compete with far fewer boats than in the morning. This reason alone often leads to more fish—sort of like how sharing a pizza with one person instead of a crowd leaves you less hungry.

Can you catch kings in the afternoon? Yes! I run a fairly equal number of morning and afternoon trips each year. Over the course of the season, some weeks, the morning bite is better, and other weeks, the afternoon trips produce better action. This is often the result of local weather patterns and moon phases. During a full moon, fishing between 10 a.m. and 3 p.m. is usually excellent. I believe the fish feed all night, helped by the moonlight, and then have a second feeding period when the sun is high in the sky. Also, an approaching weather system can really turn on fish during the afternoon. My favorite time to chase kings is hot summer afternoons when a low-pressure system is moving in and storm clouds are brewing on the horizon.

If you head out early in the afternoon between noon and 2 p.m., you want to follow the suggestions made for the previous three options to help you determine where to begin fishing and how to set your lines. If it is really bright and the water is super clear, fishing deeper in the water column will usually produce more fish—then Options 2 and 3 will be your best choices. If some cloud cover and wave action are happening, consider Option 1. I've had many charters where the afternoon king bite is excellent in the exact location where we caught them at sunrise.

No matter where you fish, pay close attention to your sonar when you run to the spot where you want to set up. Once I hit the area that might hold kings (cold water + bait fish + structure), I often slow down, and adjust my sonar, and start looking for bait and game fish marks. I may run parallel to the shore looking for fish or work deeper looking for signs of life. This will save you valuable time if you can eliminate unproductive water before setting lines.

Late afternoon and evening are the prettiest times of day to be on the water. The evening period is really a reverse of the morning. As the sun is setting, kings begin to move up in the water column. Some fish head toward shallower water, although I really think the big horizontal moves occur later in the night.

Afternoon fishing is not complicated. Set a mixed spread of stealth and aggressive presentations. As the sun settle on the horizon, start moving your spread higher in the water column. Adjust your presentations and colors to a low-light scenario. As night descends, slide into the zone that produced at first light. It usually comes to life as kings go on a feeding frenzy. Keep an eye on your graph and hang on!

Keating on Kings: Great Lakes Chinook Tactics Way Beyond the Basics has 256 pages packed with detailed information on specific tactics and strategies used to catch king salmon in the spring, summer, and fall.

Anglers are fishing deep water late into the fall and finding they can catch immature kings across a broad section of the water column.

CHAPTER 9

Steelhead—Chrome Thunder Near and Far

Pound for pound and ounce for ounce, few species can surpass steelhead as a game fish. These magnificent creatures strike like a freight train and explode from the water like a Polaris missile launched from a submarine. Best of all, Great Lakes trollers know that steelhead are aggressive and readily strike during the bright mid-day hours. This makes them a great alternative target when salmon disappear.

Whether you pursue steelhead in a river winding through snowy banks or chase them across the horizon on big water, a certain mystique surrounds this great fish. When my dad and I bought our first boat back in 1972, one of the first fish we hooked was a giant steelie. I will never forget that fish. We were trolling northeast of Waukegan harbor (north of Chicago) on a hot summer morning. To be honest, we didn't have a clue what we were doing, and our empty cooler proved it; we had not had a single strike!

Minutes turned into hours as the steady, rhythmic hum of the 50-hp Johnson outboard put my dad into a coma-like state in the bow of our 17-foot Whaler, the *Frick N Frack*. Me? I had tried every lure we owned at that point in our young salmon career, but nothing coaxed a fish into striking. I even began sacrificing my sacred supply of M&M candies over the side, hoping to appease the dormant fish gods!

With the sun beating down, I was in a Zen-like trance as I stared blindly at the rods, hoping beyond hope that somehow, I could will a fish to strike. Suddenly, something slammed a downrigger line! Before I could rouse myself out of my dream-like state, an enormous silver creature exploded from the water! For what seemed like an eternity, the great fish just hung in the air—my mind's eye still sees it in slow motion—before falling back into the lake and continuing on his way. We lost that fish, but I will never forget the sight of that silver torpedo, glistening in the sunlight, and the excitement that my dad and I shared for a moment.

Welcome to the world of steelhead fishing! This world is characterized by periods of pure boredom as we hunt for schools of fish, but once fish are located, hang on to your hat! Action can be nothing short of explosive. My early steelhead strategies were rather random; nothing more than an incidental catch as my dad and I pursued kings, coho, and lake trout. Over time, and after countless hours on the water, we learned that we could successfully target steelhead.

Sure, steelies are the great nomad of the Great Lakes, but today, the steelhead population throughout the five lakes is as strong as ever. With modern stealth tactics, a plethora of great lures, modern electronics, and decades of experience, we can now head offshore with reasonable certainty that we will catch numbers of these hard-fighting fish. And, each season, anglers of all experience levels catch some real monsters.

STEELHEAD BASICS

Steelhead are lake-run rainbow trout on steroids. They are highly unpredictable, prone to wander, love wide-open spaces, and are opportunistic feeders devouring almost anything that crosses their path. Their large eyes certainly help them when it comes to finding a meal. From tiny-winged insects to beetles and moths to alewives, shiners, gobies, perch, shad, and sticklebacks, we have to ask, "is there anything they won't dine on?" I have even pulled three cigarette butts from one fish and a 14-inch king from another!

Historically, a variety of different strains have been stocked in the Great Lakes, including Shasta, Kamloops, Arlee, Ganaraska, Chambers Creek, Skamania, and domestic rainbows. The various strains have many similar features, but they are on different biological clocks. Some are spring spawners; others return to spawn in the fall or winter. Also, a few strains tend to favor shallow water while some orient themselves to deep, open water.

Steelhead are found in all five Great Lakes. They are opportunistic feeders and can be caught year round.

These variations give Great Lakes anglers a variety of seasonal angling options and opportunities throughout the region.

Our steelhead tolerate a wide range of water temperatures and utilize the entire water column much of the season. During the spring, they are most commonly caught in the upper layers of the water column. Once a thermocline sets up, they are often found suspended in and just above the thermocline. If kings, coho, and lakers are present, the steelhead will usually be found above and outside—more towards the middle of the lake—than the other species.

Steelhead are a finicky fish. They are directionally oriented, and some days, you will only catch them trolling in one direction. I don't care if you are Superman on the water; some days they just defy explanation. Savvy tournament anglers have learned that steelhead school by size. If you are into a school of 4- to 6-pound fish, you may need to move to another location to find larger fish. The really big jumpers, those fish weighing more than 15 pounds, tend to school shoreward of smaller and medium size fish.

While steelhead do strike at first and last light, some of the best action is found during the mid-day hours. They have large eyes and frequently cruise the upper layers of the water column. Bright light allows them to see their prey at a great distance. Because of their aggressive nature during the mid day-hours, they are great alternative targets to consider if salmon action slows down. Many anglers target kings or coho at dawn, and transition their presentations toward steelhead as the day advances. Many charter captains have turned a slow afternoon trip into a huge success by targeting steelhead.

As we unpack a methodology of catching *chrome thunder,* we must remember steelies are like teenagers—they don't always follow the rules. In fact, they break the rules, time and time again. Schools of them can appear out of nowhere and disappear just as fast. While we can target them in the layers around the thermocline, some days, you might catch them 100 feet down or just off the bottom hanging out with lake trout.

If you have true grit, a set of waders, and a boat capable of making long runs, you can catch steelhead every month of the year. Let's begin our look at this fish with a seasonal approach to locating fish and the presentations and lures we need.

SPRING STEELHEAD A-Z

Spring steelhead anglers have two options: to target pre-spawn fish staging to run up creeks and rivers or to run offshore and fish open water. Let's look at open water strategies first.

Offshore fishing is a hunting game. From the moment you leave the dock, it is all about the hunt. Historically, anglers often had to make long runs offshore to find clear water and fish. Remember, steelies like clear water. With the advent of zebra and quagga mussels, clear water and steelhead are found much closer to shore than in decades past. Just how far out you have to run varies by region and depends on how close to shore you find deep water, bottom composition, and local wind velocities. Typically, you will find greater concentrations of fish beyond the 70-foot mark. In some areas, you will find the largest concentrations eight miles or more from shore. Spring steelhead also tend to school farther out than concentrations of coho and king salmon.

While the thought of blazing a trail offshore over miles of open blue water is a bit daunting to many, technology and a thorough understanding of how wind, waves, and spring warming influence the water and fish will narrow your search parameters and save you valuable time and fuel.

Water Warming Dynamics

As winter releases its grip on the Great Lakes, a gradual warming process takes hold of the water from south to north. During late winter and early spring, the entire water column is of a relatively uniform temperature. As days lengthen, solar radiation begins warming the shallower and darker, murkier, shoreline waters. This band of warming surface water begins to spread horizontally out into the lake. Over time, this warming transfers energy down into the water column and horizontally out into the lake. As the warming water moves out into the lake, it forms an edge or a break. This is where the warm surface water encounters the colder surface water.

These breaks, or transitional zones of confrontation, set up in bands running roughly parallel to the shoreline. Depending on the weather and region, a series of breaks sets up. As the lake warms, you can find progressively colder bands of water as you move offshore.

Surface temperature breaks are the key to locating fish in open water. These breaks are highways beneath the waves. They are a point of reference where a variety of factors concentrate currents, debris, plankton, bait, and game fish.

Along with being a boundary between two masses of water with different temperatures, surface breaks often represent current lines on the lake's surface. In other words, the water on one side of the break may be *flowing* at a different rate. If some form of bottom structure is in the vicinity, the break may also be accompanied by a mild upwelling. Even structure 100 feet deep or deeper can create upwellings, which concentrate debris, insects, and plankton. This in turn will attract baitfish. All of this spells opportunity for Mr. Steelhead.

Off Winthrop Harbor, Illinois, we have a rocky hump that rises from 140 feet of water up to about 100 feet and back down. Similar features can be found in other areas as well. Despite its depth, this hump has a big impact on surface breaks during the spring. The northeast face of the reef is steep and creates an upwelling any time the bottom current is running into and colliding with the drop off. Features such as this are steelhead magnets in the spring and early summer.

With the Internet, you can locate surface breaks before leaving port.

Satellite-generated images depicting the surface temps give you a general idea of what to expect when you head offshore. To find these sites, simply Google "*Lake Name* surface temps." Accurate readings are only possible when there are no clouds blocking the satellite's view. Some days, these images won't give you exact locations where you'll find fish, but they will help you identify which areas to begin looking for more pronounced breaks.

You can also combine a plot of seas-surface temps with the Great Lakes Coastal Forecasting System (GLCFS) surface current charts. Areas of strong current often have a pronounced temp drop during the spring. By combining the data from a surface temperature plot with surface currents, you can narrow your search parameters and locate concentrations of fish.

If you do not have access to these charts, or cloud cover obscures satellites from providing accurate readings, just head offshore and look for breaks the old-fashioned way. When my clients want to focus on spring steelhead, I often just run offshore, watch my surface temp gauge, and begin fishing when I find the breaks.

Which breaks hold the most fish? While any break can hold fish, my logbooks show that the three most productive breaks include the 42- to 44-degree line, the 39-degree edge, and the 47- to 48-degree line. These three edges are steelhead-feeding zones during the spring. A quick note:

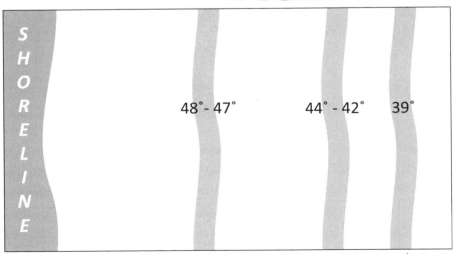

Target spring steelhead on surface temp breaks. This diagram illustrates the 3 most productive breaks.

some breaks also feature a slight color change or variations of the surface texture. One side of the break may have a subtle, glassy look, and the other side may have a bit of a ripple or chop on the surface. *Any* break can be a reference point used by fish to feed and travel along.

You may be thinking that steelhead fishing is too complicated and is reserved only for those with a six-figure battlewagon and all the latest technology. Not True! With a little courage and a few tips on how to read the water, you will soon be catching loads of chrome thunder. My old buddy Jim Flickenger (you can read about *Crazy Jim* in my book *Angling Life*) had primitive instincts. There wasn't a touch of the modern age on his 19-foot boat. He would race across the surface of calm water at 40 mph and sniff out the steelies just by looking at the water. He would pay no attention to where the fleet was fishing, he just took off! More times than not, he would motor miles from shore and just stop, put his lines in the water, and begin catching steelhead. This is an example of the subtle art to steelhead fishing that I hope to teach you!

Surface Breaks

The seasonal warming of surface water creates spring surface breaks. This warming is generated by the sun. The interplay of sunlight, wind, warming, current, and bottom topography dictate the size, texture, and duration of breaks. There is tremendous variation between the types of breaks you may find. Some breaks are very distinct and feature a rapid temp drop in a distance of 100 yards to a quarter mile. For example, over a horizontal distance of 300 yards, the surface temp will drop from 45 to 41 degrees. Sharp breaks often represent a clear separation of two distinct masses of water.

Some breaks will be more diffuse, and as you move horizontally out into the lake, the temperature will drop gradually, maybe a degree of change for every half mile of horizontal distance. For example, in 70 feet of water, the surface temp is 54 degrees. Two miles beyond that level, the water is 49 degrees. Over that two-mile distance, the drop in temperature is very uniform. On either side of that two-mile band, the surface temp will be very uniform. A third type of break really isn't a break in the true sense. The water just gradually drops off in temperature as you move out into the lake.

The rate at which the temp drops may not be any different from one level to the next. All breaks *can* hold fish, but the more pronounced breaks will usually feature current lines and greater concentrations of fish.

Impact of Wind on Surface Breaks

Surface breaks are transitory in nature. Rarely will you find the same break at the same waypoint for more than a couple of days. The duration, location, and texture of breaks are ultimately dependent on the intensity and direction of wind, sunlight, and the overall warming pattern of a lake. Honestly, some years, an individual lake warms really fast. Other years, it seems to take longer to warm the water column. A shifting wind regime tends to mix the water and slow the overall warming process of an individual lake. Periods when the wind changes direction daily tend to keep surface waters cold.

During the spring, the surface waters of the Lakes are gradually warming. As the water warms along the shallower shorelines, it will move horizontally out into the lake, forming an edge or a break at the intersection between cold water and warmer bands of water. Since these breaks are on the surface, their location is directly influenced by the wind.

A strong, onshore wind will push colder, surface water toward shore. This will push any breaks and warm water shoreward and concentrate the lines of horizontal temperature variation. If a gradual break existed prior to a strong onshore blow, the wind would make the break more pronounced and push the temperature contours closer together horizontally.

For example, let's say a gradual break has set up offshore. The outside of the break, nine miles from shore, is 39 degrees. Six miles from shore the temperature is 48 degrees. After a strong onshore wind, the 39-degree edge is now less than six miles from shore and the 48-degree water is five miles from shore. The distance between the 39-degree water and the 48-degree band is now only a mile. Application: some of the best spring steelhead fishing occurs on the days following a strong onshore wind regime. Breaks are more concentrated, and the steelhead, which school just under the surface, will likewise be bunched up along the breaks. Strong onshore wind brings schools of steelhead within range of small boat anglers during the spring.

An offshore wind pushes the breaks out and tends to make the breaks more diffuse. Likewise, schools of fish will be more scattered during an offshore wind regime. For example, a strong five-degree temp break sets up 10 miles offshore. After two days of a strong offshore blow, this sharp break might no longer exist. What you find in its place is a gradual drop in temperature that now occurs over the horizontal distance of three miles. Prior to the wind, the cold edge was 10 miles from shore. After the wind, the cold edge may now be 14 miles from shore. One caveat to this scenario is water clarity. Often, warmer water will be darker or stained. There is often more life in the darker water. An offshore wind will blow that band of murky water out deep. If roaming schools of steelhead and baitfish are offshore, these bands can turn into fish magnets with hot fishing opportunities for anglers who find them.

Before we go any further, let me just say there is no "normal" when it comes to the nature of breaks. Regions with deep water and sharp drop-offs tend to feature more pronounced breaks. This is the result of currents colliding with drop offs and ledges and creating upwellings. Areas with gradual drops tend to have more diffuse breaks, and with the right combination of swirling winds, sharp break lines never set up some years. In this scenario, gradual or diffuse breaks will be all you have to work with. You just need to learn how to analyze the water you are fishing. With a little experience and the right tools, which we will discuss below, you will catch loads of *Chrome Dynamite*.

How do Spring Steelhead Relate to Surface Breaks?

Experience teaches us that rainbows school in relation to break lines. To help us come up with a strategy for targeting break lines, we must address two questions: first, what are the schooling patterns of steelhead in relation to break lines? Second, how close do fish hold to break lines? Remember, breaks are highways within a vast, open lake. They concentrate food for the lower end of the food chain, which draws predators. I think the fish often roam between breaks, eating what they can find. When a concentration of bait sets up, it holds them in the area until a weather change re-orients the break.

The exact location of fish in relation to individual breaks varies from day to day, but a few principles will guide us to fish. While any break *could* hold fish, the more pronounced or defined that a break is, the better the

Steelhead often strike in pairs.

odds that fish will hold close to it. Also, larger schools of fish tend to form on well-defined breaks. On less-pronounced breaks, steelhead tend to scatter and travel in smaller pods.

Pockets of steelhead tend to school parallel to breaks. They may travel tight to the edges of a break line, or they may hold off the break anywhere from a couple hundred yards out to a mile or more. Steelhead are nomadic by nature and often travel up and down these zones of variation. These zones are usually aligned parallel to the breaks, which generally run parallel to the shoreline. These zones may be a few hundred yards across or several miles wide. While fish may be found on the warm or cold side of the break, I usually find more steelhead on the cold side.

When chasing rainbows across the horizon, you need to be flexible. Because you might find fish on either the warm or cold side of a break, you want to implement a trolling pattern that allows you to thoroughly explore the entire break before moving on to bluer pastures.

Getting Started

All steelhead trips to the deep begin with the hunt. A well thought out-trolling pattern that allows you to cover maximum water as you explore a series of breaks is step one. Once you locate fish, you can adjust your trolling direction to stay on top of active fish for maximum periods of time. Since you often find a series of breaks as you head offshore, it is best to start at the breaks closer to shore, and if fish aren't there, you continue working out into the lake from one break to the next. This avoids the dilemma of running past good-looking water, setting up, not having any action, and then wondering, "should I troll out deeper or head back to shallower water?"

While searching for fish, my overall trolling pattern is at angles perpendicular to breaks. This allows me to cover maximum territory. Before going any further, let me spell something out. When trolling across breaks, you need to pay very, very close attention to the water, currents, and how your boat and gear are interacting with the water. You are not just randomly trolling across the surface. When crossing breaks, I don't troll at an exact 90-degree angle. I constantly tweak my course, trying soft and sharp angles in relation to the breaks. I pay ultra close attention to my Course Over Ground on the GPS to analyze trolling speeds and angles. (See Chapter 13.) If I am not catching fish, or my lines don't look right, I make gradual course adjustments as I search for fish.

Once I find a temperature or depth band that holds fish, I often level

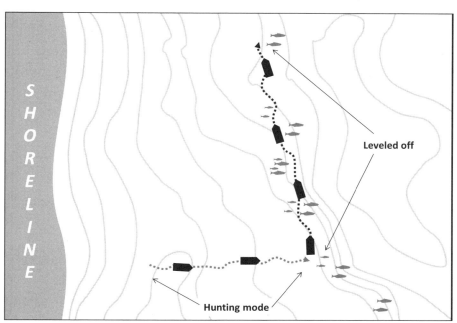

Chasing steelhead over deep water requires anglers to hunt for fish. Making a pass out into the lake, working across temp breaks, is the best way to find fish. Once you locate a band of fish, set up your trolling patterns to stay on the fish.

off and troll parallel to the breaks. Sometimes, the fish randomly scatter across a two- or three-mile band of gradual temp breaks. In this scenario, the fish often keep biting if I make long passes at soft angles (horizontally aligned to the shore) through the fish. To maximize this situation, you should determine the most productive course (COG) and then follow those lines through the fish. Pay attention to speed, too. You may have a good pass trolling in one direction. When you turn around and work back through a school of fish, you may need to tweak your speed and angle going in the opposite direction.

Locating Near-Shore Spring Steelhead

Many steelhead across the Great Lakes region return to rivers and streams to spawn in the early spring. The first step to catching these staging prespawn fish is to determine which rivers have a run of spring fish. Key your near-shore fishing off these sites. Along with spawning steelhead, some non-spawning steelies, plus other species, will be attracted to the warm water flowing out of local rivers and streams. Generally speaking, you can find staging fish from a few feet of water out to about 40 feet.

How big does a river need to be to attract fish? While it is true that larger rivers have more to offer, I have caught steelhead in shallow water off creeks that a good athlete could leap across. Spring rains increase river flow, and some of the best fishing comes following a heavy rainfall.

One of the simplest strategies involves targeting areas where the river's discharge plume intersects structure. This could be changes in the bottom (drop offs, humps, wave troughs) or man-made features such as break walls and jetties. Color lines marking the transition between darker, warmer river water and the lake are excellent breaks to troll along. You may find fish on the clear or murky side of a break.

Wind direction and velocity influence river-mouth fish. The river plume is flowing along the surface, so its direction of flow will be steered by the wind. Concentrate your trolling efforts on the leeward (downwind) side of the river. Even though you may be fishing right next to the beach, anytime steelhead are the opponent, you must consider your trolling angle. When working river-mouth structure in conjunction with the river plume, you will find some days when a troll parallel to the shoreline is best, and on other days a perpendicular troll will produce. While most anglers troll off river mouths, others looking for some crazy fun will drift and cast. (For possible line spreads, see Chapter 10)

TRICKS AND TACTICS TO CATCH SPRING STEELHEAD

Courage, flexibility, and patience are keys to success! Head offshore with a game plan, but pay close attention to the subtle nuances and clues that the lake, weather and fish give you. Keen observation skills, more times than not, will lead you to fish. This is exactly what saved a slow charter of mine in the bottom of the ninth inning. We were randomly wandering around in the middle of nowhere. Nothing felt right. With nothing to turn on, I just kept trolling further and further out into the lake. Time was running out, and I decided that we should turn around and troll back toward the harbor. As I turned, I spotted a handful of sea gulls sitting on the water just outside of us. Rather than turn, I decided to loop back out and work past the birds. Sure enough, we found fish—lots of them! Sea gulls will lead you to baitfish. When you see them in the middle of nowhere, you can be assured something to eat is near-by.

If you head offshore and are confronted with a series of well-defined temp breaks, begin fishing on the shoreward side (warmest) of the best break available. If action is slow, you have two options: you can move up and down the break looking for fish, or you can troll out into colder water. Generally, I won't troll toward shore at the beginning of a steelhead trip. The thought of "what is out deep" drives me nuts!

Some days, you won't find any major breaks. What you often do find is a gradual progression of lesser breaks stretching from warmer to colder water. It's not uncommon to find three or more gradual break lines extending across an area. Do all the breaks hold fish? Maybe, maybe not. In this scenario, set up a trolling pattern that works perpendicular angles to the shoreline. This allows you to troll across all the breaks looking for fish. Often the 42- to 44-degree edge will hold the most fish, so I often start just inside of this break.

If you are in an area and everything looks especially fishy, before you leave the area, work the water from every trolling angle. Offshore steelhead are extremely sensitive to speed and direction. For example, you may not catch any fish on a west troll, but they'll bite the props off on an east troll. Often it is just a matter of discovering the hot speed and angle. If you just make looping passes, pay attention to inside and outside lines as steelhead are super speed sensitive. If outside planers get hit on a turn, speed up. If inside planers pop on the turn, slow down.

Trolling Strategies and Presentations

Steelhead are a psychotic fish! Of all the salmonids, they are the most sensitive—and selective—when it comes to color. They often have speed issues and will only hit if you're trolling in a specific direction. These fish are a mess! This makes them all the more exciting to fish for because you never really know what to expect from them.

In spring, concentrate your efforts on the top 20 feet. Side planers, (mast-and-ski and mono inline planers such as Yellow Birds or the Church TX-12), divers, Slide Divers, and light line flat lines are productive. Side planers are the most productive spring presentation when exploring a series of temp breaks. They allow you to cover a wider path, place more lures in the strike zone, figure out the best speed, and reach fish spooked by your boat.

Since you can encounter aggressive fish and negative fish when offshore, you should run several different presentations to help you dial into a hot bite. Surface planers, segmented leads, and light line applications will be best for negative fish. Divers, riggers and side planers will work best for aggressive fish. There will always be a few fish with a chip on their shoulder. These fish are attracted to a spinning propeller: a diver out on 25 to 45 feet of mono will be too much for Mr. Attitude to resist.

When setting a spread of surface-oriented boards, the overall pattern should resemble an inverted V going through the water. The point of the V is the bow of your boat, moving forward. The legs of the V represent your side planer lines. The longest leads will be on the outside planers, and as you move in toward the boat, the lead lengths will be progressively shorter.

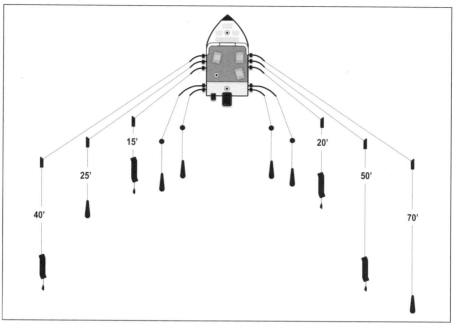

When spring steelhead are feeding close to the surface, a mixed spread of red flashers/flies, and clean spoons, draws steelhead into your spread and triggers strikes.

This pattern reduces tangles on turns and when fighting fish. When a large fish hits an outside planer, it will pull toward the stern and clear the other lines. If you set an inside planer with a long lead and hook a fish on the outside planer with a short lead, the fish will likely tangle the inside planer as it comes across the inside line.

Setting a spread of side planers on the surface is similar to setting a spread of riggers, coppers, and lead cores in the summer—every line you put in the water is impacting the lures around it. For summer fishing, the focus is on the vertical relationships between rigs. In spring, you must pay close attention to the horizontal relationships.

When setting side planers, keep three horizontal variables in mind: distance behind boards, distance from boat, and distance between lures. These three variables are interwoven and influence whether fish strike or take a pass. On some days, the planer closest to the boat with a short, 10- to 20-foot lead produces best. This rig might be catching fish pushed out by the boat, or attracted to the propeller, or as your shallowest lure, it might be highly visible to fish feeding just below the surface. Other days, Mr. Steelhead will be overly sensitive to your presence, and the best rods will be your outside planers, set on long leads (in excess of 70 feet) and run way outside your other planers.

Some days, a team of three or four planers tightly spaced (horizontally) on a side will draw more attention. Other days, you need more horizontal separation between individual boards. Think about how adding a flasher to a group of spoons will change the overall appearance of the spread.

Staggering the lead lengths on your planer boards will help you dial into the fish. For example, when running three planers a side, run your port planers on 15-, 35- and 50- foot leads. Set the starboard side back 20, 50, and 100feet. As the fish start striking, you can adjust your lines accordingly.

Variables that impact lead lengths off planers include light intensity, water clarity, wind, wave texture, and fish temperament. If the water gets rougher or calmer, you might have to adjust your leads. If the sky brightens or darkens, you may have to adjust your lead lengths. Flat, calm days and rough days often require extreme measures on your part. There's really no method to the steelhead's madness. Sometimes, they want the leads longer; sometimes, they want them shorter.

Observe all of your lines collectively and make adjustments based on results. For example, if your side planers are hot and divers are dead, switch to a Slide Diver or Torpedo. Try adjusting your diver to run shallower and put it farther out to the side on a 3.5 setting. If divers and shallow riggers are producing and planers are dead, you might need to adjust your planers to get the baits a few feet deeper. Add a larger keel sinker or set the rig back on a longer lead, and you might trigger strikes.

Segments of lead cores can be devastating on spring steelhead. Setting a two- to six-color lead core is often the perfect compliment to a spread of mono boards. I often set one of these shorter leads on the inside planer. This rod takes the lure 10 to 20 feet down, just below and behind the other baits.

Trolling speed is a variable that is constantly in flux. The general range is 1.9 to 3.2 kts. (2.2 to 3.7 mph). Faster speeds of 2.3 to 2.8kts. allow you to cover maximum amounts of water as you hunt for fish. If you think fish are present or you start marking bait, adjust your speeds. While steelies are speed junkies, some days a slow troll draws more strikes. Bottom line? Don't be afraid to experiment with trolling speed.

Downriggers and divers also produce. For divers, use 6-to 10-foot, 20-pound fluorocarbon leaders. Spoons, cranks, and 00 red dodgers with flies all take plenty of fish. For riggers, spoons set back 40 to 150 feet on 12-pound test line or SWR's work equally well. When targeting breaks, stagger your riggers from 10 to 40 feet down. When hunting spring steelhead, I often set one or two riggers way deep for kings.

Irresistible Lures for Chrome Dynamite

Mr. Lake-run Rainbow is an opportunistic feeder who will hit just about anything on the right day. Spoons, flies, and body baits can be mixed together into a steelhead spread. Speed tolerant lures that work at higher speeds of 2.3 to 3.2 kt. are preferred. This smorgasbord approach to lure selection helps us dial into the fish's palate.

One of the best all around spring steelhead lures anywhere is the 00 Alderton Action Flasher in red or orange followed by a two-inch tinsel fly. If you are serious about steelhead fishing, you need both the red and the orange ones—more than one of each. Even though the red and orange look really similar to our human eyes, fish apparently can tell the difference. Some days, they'll only hit the red flasher, and other days, it has to be orange. Don't ask why—just figure out what they want on any given day and give it to them! I usually begin all steelhead trips with at least one of each color in the spread. I've done *taste tests* when the fish started hitting the orange flasher: I have run the red flasher identical to the orange one, but they never took a hit. Color makes a big difference!

These small, metal Action Flashers (Dreamweaver makes a similar one called the Coho Dodger available in red as well as chartreuse versions) work well with peanut flies and 2- to 4-inch flies. Productive spring fly colors include all shades of blue, either plain or mixed with copper, silver, gold, white, or mylar. Purple, pink and red flies also take loads of jumpers. If fish are feeding on flies under a bright sun a purple-black-gold fly, a black-gold or black-green peanut flies are productive. On bright sunny days or when green beetles are floating on the water, green flies get the nod. Lead length for flies varies from 14 to 20 inches. When trolling fast in cold water, longer leads will slow the fly down and trigger strikes.

When choosing spoons, it really is a color bazaar. Traditional spring colors are orange, red, gold, gold with strawberry, gold with orange, silver with orange, orange with yellow, and blue with yellow. Popular patterns include gold with orange cracked ice tape, silver with orange cracked ice tape, red, Blue Oz, and Blue Thunder.

Spoon size also should be considered. Begin with a variety of sizes and adjust based on what the fish are hitting. Typically, you can determine a pattern each spring, based on the size of bait in a region. There are many great spoons on the market. Some time honored favorites for spring include Mauler's, Fuzzy Bears, Super Slims, Stingers, Silver Streaks, and Finn Spoons. But again, spoon brand's and colors are as varied as the opinions of a group of human beings. What's my point? If you think fish are in the area and you are not getting bites, be aggressive with changing spoon brands and colors until you dial into what the fish will bite.

When fishing ice-cold water, 42 degrees or cooler, body baits produce well. Productive plugs for offshore steelhead include Brad's Thin Fish in Red Tiger, the Cordell Wally Diver in the Orange G-finish, J-7, J-9, and J-11 Rapalas, jointed Rebels, Reef Runner Little Rippers, Reef Runner Ripsticks in Oahe Red, Bare Naked, or Fire Tiger, and the Bomber Long A's.

Often, an integrated spread of clean spoons and red or orange flashers produces best. Steelhead look up as they feed. When setting a spread to target the top 20 feet, try to visualize what the group of lures looks like as they move along just below the surface. Just like setting a spread of downriggers and divers, your group of surface planers can be run as a group, working together, or you can set the baits to run more independently.

Fish might come at lures from the side or from below. Think about how light and water clarity affect the visibility of your spread. Several swishing or spinning red flashers mixed in amongst a group of spoons or plugs often draws the silver torpedoes into your spread, and the clean baits will trigger strikes. Remember, a spread of surface side planers typically will run in the top 10 feet. By adding a few segmented leads, you can easily extend your strike box down to 20 or 30 feet.

Steelhead hit well on sunny, calm days.

On the flip side, some days, a full spread of flashers and flies or a spread of only spoons works best. Every day is different. Just remember, the location of individual lures within a group spread is just as important as the lure itself. When you determine what the fish want, set the lures back in their exact (horizontally and vertically speaking) location!

Chasing spring steel over the horizon is one of the most exciting games in town. While you can leverage your strategies and lure selection, sometimes, it is just all about being in the right place at the right time, and the best way to have that happen is to be out there trying.

SUMMER STEELHEAD

Steelhead have saved many slow, summer outings. While spring anglers focus on the surface layer, summer strategies require you to recalibrate your vision and focus on the sub surface zone from 20 to 70 feet down. This requires different presentations and some modifications to your lure selection.

By now, you realize that steelhead are the nomads of the Lakes. While it's true that you can run into fish just about anywhere, the deep, open spaces far from shore provide more opportunities for summer success. Often, the largest concentrations of steelies are often found outside the other species. To many anglers, this seems like a very random approach—because it is! So goes the nature of steelhead fishing! Plus, we can do many things to reduce the randomness of our steelhead encounters.

Spring steelhead favor the coldest water available. In the summer, it's just the opposite. You frequently find the largest concentrations of fish higher in the water column above kings, coho, and lakers. For this reason, summer anglers concentrate their firepower on the thermocline and the zone immediately above the thermocline. While the 50- to 58-degree zone is considered the ideal temp zone for Mr. Steelhead, these fish are notorious for dashing up into warmer water in pursuit of a good snack. Steelhead are opportunistic predators, so if lunch is more readily accessible down in deeper, colder water, you might find them down in the zone where kings and lakers frequent. In other words, when steelhead are your target, head out with a plan, but be ready to adapt your presentations.

When setting a spread of lines for summer steelhead, first ask yourself how far down in the water column you want to target. When mining the upper layers of the water column—the top 30 feet—segmented lead cores and coppers, Slide Divers, diving planers, Torpedoes, and Dive Bombs on in-line planers are all good delivery devices. If you target the 30- to 60-foot level, downriggers, copper, lead core, Slide Divers, and diving planers are effective.

There are no guarantees when you head offshore in search of Summer Steel. Mystery, an element of hunting and a sense of anticipation are your constant companions. Whether you fish high or low, use speed-tolerant lures. When you troll at speeds of 2.4 kts. to 3.1 kts. (2.8 to 3.6 mph), it is amazing how much water you can cover, compared to a slower troll. Really, finding the fish is the greatest challenge when it comes to catching steelhead.

Summer Strategies and Lure Selection

Some of the best steelhead action happens when we least expect it. I remember one summer when schools of jumpers seemingly materialized out of nowhere. This particular season featured steady coho and king action across a wide section of our region. But a sudden, upwelling event pushed the salmon away and anglers were left with what appeared to be a tough fishing scenario: freezing cold water on the shoreline, no bait, and no fish for miles.

Well, you don't survive in the charter fishing business for more than 30 years by telling your clients, "you should have been here yesterday!" *You go fishing*! Rather than follow everyone around waiting for the next wave of salmon to show up, one morning, I put on my Christopher Columbus hat and headed for the horizon in search of whatever was out there. My group on this particular day included a father, his four children, and an uncle. We'll save the story that unfolded at the dock for another book.

Since fishing *had* been so good the past few weeks, no one had ventured beyond the 180-foot mark, which out of North Point Marina is about 7 miles from shore. On this day, the lake was flat calm, so I set up on the outside of the known world and plotted a course into the deeps. By the time I had the downriggers, divers, and all the planers out, we had taken a pair of fish! Since yesterday was so slow my first thought was, *maybe I should turn around?* But off in the distance farther out, I thought I saw a fish swirl on the surface.

We continued trolling toward the deeps, and the farther out we got, the more fish we saw breaking the surface. It appeared as if they were chasing baitfish. Action went from an occasional bite to non-stop doubles and occasional triples as we stumbled across a huge school of steelhead that stretched for miles! We made a huge haul of big steelhead on this day and for many days afterward!

What drew the fish? The upwelling had shifted the currents, raised the offshore thermocline higher in the water column, and brought huge schools of young-of-the-year baitfish into our offshore waters. Alewives and perch spawn in the spring and early summer. After hatching, these young fish prefer warmer water than adults and live in the highly-fertile, upper layer of the water column, above the thermocline (typically the top 50 feet). Sunlight makes this zone nutrient rich and perfect for young-of-the-year bait. These tiny baitfish are not strong swimmers and drift with the currents. The schools often show up on sonars as clumps or clouds hanging down from the surface.

When steelhead feed on bait balls in the upper water column, an integrated spread of segmented leads, divers (or Slide Divers), and riggers is super productive. When the bait is in the top 20 feet, the steelhead will only strike lures above 20 feet. Two- to five-color lead core segments are the most productive rods for fish in this range. I've seen many days where big rainbows will strike these short leads and never touch lines running a few feet deeper. When they feed 20 to 40 feet down, try 5- to 10-color leads.

Steelhead can be a bit like tuna when they aggressively feed on particular size bait. In late summer, you often find schools of young-of-the-year alewives and perch less than one-inch long. When steelhead focus on eating small baitfish from ¼ to 1 inch long, they will only hit small lures. Larger spoons are ignored. They get so keyed in on small baits that the larger spoons just look unnatural. It is imperative to use a small, ball bearing swivel and fluorocarbon leader on lead core and copper rigs. Use 20-pound, or lighter fluorocarbon. Typically, you will be fishing clear water under midday brightness, and steelhead have great eyesight.

Smaller spoons such as Stinger Scorpions, Mini Silver Streaks, and the Savant Jake 45 are favorites. These small spoons are super effective on flat, calm days. When fishing in a slight chop, then Super Slims and the standard size Stingers are also strong producers.

Another ancient secret from the *Blue Horizon* that will increase your steelhead catch is to use spoons that have lost much of their paint. Michigan Stingers are notorious for losing paint as they catch fish. Spoons that only have a *splash* of color left on their front are the best for fish that are feeding on micro-bait. I think that as the fish are busting through a school of bait, the flash of the spoon gets their attention, and in their instinctive way of making split second decisions, the small flash of color resembles a tiny baitfish and *wham!* Fish on!

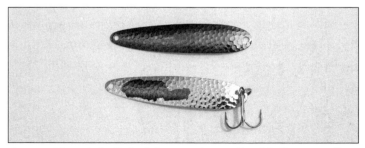

Spoons with a splash of color left are candy to steelhead feeding on small baitfish in the upper levels of the water column.

When the fish feed high in the water column, try to determine what they are eating. If it is alewives, then silver, silver/blue, silver/green, and silver/purple spoons work best. If it is perch, then greens, gold, yellow, and blends of those colors are best. Some days, a little red, orange, or yellow on the spoon will trigger strikes. Two of the tried and true color patterns for this out-of-temp fishery are the Ludington Special and the Green Puke patterns.

Let's look at some typical rod spreads to target summer steelhead. When fish are feeding in the top 15 to 30 feet, a spread of segmented leads is dynamite for these high-running summer steelies. A typical six-rod planer spread (starting with the outside planer and moving in) would include a three-, five- and seven color-lead core, or you might try a two-, four- and six-color core. If the fish are slightly deeper, say from 20 to 50 feet down, then a five-, seven-, ten-color spread (six, eight, ten colors) can work. For a shallow copper spread try 50, 100, 125, and 150 segments.

You can use your downriggers to target steelhead, or you can drop them down deeper for kings or lake trout. When setting riggers for summer steel, I like to run an SWR off one corner and a 12-pound test "light line" rod off the other corner rigger. The light line is set back 30 to 50 feet, and the

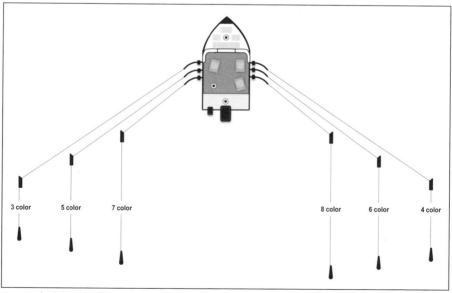

A spread of short lead core segments targeting the top 30 feet of the water column is an excellent way to target summer steelhead.

SWR has three colors of lead. The SWR and light line rig can run though the entire water column, depending on where the fish are suspending. If 5- to 8-color lead cores are hot, set the SWR on a corner rigger 20 to 30 feet down. Often I run my boom riggers with the 0 metal dodgers in chrome, silver glow, or yellow. The dodgers are set from 35 to 75 feet down. Yes, the big metals will be spinning, but steelhead frequently smash these rigs all day long. Remember, never try and understand *why* a steelhead does anything.

Fly colors change from day to day, but what is often more important than color is the density of the fly. When steelhead feed on smaller baitfish, a well-worn fly will catch more fish. Many of my best steelhead flies are very sparse, only having a few strands of short tinsel left. I only run one or two beads under these flies. A short-shank #No. 2 treble will assure that more fish make it to the smoker.

Divers rigged with flasher and flies or spoons take plenty of summer steel. If I am running all spoons on my riggers and planers, then a flasher and fly off each diver are perfect complements. They catch fish, and the flasher draws fish to your boat and into the spread. If the big dodgers get hit on your boom riggers and the divers rigged with flashers are dead, try a spoon on the diver just outside your riggers. Because the fish are high in the water column, you can run wire, braid or mono divers. I prefer wire or braid. Tweak the setting on the diver until you find what the fish want.

There is nothing more exciting on the Great Lakes than a big, summer steelhead crushing a diver, launching itself from the water, and charging for the horizon! Heading offshore late in the summer or fall is a great time to load up on 6- to 15-pound fish. The filets off these fish are perfect for winter smoking projects. I vacuum seal the filets and thaw them to smoke. Smoking a fish you caught brings a touch of summer to your soul on a cold winter day. The great flavor of smoked steelhead paired with Gouda cheese, crackers, and your favorite beverage, consumed by the fireplace, brings our memories of summer's victories on the water to life when the snow is falling outside.

CHAPTER 10

Lake Trout Wisdom

Mysterious, underrated, and big are a few words that come to mind when I think about lake trout. When I was younger I was fascinated with lake trout. Maybe it came from walking the aisles of the once glorious Chicagoland Sport Fishing show at the old Amphitheater. I can still remember the mounted fish hanging in the booths of the Canadian outfitters. I would look at their photos of huge trout and dream of one day slugging it out with a deep-water monster. To a kid growing up in the suburbs of Chicago, these behemoths took on a mythical quality and seemed totally out of reach. Maybe it came from a youthful imagination that wondered, every time my dad and I dropped a line into the depths, if the next fish would be a world record lake trout.

Like the veteran relief pitcher that steps in and saves the ball game in the bottom of the 9th inning, lakers are as much a part of the Great Lakes fishery as hot, buttered popcorn is a part of any movie going experience. They are a true Great Lakes native. Once lake trout were the dominant predator, but a perfect storm of exotic invaders and commercial overfishing decimated their population. Once the sea lampreys were brought under control, stocking programs and natural reproduction have restored lake trout to the system.

Today, thriving populations of lake trout can be found in Lakes Superior, Huron, Michigan, and Ontario. Limited numbers are found in much shallower Lake Erie. Like many species, yearly catch rates fluctuate from region to region. In the early days of the fishery, lake trout were caught primarily by anglers dragging wire line on the bottom. Today, anglers utilize a wide variety of presentations and lures to catch lakers throughout the water column. Lake trout are a vital part of the Great Lakes fishery. They grow to gargantuan sizes and can often be located and caught when other species are not available. From jigging in kayaks to trolling the bottom with wire line, there are a tremendous amount of opportunities available for those anglers who set their sights on capturing Great Lakes lake trout.

LAKE TROUT CHARACTERISTICS

To help us more efficiently target lakers, let's spend a few minutes studying the creature. Lakers don't need any blankets, hats, or survival gear at the tailgate party. Their bodies are designed with layers of insulating fat (great for the smoker!), making these fish perfect for cold water. Their peak operating temperature is 42 to 54 degrees, but you may find them in much colder water. They are slow growing and structure oriented. They spawn in late fall. Some strains spawn over rocky, deep water reefs. Other fish come in and spawn along near-shore structure. In some areas, mature lake trout will migrate up rivers late in the fall.

Like the other trout found in the Great Lakes, lakers are opportunistic feeders. Prior to the arrival of exotic species, they survived on a diet of smelt, sculpin, herring, and chubs. Today, lake trout commonly dine on alewives,

Lake trout grow big on the Great Lakes!

gobies, smelt, emerald shiners, sculpin, chubs, herring, sticklebacks, and gizzard shad. I've even found young salmon up to 11 inches in their bellies!

In the past, we thought lakers spent all their time on the bottom. Today, anglers catch lakers throughout the entire water column. Yes, there are times when you need to drag your lure across the bottom to trigger strikes, but there are many days when you can catch more and larger fish suspended. This may have to do with the improved water clarity of the Lakes or the impact of invasive zebra and quagga mussels on the lake's bottom. Or it may just be that modern anglers are better equipped to locate and catch them.

When I began chartering, lake trout were the most predictable and dependable species that we targeted. There were always a few key locations that would produce a good catch of fat trout. Those days are long gone! Lake trout have borrowed a page from their speedy, more glamorous cousin, Mr. Steelhead, and have learned how to seemingly vanish overnight. Today, anglers often have to *hunt* before the catching begins!

While loads of lake trout are caught from deep water every year, many anglers are finding that they can catch big fish close to shore and, at times, lurking in the upper layers of the water column. For light tackle enthusiasts, this is good news; for shallow water lakers fight much better than fish dragged up from the depths. How close to shore will trout go? In Indiana, lake trout spawn on reefs less than a mile from the shore. On Lake Ontario, lake trout provide great small boat action in the Niagara River, and in Milwaukee, Wisconsin, lake trout provide action for hardy, small boat anglers fishing just beyond the break walls from late fall to early spring.

One last observation: when Mr. Lake Trout is hungry, he is easy to catch. When lake trout are not feeding, they are one tough creature to catch. Negative trout require finesse, a keen eye when choosing lures, perfect boat control, and a bit of luck never hurts! Let's look at some of the tactics used to catch this great All American game fish!

LOCATING AND CATCHING SPRING LAKE TROUT

During spring and prior to the development of the summer thermocline, you can potentially run into lake trout just about anywhere. On the surface, this that might seem like a good thing, but it really makes finding lake trout more of a challenge. As you travel across the Great Lakes region, you will find some areas have good early season laker action close to shore, but in other areas, the fish stay in deeper water. Captain John Tomczyk of Daybreak charters trolls the south shore of Lake Superior in 15 to 40 feet of water in spring. Off Chicago, Illinois, huge schools of hungry lake trout take up residence off the city skyline in 40 to 55 feet of water. The Chicago fish are feasting on gobies.

As winter loosens its grip on the lakes, lake trout are drawn to warming water along the shoreline. Some fish will also follow schools of spawning bound baitfish such as smelt or alewives into the shallows. River and stream outflows, harbor mouths, and any rocky structure will attract fish. Large rivers wash lots of warm water and nutrients into a lake. Trout are a detail-oriented fish, so any thing different along the bottom can be considered structure. Some of the more prominent features include boulders, rip rap, or a drop off paralleling the shoreline.

Not all trout head to the beach for spring break. Plenty of lake trout will remain in deep water across the region. These deep water fish do roam the entire water column. History, however, suggests that some of the most consistent action over deep water (in excess of 150 feet) will be found by targeting either the bottom 10 feet or the top 20 feet of the water column. I know this sounds a bit extreme, but when targeting Mr. Lake Trout in April and May, sometimes it is best to focus on the boundaries of his home, the bottom, and the surface. Some of my biggest, career lake trout were caught in May off mono side planers targeting offshore steelhead.

There are a tremendous amount of options available when it comes to catching lake trout during the spring. Every year is different, so gathering local intel and being familiar with all available structure, both shallow and deep, will be helpful when you get out on the water and begin looking for fish. Visit some of the more reputable angling forums and inquire from the more experienced guys where the historical laker fisheries are located. In some regions, large schools will take up residence in 40 to 60 feet of water during spring. Some of these fish will even make feeding forays into less than 20 feet of water. In other areas, you will need to be in 100 feet of water or deeper to find bottom oriented lakers. Off of my homeport I've caught plenty of spring lake trout suspended in over 200 feet of water.

Tactics used to catch lakers from shallow water are very similar to fishing for brown trout. Mono side planers, segmented lead core, and Slide Divers are the most productive presentations for shoreline shallows. Keep it simple with side planers. A 10- to 20-pound test fluorocarbon leader is a must. Keel sinkers of ¼ to 1 ounce are standard. Lead lengths off the planers will vary each day, but the general range is 10 to 100 feet off the boards. As you dial into the bite, adjust your lead lengths and vary the horizontal distance between individual planers. On flat, calm days, planers run way off to the side are best. Trout will utilize the entire water column, so the length of lead core will depend on how shallow you plan on trolling. The depth principles for setting a spread of shallow-water planers outlined in the brown trout chapter can be applied for lakers as well.

Laker Legend, Capt. John Tomczyk, has two favorite spring presentations that can easily be run from small or large boats. John sets Slide Divers back 50 to 70 feet and runs them just a few feet below the surface and off to the side. This adds an element of stealth just outside your boat's trolling path. One of John's favorite early season rigs is a Musky Torpedo run down the chute. John sets the spoon back 50 feet, clips on the Torpedo, and then drops it right behind the boat. It doesn't get any simpler! When chasing trout up into the shallows, Capt. Tomczyk also runs a spread of planer boards (mono or short lead core segments) off the sides. John's favorite shallow water spoons are the willow leaf shaped Finn Spoons.

When picking shallow water lures, determine what the trout are eating. If fish are following smelt into the shoreline, minnow style crank baits such as jointed Rebels, Rapalas, and Bomber Long A's are steady producers. If you are not sure what they are feeding on, your favorite lake trout spoons will work. Shallow water trout are aggressive, so you just might be surprised at how fast you can troll for them.

When targeting spring lake trout over deep water, you can use a variety of presentations, techniques, and lures. Since it is often easiest to find fish in the top 20 feet and the bottom 10 feet, big catches are made when you weave spring and summer styles into your spread. If you find that fish are more concentrated shallow or deep, you can narrow your focus. When targeting spring lakers, it is not uncommon to catch kings, steelhead, and coho as well.

With all that water beckoning you forward, where do you begin? While it may feel like looking for a needle in a haystack, you greatly increase your odds of finding fish by targeting surface temperature breaks. Any temp break might attract lakers, but colder breaks of 38 to 48 degrees will hold more lake trout. The methods for locating breaks and the trolling strategies discussed in the steelhead chapter can be applied to lake trout.

The best presentations for plying surface breaks are mono side planers and short segments of lead core or copper. Deep water is generally crystal clear, so 14- to 20-pound test fluorocarbon leaders and small swivels are a must. A variety of spoons will work on side planers. As you select spoons, consider not only the color but also the size and brand of spoon. If trout are feeding on sticklebacks, they will want a small spoon. When I am offshore randomly hunting for fish and not marking bait, it seems magnum spoons will draw more strikes.

If the trout are right up against the surface, then mono side planers with ¼ to 1-ounce keel sinkers are perfect. You can easily run two to four mono inline planers a side. Set the outside planers back 80 to 100 feet. As you move into the boat, begin to shorten the leads. Most days, 40 to 60 feet leads are productive. You would be surprised at how many lake trout are up feeding just below the surface.

When trout are holding 5 to 20 feet below the surface, short segments of lead core or copper are the best presentations. Try setting one or two leads (3 to 6 colors long) inside a spread of mono boards. If the lead cores are firing, you can either add more weight to your mono planers or put out more lead core lines. For copper lines, try 50- to 125-foot segments. Slide Divers, diving discs, or a Torpedo angled off the side can easily be added to a spread of side planers.

On southern Lake Michigan, we run a lot of 00 red flashers and dodgers with flies for steelhead and coho offshore. On some days, the lake trout hit these flies better than spoons. I would not be afraid to try one of these coho rigs for lakers. Sometimes, just running one 00 red in a spread of spoons will draw attention to all the other boats. You can learn more about how to run these great lures in the coho chapter.

With a spread of planers focused on the upper layers of the thermocline, you can easily run your favorite deep water trout baits on downriggers or wire line below the boat. Depending on boat size, experience, and sea conditions you can target the deep zone with one rod or as many as you can fit down there. If I know I'm going to be trolling at higher speeds, I may set an SWR with a magnum Moonshine down deep. Spring lakers love clean spoons in the depths. If I want to run a dodger or flasher deep and still troll at higher speeds, I will run longer leaders between the dodger and fly or Spin-N-Glo. Essentially, the longer leader slows the *whip* of the fly down. For 8-inch attractors, I will run 24-to 32-inch leads. For the 10-inch paddles, I will go as long as 48 inches at times!

When randomly trolling over deep water, watch the graph. If I suddenly mark bait or fish down deep, I slow down and allow my deep lines to

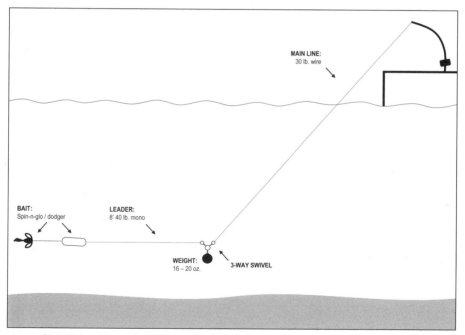

A wire line with a 1-pound or 20-ounce sinker, dodger, and Spin-N-Glo run along the bottom is a time-proven method for catching lake trout. This same rig is just as effective when run suspended as well.

swim tantalizingly past Mr. Trout. When targeting trout on the bottom in spring, the lures and presentations are no different from summer strategies.

Before talking about summer fishing, I need to tell you about the number one trout lure to run behind metal dodgers or plastic flashers. In spring, summer, or fall, or any time trout are on the bottom (or suspended), it is hard to beat "Ole' Moe." *Ole Moe* is a number 4 or number 2 Spin-N-Glo run with a half-cut fly (tinsel or Mylar) on the tail. I think lake trout are genetically engineered at the hatchery to hit this rig. To make the rig, simply run your leader through the Spin –N-Glo body, then a single bead, then the fly, and tie a No. 2 short shank hook on the end. You are now ready to mop up on lake trout!

My favorite dodger to run with Moe are silver, yellow, and silver glow Luhr Jensen dodgers in the 0 size. Opti Dodgers work well, too. Favorite Spin-N-Glo colors include green/white, yellow with red spots, green/yellow, glow, and pearl. Traditional tail colors include white, pearl/blue, and yellow. Does color really matter on the bottom? Some days, they sure seem to pick on one color over another, so shuffle through colors until you find what works.

SUMMER LAKER TIPS

Summer lake trout strategies have changed tremendously over the years. In the past, it was simply a matter of going out to the local lake trout stomping grounds, dropping wire line and heavy sinkers to the bottom, and grinding out a catch of trout. This method still works, sometimes, but today, just as many lakers will be caught suspended as on the bottom. In fact, Capt. Tomczyk believes that most anglers troll their lures *below* the fish! John makes a living catching lake trout from Lake Superior, and more than half of his fish are caught suspended each season!

Before setting lines, let's look at a few key principles that will help us locate fish. Cold water is a must. Second, lake trout love structure. Structure on Lake Superior looks very different than structure in southern Lake Michigan or the eastern reaches of Lake Ontario. To catch more trout, you need to do a little homework before leaving the dock. Find a good chart of the water you fish and look for features that stand out. If you fish in an area that is structure rich, then you need to locate structure that has drastic depth changes and jagged edges.

If you fish in an area that is relatively flat, like the southern basin of Lake Michigan, then even a shallow hump rising only several feet off the bottom will attract fish. My buddy Capt. Arnie told me a great story about *structure fishing* during the big spring tournament out of Michigan City, Indiana. Arnie was tipped off about a great *reef.* When he found it, he said, "it was like looking for a skull on the bottom of the lake miles from nowhere." Obviously, this was not a large feature, but Arnie found plenty of fish around that particular feature because the surrounding water was so flat.

The glaciers that carved out the Great Lakes left many ledge-like drop offs, and rocky reefs, that can be found in the 90-to 180-foot range. This is the summer trout zone. Once you locate good structure, start paying attention to how sub-surface currents interact with individual structures. According to Capt. Tomczak, Lake Superior has a plethora of rocky, jagged humps and ledges. He targets structure where the bottom current runs into the steep face of a drop off. According to John, this creates an upwelling. John says you can see the bow in the thermocline (on your graph) when an upwelling is at play. Because on Lake Superior there is so much good looking structure, John has learned to identify which features hold fish, based on the wind direction (and resulting current flow). Remember, currents are wind driven, and each wind regime will create sub-surface currents that will interact with bottom topography. The chapter on Currents at the end of this book unpacks a strategy for how to analyze wind patterns, interpret currents, and match conditions with productive structures based on the weather.

Another form of structure many anglers ignore is bottom composition. The bottom composition of each lake varies from one area to another. In some areas, you will have muck, interspersed with rock and clay bottom areas. Lake trout are not everywhere! You must find the features that are attracting fish because lakers will return to the same locations, under the same conditions. Also, if you have a rocky formation in 80 feet of water, look for additional, similar rocky features in deeper water directly offshore.

Lake trout often move perpendicular to the shoreline. In some areas, lakers will feed over clay bottoms. In another area that has predominantly a muck bottom, areas of rock will attract lakers. Anything different about the bottom topography or the water can attract lake trout. Capt. Ralph Steiger has an excellent fall program jigging blade baits for big lake trout in southern Lake Michigan. The southern rim of this lake is known for its sand. Ralph targets areas along the shoreline where steep breaks combine with gravel or rocks on the bottom. Ralph trolls until he finds fish, then sets up and jigs.

Some days, lakers don't seem to be relating to anything. I've seen plenty of days when we are chasing salmon between 200 and 300 feet of water, and we'll mark plenty of trout suspended and down on the bottom. These *drifters* are tough, but not impossible, to catch. Even in the middle of nowhere, subtle areas where the bottom drops off faster will attract open water trout, even when they are over 200 feet deep. In the Great Lakes, you will find rocky humps that rise up off the bottom in over 200 feet of water. One of my favorite deep humps goes from 235 feet up to 220 feet. It's less than a ¼ mile long, but it attracts trout in summer like the music on the ice cream truck attracts kids in the neighborhood.

Setting a spread of suspended lines targeting lake trout is not that different than targeting kings or coho. A variety of presentations including

downriggers, diving discs, copper, lead core, and Torpedoes are productive. Target depth will determine which presentations to run. Setting coppers and lead core is pretty straightforward. You can run meat, flashers and flies, or spoons on these rods. My favorite copper spoon is the magnum and regular size Black Fin Tuna Silver Streak. Spin Doctors in shades of yellow and green are my favorite flashers for coppers and lead core targeting lakers. When lake trout drop deep and go completely shut off, my best rod is a Musky size Torpedo SWR with a clean Stinger or Super Slim. The Torpedo is clipped to the braid backing in front of three colors of lead core, then let out anywhere from 250 to 500 feet, then attached to a Church TX-44 planer. Some days, it takes all the fish.

Setting downriggers and divers requires a little strategy when it comes to lake trout. Lake trout are drawn to the color yellow, which makes the chartreuse Dipsy Diver one of my favorites. My second favorite diver color is pearl or white. At times, the magnum Lurk Disco Diver will produce more trout than the standard divers. Plastic flashers, metal dodgers, meat rigs, and clean spoons all produce on divers. Suspended lake trout can be discriminating eaters, so aggressively change diver baits until you connect. Adjust how far out you run divers and what angle you set them on. If fish are spooky, then switch to Slide Divers.

Downriggers are my best lake trout rods. When running metal dodgers, shorter leads of 5 to 10 feet work best. Eight-inch flashers work best stretched back 10 to 20 feet. The larger 10 and 11-inch paddles should be run 20 to 40 feet off the weight. Magnum spoons such as Silver Streaks, Stingers, and Moonshines work best off riggers when they are only 20 to 40 feet back. When you are marking suspended trout but they are not hitting, try changing your lead lengths off downriggers. Simple adjustments can make a big difference on moody fish.

Trolling speed is an unknown variable that you must isolate daily. I catch many lakers at salmon speeds, but when the trout are on the off, you might have to idle way back and creep along to draw strikes. If you can see fish on the graph but action is slow, make frequent speed adjustments. Trout are known to follow lures, so sudden speed changes often trigger strikes.

One of the oldest tricks in the book is the neutral drop. When I'm trolling deep, open water with a full spread of lines targeting anything with a tail, I like to run one rigger, with a 15-pound weight, well below all the other lines. This rod usually has a yellow Jensen dodger with a yellow Ole Moe. When I mark a deep trout, I will drop (or raise) the lone rigger toward the fish, then drop the boat into neutral. I cannot remember how many times that has triggered strikes! These strikes are often very light, and if the rod is not loaded, they are easy to miss.

Lure selection for summer and fall lake trout is pretty broad. When trout are on or near the bottom, dodgers or flashers work best. My favorite metal dodger is the 0 size Luhr Jensen, followed by the Opti-Dodger. Capt. Tomczyk favors the smaller, 00 Jensen dodgers. He believes the smaller dodger allows him to troll at faster speeds. Top dodger colors are silver, silver glow, and yellow. A number of plastic flashers work for trout; my favorites are Spin Doctors, Hot Spots, and Dream Weaver Paddles in the 8-and 10-inch sizes. Productive base colors for flashers include white, yellow, green, and silver. A variety of tapes (UV and glow) are added to flashers. Flies in shades of green are the most consistent laker takers. Spin-N-Glos and Peanuts should also be used. When using Spin-N-Glos some days the trout will hit just the plain Spin-N-Glo, no skirt. Other days, running it with the skirt, AKA *Ole Moe*, will take more fish. Small details make a big difference with Mr. Lake Trout.

I used to think that when it came to catching laker, lure color didn't make much difference. One day my friend, Capt. Caleb Weiner, reminded me that lake trout can be totally keyed in on a particular color. I just wish he didn't have to *kick-my-arse* on the fish to make the point! After a morning charter, I returned to the dock to learn that *my buddy* had pounded the trout. Funny how sometimes you don't learn the hot tip until all your lines are out of the water. After all of our customers had left, I simply walked over and asked Caleb what he did differently. We were fishing the same level, running, or so I thought, pretty much the same gear. But then Caleb pointed to his dash—it looked like he had dumped a tackle box on it! It was covered with an assortment of plastic flashers, metal dodgers, flies, and Spin-N-Glo's. He then said that he just kept changing lures until he found the hot rig for the day.

On this particular day, I had become complacent. In my little world, I thought that when it came to catching a laker off the bottom 150 feet down (or deeper), color didn't matter. Caleb loves fishing for trout. He changes lures more than anyone I know when it comes to trout, and he has proven that a systematic approach to shuffling through productive color patterns is better than merely dragging your favorite lure around clinging to ancient ideas. When targeting deep trout, lure selection matters.

There is an art to catching bottom-oriented lake trout. The greatest challenges in catching trout off the bottom are speed and lure control. For this reason, when you are targeting the bottom, you might want to only run a few lines. The deeper in the water column you are targeting, the truer it is. This will allow you to focus on what matters most. I had to relearn this lesson on a recent charter. Fishing had been good all week long for a nice mix of kings, steelhead, and lake trout. We were fishing the entire water column, from just below the surface all the way down to the bottom in 140 to 220 feet of water. On this particular day, the silver fish had vanished. I was running a complete spread of riggers, wires, lead core, and copper. Another

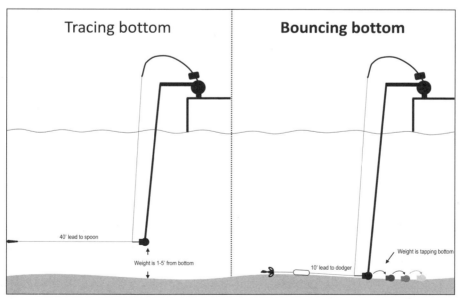

When tracing the bottom with a spoon on light line, you want to run the spoon within 1 to 5 feet of the bottom. When bouncing the bottom, the downrigger weight should occasionally tap the bottom.

captain had decided to focus on the bottom and just try to catch trout. He ran two downriggers and two wire lines with 20-ounce ball weights. He got everything rubbing on the bottom just right. Nice and slow. Then, he just kept adjusting his angle (COG) over the bottom until he found the hot troll. He caught a limit of trout. On that day, I was *distracted* by all the other lines, so I never dialed in my deep rigs. Application: when you are trying to dial into deep water trout on the bottom, some days just running a few lines allows you to focus on what matters most—getting the speed, angle, and rub just right.

When fishing riggers on the bottom, use a 15-pound weight. This will minimize blowback and allow you to get a better read on *where* your lure actually is. Some days, you want the weight just a foot or so off the bottom. Other days, the weight will need to occasionally *kiss* the bottom, maybe coming in contact with the bottom once every 15 to 30 seconds.

Running wire line on the bottom requires you to use a 1-pound or 20-ounce sinker. The intricacies of how to do this are discussed at the end of the wire line chapter. When tapping the bottom, you can swap out the beads beneath the fly with Lindy floats. These come in a variety of colors and function in the same way as the beads, but they add a touch of buoyancy and hold the fly off the bottom.

Captain John Tomczyk with a beautiful Lake Superior lake trout.

CAPTAIN JOHN TOMCZYK'S LAKE TROUT WISDOM

Daybreak Charters www.daybreakfish.com 906.250.1052

- The majority of John's trout are caught around structure.
- Lake Superior has an overabundance of structure, so John focuses on drastic, jagged edges that create upwellings. Look for steep, rocky humps that rise up off of the bottom from roughly 120 to 160 feet. Many of these humps are only 200 yards long. Also, bank or shelf type drop offs that parallel the shoreline hold trout.
- Never fishes flat bottom, unless it is next to structure.
- More than half of John's lakers are caught suspended well off the bottom. The largest fish are taken suspended and closer to shore. John thinks smaller fish hide near the bottom.
- Average fishing depth over the course of the season is 120 to 150 feet. John targets 15 to 40 feet of water during the spring.
- The majority of fish are concentrated in key areas.
- Favorite speed is 2.5 mph over ground. John observes many anglers trolling too slow.
- Spoons are the top bait all season. Favorites are the magnum Silver Streak Greasy Chicken Wing near the bottom, and Ol' Yellar. Finn Spoons work great in the upper levels of the water column. Favorite Finn patterns are the Tequila Sunrise (pink and gold stripe on gold plate) and the plane gold Finn. When fishing deep, magnum spoons take over 80 percent of his fish.
- The 00 Luhr Jensen dodger (half green/half glow) followed by a green/yellow or a white Peanut (or Spin-N-Glo) on a 15 inch leader is hot bait. Sometimes, John tips the Peanut with a 1 inch by 1½ inch sucker strip. Smaller dodger lets him keep his speed up. He runs this 3 to 5 feet off ball. Leads below 100 feet are rarely longer than a rod length.
- Slide Divers are his favorite diver for shallow and deep applications. He runs spoons on the Slide Diver but his best Diver rig is a Frog Spin Doctor and green/glow Mikes Eye Fly with a Spin-N-Glow in front of the fly.

CHAPTER 11

Brown Trout Logic

When I was young, I used to read every fishing article I could get my hands on. I remember an article about monster brown trout from Flaming Gorge reservoir in Utah. In my mind's eye, I can still see the photographs of those giant fish and remember how badly I wanted to catch a trophy brown trout! While my dad and I got pretty good at catching coho and king salmon, browns were a rare visitor aboard our boat. We caught some browns, but not in any great numbers—and certainly none of the trophies I so desperately wanted to catch.

When I turned 16 and acquired a driver's license, my fishing horizons expanded, and the one fish that was within reach of my buddy's canoe and a few paddle strokes was—none other than Mr. Brown Trout. One of my favorite memories involved a snowy January morning. My buddy Paul Jaros and I took his green canoe, strapped it onto the roof of my parents' white station wagon, drove up to the Zion Nuclear Plant, and carried that little watercraft down to the gravel beach. And yes, we headed out into the freezing cold winter waters as only two teenagers who thought they were invulnerable would do. After paddling about 180 yards into the lake, we found ourselves floating and alone, the lake eerily calm. With mist rising off the turbulent discharge water, we were absolutely surrounded by browns. Cast after cast, we caught fish. It was like fishing in an aquarium!

Over time, I learned that to catch browns, I had to do things differently compared to the other salmonids. Brown trout don't behave like kings, coho, steelhead, and lake trout. For starters, browns are a shoreline-oriented fish that prefer water that's warmer than their cousins like. This makes them ideal targets for small boat anglers and shore fishermen. When Dad and

Brown trout are great small boat targets. They live near shore and grow to massive sizes.

I would trailer our 17-foot Whaler up to ports in Wisconsin for the late summer king bonanza, brown trout turned several slow adventures into great successes. Quite by chance, we learned that we could catch big, staging browns when the water warmed up and got murky enough to chase the kings out into the deeps. The browns would hang close.

While salmon and steelhead think nothing of packing their bags and roaming vast stretches of open water, browns are homebodies. They are opportunistic feeders that look for areas with good structure. When they find their comfort zone, they don't leave! (I think my parents thought that about me when I was in my 20s—their couch was comfortable structure and close to their refrigerator, a reliable food source).

Brown trout are one of the largest and most beautiful salmonids found in the Great Lakes. If you want to add a brown trout playbook to your angling game this season, you must adjust your thinking and tactics. You might have to venture into new territory, adjust your trolling spread to skinny water, and add a few lures to your arsenal. Before diving into the nitty-gritty of how to locate and catch Mr. Brown Trout, let's spend a few minutes studying the patterns and characteristics of this magnificent creature. A thorough understanding of browns will narrow your search parameters and lead you to success.

THE BASICS

Browns prefer warmer water than the other salmon and trout species. The general temperature range of browns is 47 to 65 degrees. Their optimal feeding range is 54 to 62 degrees. In some regions, they remain fairly active in temperatures up to 65 degrees. Excessively warm water will drive browns offshore, but they will return to the shallows when temperatures cool down. There are exceptions to all things fishy, so yes some browns are randomly caught from deep water every season. While kings and coho prefer to dine on alewives, brown tout are opportunistic feeders. They love the invasive round gobies and will feed on just about anything else that crosses their path, too.

Brown trout are a shoreline and structure-oriented fish. While other species seem to randomly roam the lakes, browns spend much of their time holding on near-shore structure. Some of the best fishing each season takes place from the beach out to 50 feet of water. How shallow do browns go? They venture into shallower water than you can imagine. Structure features that are magnets to browns include drop-offs, humps, boulders and rocks out on the lake bottom, piers, breakwalls and jetties, points, rivers, power plant outflows, waste water run-offs, industry discharges, harbor mouths, and any rocky areas along the bottom.

Their preference for warmer water, along with their love for structure, keep browns near the shoreline for much of the year. This makes them ideal targets for small boat anglers. Many charter captains have developed strong brown trout programs for days when the winds keep them from making long runs offshore, so they can target browns in more comfortable waters. Recreational anglers that trailer their boats for hours to fish for salmon and arrive at a rough lake should pay close attention to the following material, as they can often find some fishable water in brown trout country on those days.

Water clarity is a key variable. Browns usually are extremely difficult to catch in gin-clear water. This may be because boat noise gives them lockjaw in their shallow environment. For sure, like many fish, they are extra wary in shallow water. I think the most likely reason they can be tough when they're in clear, shallow water is their great eyesight. I believe they see the lures too well and sense something wrong with them. Fact: they are much easier to catch if the water has some color. I'm not suggesting that you target muddy water, but rather that you look for "stained" or slightly murky water. Shoreline water is more easily impacted by wind and wave action, currents, and rain runoff. For this reason, experienced brown trout anglers have learned to analyze water texture. Water clarity changes significantly over the course of a week or season and from one region to another. On Lakes Ontario and Erie, finding murky water is much easier than on Lakes Michigan and Superior. No matter where you fish, your action will greatly improve when you incorporate water clarity into your brown trout targeting matrix.

One particular late summer charter trip really helps clarify this point. On this day, I ran the *Blue Horizon* north to fish off the Port of Kenosha, Wisconsin. Capt. Brian had fished this area the previous day, and he told me that his best action had come in the murky water. We left the harbor before sunrise, ran 5 miles to the north, and set lines in about 30 feet of water as the sun was breaking through the morning fog. I had told my clients that we were going to pound the fish (always a mistake) and the lack of action greatly disappointed.

Once it was light and the morning fog lifted, I realized why fishing was so slow. The water was crystal clear! Overnight, a light south wind had pushed a band of ultra-clear water into the area. Water temps were perfect. I was marking bait, but either the browns had moved, or I couldn't catch them. At 8 a.m. I received a phone call from another captain who was fishing several miles north of me. Capt. Rich had slid up into 8 to 12 feet of water and had found the same, slightly cloudy water they had been fishing the previous day, and he said the fish were biting! I bumped up my trolling speed, turned the boat to the northwest, and slid into the beach. We were soon into fish. In the next two hours, the action was non-stop, and we took a limit of browns and some nice kings, as well. On that particular day, the catchable browns followed the murky water up into the shallows. The previous day, the murky water had extended to the south. You will be amazed at how shallow you can catch browns if conditions are right!

Before moving on, here's a warning: browns are downright goofy and moody. One day, they can be the easiest fish in the world to catch, hitting wire divers 20 feet off the rod tip, and the next day you can pass a perfectly presented stealth lure past a thousand fish and not get a single strike. Some days their response doesn't make sense. Muskies are called the fish of 10,000 casts. Some days, browns are the fish that require you to try 100 different lures. Call them *finicky*. Honestly, some days you just need to figure out the exact size, color, and brand of lure they want.

Despite their unpredictable nature, browns can be caught throughout the day. Just because they don't hit at sunrise doesn't mean you can't catch them later. This is especially true when browns hold in extra dark or murky water. On these days, the best action often occurs in the middle of the day. During low light conditions, it may just be too dark for the fish to see lures. The increased sunlight makes lures more visible in murky water.

Since browns live close to the shore, you must refine your techniques to catch them. Unlike deep, open water, the shallows are totally unforgiving of angler error. Fish in shallow water are more sensitive and moody than the same fish found in deeper water. Their environment, their *world* so to speak, is very restricted. The vertical boundaries from the surface to the bottom may only be 10, 20, or 30 feet. This alone heightens their already spooky nature.

HOW TO FIND BROWNS

Step one is to identify areas that have received good plantings of browns. Browns are homebodies. While browns can be found just about anywhere, you greatly increase your odds of success when you key on regions that receive heavy stockings or where browns naturally reproduce. Next, spend a little time studying a topographical chart or consult the local fishing guru and seek out areas from the beach out to 50-foot depths that are structure rich. Browns are usually far more concentrated on structure adjacent to stocking sites.

Structure really matters. Off my homeport, there is little significant, shallow water structure. Run 6 miles to the north or 14 miles to the south and shallow water humps, drop-offs, and rocky formations are plentiful. Loads of browns populate those areas. I catch few browns close to my harbor, but if I venture to the north or south, browns start hitting our landing net. Structure matters.

When targeting spring browns, look for the warmest water available. You'll often find it around river and power plant outflows, industry and waste-water discharges, harbor mouths, or stretches of shallow water. Cities with large break wall structures, such as Milwaukee, Wisconsin and Oswego, New York are brown trout havens during the colder months. The best spring brown action is often found in 5 to 20 feet of water. I've caught many browns when my boat was in only 8 to 10 feet, and my planers were up against the beach!

When trolling in less than 10 feet of water in spring (or any season, for that matter), pay attention to any subtle nuances in the shoreline. Old jetties that extend into the lake attract browns. Fish any shoreline abnormality: a spit of sand, a slight point extending as little as 50 feet out into the lake, or even a slight bend in the shoreline. Currents are more intense along the shoreline and even minor shoreline abnormalities and structure alter water flow. Abnormalities also attract baitfish, and browns will hunt right up against these shallow water features. They also hold outside these features in 15 to 25 feet of water.

As the shallows warm in summer, browns retreat off the shoreline and drop down into 30 to 50 feet of water. Their movements continue to key off structure and their water temperature preference of 54 to 62 degrees. Want to know the secret to catching browns? Locate the intersection of 54- to 62-degree water and bottom structure.

Three highly productive features when it comes to browns are humps, drop offs, and large boulders scattered across the lake bottom. Any hump could hold browns, whether it rises 2 feet or 10 feet higher than the surrounding bottom. Drop offs vary tremendously, so isolate which drops in your region offer the most drastic change. Browns utilize the entire water column, so you might find them holding on the bottom or suspended. When feeding on gobies, they are tight to the bottom. They typically will not stray far from their favorite areas. If water becomes excessively warm in the 30- to 50-foot range, then browns move farther out into the lake seeking cooler water.

Anytime cold water rolls into the beach—which happens a lot in the summer—you can find browns feeding up in less than 10 feet of water. My friend, Jim Brooks, caught a 27-pound brown one summer trolling in 8 feet of water off Port Washington, Wisconsin. The massive brown hit a Bomber Long A off his outside side planer board, which was running up against the beach. Jim believes the fish was in only 2 to 3 feet of water when it hit!

Browns spawn in the fall. Some of the best big brown action occurs when browns stage off spawning rivers and harbors during July and August. These pre-spawn fish are as moody as a Dutch wife. They will seemingly sit all day, staring at the bottom, counting zebra and quagga mussels, and then, without warning, go on massive binges. During these frenzies, you can catch great numbers of fish. Success during the late summer and fall is all about being in the right spot at the right time. Key your late summer fishing efforts in regions where spawning bound fish stage. Browns follow the same seasonal patterns year after year. Once you determine which areas they like, you can go back to the same coordinates year after year.

Just because many harbors close and many anglers pick up their shotgun and head to fields and deer stands, you can fish browns through the winter. In many locations around the Great Lakes, anglers with small boats will fish for browns in the winter until ice prevents them from launching boats and kayaks. Many harbors, river mouths, and warm water discharges provide fishing opportunities through much of the winter.

STRATEGIES AND TACTICS FOR BROWN TROUT

Stealth presentations are super productive for shallow water browns, and they allow you to run additional lines in the shallow strike zone. When engineering a shallow water brown program, you must constantly be aware of the depth you are trolling. Let's unpack our methodology based on two zones—the beach out to 25 feet and the 25- to 50-foot level. We'll look at the beach zone first.

Most anglers struggle to catch fish off the beach. Fact: the shallower the water you troll, the less room you have for error. When fish move into 5, 8 or 12 feet of water, they are living in some tight quarters! With the surface a few feet above and the bottom right there, they are extra spooky, easily agitated, and highly aware of everything going on around them. Engine noise is magnified, and the echo of your boat's signature announces your presence before you arrive. The immediate environment has a huge impact on how a fish behaves and whether he will strike. If you take the same fish and put him in deeper water, he behaves very differently than when he's in super shallow water. When the shallow water is clear, fish get extra spooky.

To help you capitalize on this super shallow fishery, lets further divide the beach zone into three levels—the beach out to 10 feet, 10 to 15 feet, and 15 feet out to 25 feet. Pulling fish off the beach is an art, and you must be precise with which rigs you run and how you run them. Some days the fish will suspend and hit lures throughout the water column. When browns are negative, however, the most productive rods are often planer boards with lines riding just above the bottom. I know what you're thinking, "but the water is sooooo shallow, won't they see the lure overhead and swim up and strike?" No.

You can effectively target these negative fish with monofilament side planers, short lead core segments, and super short coppers. If you want to run lead core or copper off side planers, you must maintain a minimum trolling depth; otherwise, you will snag the bottom. The presentations you use really must be adjusted to the minimum water depth you troll. If you are running short coppers, you cannot slow down! They will hang bottom fast.

What does this mean? When targeting the shallow zone, you must always be cognizant of where your deepest planer line is running. If you go in shallower than the depth it is running, bad things can happen.

If you want to troll in less than 10 feet of water, then you should only run monofilament planer boards and lead segments up to one color. If you stay outside of 12 feet, you can safely run a two-color lead core (20 yards) without snagging debris off the bottom. If you stay deeper than 15 feet, then you can run a three-color lead core (30 yards). As long as you troll in a straight line, it will stay off the bottom. If you troll in the 20- to 25-foot level, you can safely run up to four-colors of lead core off planers (40 yards). If you stay outside of 25 feet, then you can add up to five-colors (50 yards) of lead core.

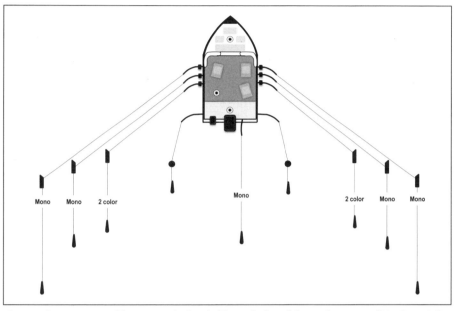

At times brown trout will go up on the beach. To catch these fish, you have to troll in 6 to 12 feet of water. Mono side planers are the best presentation for presenting lures to fish holding in super shallow water. If you stay outside 12 feet of water, you can add 1 or 2-color lead cores to a spread of mono planers.

Let's examine several planer board scenarios. You can easily mix mono and lead core side planers for shallow water. Always keep the mono planers on the outside of the lead cores. From the beach out to 10 feet of water, mono in-line planers are the way to go. You can run as many mono planers a side as you want, just set the outside planers with longer leads to avoid tangles. One warning: if you know you are going to slide your boat up into 6 to 8 feet of water, think about where your shore-side planer board will run. It very well may be in only 2 or 3 feet of water! In this case, you only want the lure back about 15 to 30 feet to avoid hanging bottom. Also, make sure the bottom is free of snags and weeds. Because of wave action, you often have very clean bottoms against the shoreline. If you are going to hold 10 to 12 feet of water, then you can run a one-color lead core as well.

When trolling in 12 to 15 feet of water, run mono planers with a 20- to 100-foot lead on the outside boards. You can then run a two-color lead core inside the mono boards. If you are holding the 15- to 20-foot level, you can add a three-color lead core inside the two-color. For the 20- to 25-foot level, I like to run a mono planer on the outside and a three and four-color lead core inside. When I know I will be trolling outside of 25 feet, I like to run a five-color lead core on the inside planer.

A few words of caution: avoid sharp turns! I often reel in my lead cores when making 180-degree turns in shallow water to avoid snagging bottom and debris. Remember, when you place a lead core out off the side on a planer board, every slight turn or course adjustment you make, the line and lure greatly speed up and rise, or slow down and sink. Spoons easily sink and grab mussels or weeds off the bottom without you knowing it got fouled. When setting lead cores or long mono planers, make sure you don't free-spool haphazardly and let the spoons hit bottom.

The second shallow zone, 25 to 50 feet of water, really feels like deep water if you've spent time trolling along the beach. When trolling in this range, longer lead cores and coppers get the nod. If you slow down or make sharp turns, coppers will snag the bottom more readily than lead core lines. The same principles for running segmented leads and coppers offshore apply for shallow water browns. You just need to keep one other variable in mind—the bottom. Offshore, our focus is to the surface and down. Inside, you need to be more conscientious of depth. Make sure that you maintain enough water depth to avoid snagging bottom with any lines you run off side planers.

Here are a few of the typical lead core spreads I run when targeting browns in the 30- to 50-foot zone. When trolling in 30 to 35 feet of water, I run the outside planer with mono stretched back at least 100 feet. Keel sinkers from ½ to 1 ounce are used on the mono board. Segmented leads from two to five colors are run on the inside planers. The longer leads should be run closer to the boat. When trolling in 35- to 45-foot depths, then segments up to 7 colors go out. Once you get past 50 feet, you can run

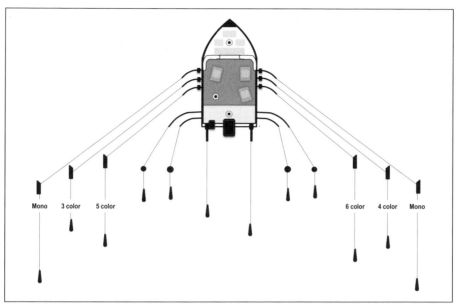

You often find brown trout holding in 20 to 50 feet of water. This is a typical spread that can be run throughout the season for browns.

up to 10 colors of lead core off planers. You want to spread your lures from the top to the bottom until you isolate at what level browns are feeding. Many days, the most productive rod is a segmented lead core that runs 5 to 10 feet above the bottom.

You can also run a longer lead core down the middle. This rod is easy to keep just off the bottom, and you easily can see if it hits bottom. If you have not trolled lead core in shallow water, consider running a lead core down the middle. Experiment with different amounts of line out and note what depth the lure hits bottom. You can then apply your findings to approximate how deep your planer boards run.

While it is challenging to run coppers in less than 35 feet of water, they can easily be used in the 35- to 50-foot zone. You cannot slow down as they do sink, and you need to exercise caution when making turns. Copper segments of 50 to 150 feet can be run in this depth range. As you move deeper, you can add progressively longer segments of copper.

On the terminal end of planer lines, 12- to 20-pound test fluorocarbon leaders are a must for spoons and crank baits. In super clear water, the lighter leader works better. A small ball-bearing swivel with spoons will produce more strikes than larger swivels. Keel sinkers from ¼ to 1 ½ ounce are recommended for mono side planers.

Divers and Slide Divers produce many shallow water browns. Running divers is easy, and they don't get in the way of planers. The murkier or darker the water, the better that divers work. I run 14- to 20-pound fluorocarbon leaders and small ball bearing swivels on shallow water divers.

In murky water, try running two divers a side. Set the inside diver at 1.5 and the outside diver at 2.5 to 3.5. I will run a smaller diver on the outside. One morning, I had a double diver pattern off each side of the boat, and all four rods hooked up in 18-feet of water at the same time! Spoons and shallow-diving cranks both work with divers. If divers are not working, try a slide diver with the lure stretched back 20 to 50 feet behind it.

Downriggers are not very useful when targeting the beach, but once you get out into 25 to 50 feet of water, they become a vital component of any brown trout spread. Because browns are weary and the water is still relatively shallow, I usually only run two of my four riggers when fishing 25 to 35 feet. If I put a third or fourth rigger in the water, all the riggers go dead. Another observation: my divers are more productive when I have just two corner downriggers in the water.

Light line rigs spooled with 8- to 12-pound test are the way to fish riggers. Stretches behind the weight really depend on water clarity. If water is gin clear, then you need 100-foot leads. If the water is murky, then leads as short as 20 feet produce. When trolling in 30 feet of water or more, then you can run an SWR. If your SWR has three-colors of lead core, then make sure you set it at least 15 feet off the bottom. If you want to get an extra line in the water, a mono flat line or a three-color lead core straight off the stern can produce a surprising number of fish.

The real secret to catching brown trout may be trolling speed. While no single magical speed guarantees success, summer and fall browns prefer lures on a fast troll, often in excess of 2.3 kt. (2.6 mph). I've had many outings where a 2.6- to 2.7 kt. (3.1 mph) troll speed was magical. Rob Wendel, who spends a ton of hours chasing browns from his kayak during the fall and spring, finds a slow troll (less 1.8-2.2 mph) is most productive. Like other fish, once lines are set, experiment with speed until you connect.

Lure selection for browns is complicated. When targeting kings and coho, certain lures and color combinations produce consistent results. Not so for Mr. Brown Trout! Spring, summer, or fall, you never really know what the day's winner will be until you go fishing. If I know browns are present where I am trolling, I aggressively change lures. Five variables to consider include brand, size, base color, overall pattern and type. Sometimes it's just a matter of shuffling through your selection of known brown killers until you find the magic bait.

Here are a list of some of the more popular spoons used for browns: Michigan Stingers, Stinger Scorpions, Super Slims, Yuks, Mini Steaks, Maulers, Savant Jake 45s, and Rattle Spoons. It would be pointless to list my favorite color patterns here as browns can want anything on any given day, and their preferences change so fast. What I can offer you are the base colors that are underlying productive spoons. The best color patterns include green, yellow, gold, glow, orange/yellow and green/glow. Now, at times, a splash of red mixed in with the yellows or gold will trigger strikes. In murky water glows and frog patterns are deadly, and then some days just a plain silver or gold spoon will be the winner. Lake Ontario brown trout expert Capt. Ernie Lantiegne employs an array of regular size Stingers and Eppinger Flutter Devils and likes color patterns that closely mimic alewives. Captains on southern Lake Michigan favor colors that mimic gobies.

Browns can be found across the Great Lakes region, and their numbers fluctuate from one year to the next. Every region has its favorite lures, so seek local guidance. When you experiment with lure selection, don't be afraid to step outside the box. One spring, my best brown trout baits were the 00 red coho dodgers and Howie Peanut flies. One recent summer, a spoon from the early days of the Great Lakes salmon fishery was one of the best baits—the small, plain gold or silver Norwegian spoon. After Capt. Arnie tipped me off on this spoon, I had to crawl up into the attic, peel off the cobwebs, and search old tackle boxes for this spoon. Creativity and a willingness to adjust your lure selection will go a long way toward helping you connect with browns.

Browns are a great alternative target to salmon and the other trout species. When the other species are hard to find or just not biting, anglers who can switch gears often turn a slow outing into a great success. Another reason to put browns on your list this season: they grow to immense proportions in the Great Lakes. As of this writing, the Great Lakes record is a whopping 41pound, 8-ounce monster. There just might be a bigger creature out there, looking to pick a fight with you!

Rob Wendel is a brown trout expert. We can all learn from his experience.

ROB WENDEL GREAT LAKES KAYAK ANGLER
10 TIPS FOR MORE BROWNS

- Browns stay in one area. If an area along the shoreline has structure and baitfish, browns will move perpendicularly in and out from shallow to deep water, all season long, based on favorable water temperatures.
- Favorite structures are large underwater boulder fields. If no natural structure exists, key your search off manmade features such as breakwalls, harbor mouths, power plant discharges, jetties, and piers.

- Browns are opportunistic feeders and will eat alewives, gobies, gizzard shad, emerald shiners, perch, young salmonids, and even dead fish.
- When targeting larger fish, pay close attention to lure size. Some days, larger fish will only strike certain size lures.
- Some days the style of crankbait is critical. For example, some days shad style baits work better than stick baits. Favorite colors are gold, green, and orange.
- Crank baits work best for spring and fall fishing. Spoons produce best in summer.
- Generally, slower trolling speeds of 1.8 to 2.2 mph work best.
- Peak activity periods are seasonal. During summer, the best bite is dawn, dusk and through the night. Spring and fall see the best action around 8 a.m. and from 3 to 5 p.m. The autumn sundown bite can be spectacular.
- Clear water situations require extra stealth. Use 10-pound fluorocarbon leaders, longer leads behind the boat. Sometimes, tube jigs will work best.
- The Church TX 6 or Offshore OR 34 for mono and 1- to 2 color lead cores. The Church Walleye Board and Offshore OR 12 for longer lead cores.

CHAPTER 12

Fishing With Meat— Lessons from Uncle Bud

By Dave Mull—condensed from his upcoming book,
King Salmon Secrets of Uncle Bud

When I asked Uncle Bud why he uses meat he replied, "I know this for sure: these king salmon didn't get up over 20 pounds by eating metal spoons or tinsel flies. They got big by eating real fish."

A retired electrician from Chicago, Bud Roche started fishing for Great Lakes salmon on Lake Michigan in the early 1970s. Now, at the age of 81, he still launches his 21-foot Grady White, powered by twin 140-hp Suzukis, at almost every chance he gets to troll the waters around his homeport of New Buffalo, Michigan from April through September. He's been a member of the Michiana Steelheaders, a smallish group of hardcore anglers for umpteen years (he really doesn't remember), and in the last decade, he has finished first in overall club standings seven times. The years he didn't get first, he got second.

It's not like he beats up on just the same group of anglers, many of whom are darn good fishermen, every year. Each July, he and two crewmembers trailer the Grady (christened "Uncle Bud) up to Ludington, Michigan, for one of the largest open pro/am events on the Great Lakes. Bud fishes the amateur side and has often finished in the money. In 2011, he achieved second place out of 75 boats, mere ounces out of winning the whole shooting match. He also has done well in tournaments out of Michigan City, Indiana. One year, Bud won the amateur side of a pro/am with a weight that was far better than the pro boats.

Many have wondered how Bud catches so many large fish, but he has kept his use of meat—partially filleted herring and alewives—a well-guarded secret. His standard answer when fellow competitors ask how he caught all of his fish has been "Blue Dolphin," referring to a popular spoon pattern. I've been working on a book with Bud for a couple of years, and one reason it didn't get done sooner is because Bud, although he hasn't come out and admitted it, has mixed emotions about the project. A former nationally-recognized dragster racer, Bud is highly competitive and likes to win. Why should he let his competition know the secrets to his success?

I met Bud back in 2003 when Great Lakes Angler Magazine, for which I was the editor, was using a 30-foot Dorado, courtesy of Running Mon Boat Works and owner Harry Glover. Harry kept the boat in one of his storage facilities in New Buffalo, and Bud rented one of the adjoining boat garages. Back then, Bud was a respected fisherman who did well, but had not yet started dominating tournaments. He started dominating next summer after he read a story on "sushi flies" written by Capt. Ernie Lantiegne. An experienced and respected charter captain out of Oswego, New York, Ernie wrote about his high rate of success with Lake Ontario fish when he wrapped a herring or alewife fillet underneath the tinsel body of a standard trolling fly and fished it behind a dodger or flasher.

I found that out when I happened to call Bud one summer day. I'd been fishing some salmon tournaments and not doing particularly well, and happened to be talking to Uncle Bud about one of his recent club tournament victories. I lamented that my own catch rate was dismal, and Bud, always direct, almost shouted into the phone, "you ought to read your own damn magazine!"

He told me how he'd been following Ernie's advice by wrapping fillets onto flies and whacking fish. He also said he'd been using herring or alewife strips pegged inside regular plastic more frequently and catching big fish on those, too.

This began our conversation about Bud's strategy of running meat, and nothing else, when he wanted to catch big fish and win tournaments.

Probably because Great Lakes salmon, steelhead, and lake trout have been fairly easy to catch with metal spoons, flasher-fly combos, and plastic

Bud out doing what he loves!

plugs, not many anglers (other than some anglers on Lakes Ontario and Superior) have spent much time learning the nuances of fishing with real fish flesh. Don't let that stop you. While fishing with meat isn't the "magic bullet" that will always fill your cooler, incorporating meat into your spread—a little bit or a lot—can help you catch more and, especially, bigger fish.

Capt. Dan Keating, my partner in Great Lakes Angler Super Salmon Schools, asked me to contribute a chapter on bait since I'm coming out with a book about the topic. In this chapter, we'll cover a lot of the basics to get you started on a tactic well-worth adding to your arsenal. For more on different bait rigs for trolling bait, watch for *King Salmon Secrets of Uncle Bud*, the book I wrote with the title character.

BAIT WORLD

Many anglers resist even trying bait because of the perceived need for specialized equipment, lots of preparation, and a high level of skill to make it run right. Those perceptions are largely wrong. When you get right down to it, running bait is as simple as adding a piece of meat to your fly with a piece of wire (sushi fly) or placing a plastic bait head over a herring strip and running it behind a downrigger, diver, copper, or lead core. That's less than five bucks worth of specialized equipment.

You can also slide a fillet into the slot of a Scarpace Plug, which is a cut-face, J-Plug-shaped plastic plug designed for the express purpose of carrying a wiggling piece of fish to salmon and trout. Even canned tuna packed into a Brad's Super Cut Plug and fished like a spoon behind a downrigger, copper line, or diving disc counts as fishing with meat. Wrapping fillets on top of a Worden's Mag Lip plug is also starting to gain acceptance in the Great Lakes angling community, after being a popular presentation on the West Coast for decades.

The bottom line is that you can present meat to salmon and trout in all sorts of ways. I've tried it over a decade of seasons and I am a firm believer that bait is a great equalizer for anglers of all skill levels. It's not a fussbudget of a presentation that needs to be finely tuned and delicately babied. The key is to put a fillet of herring or alewife down into the fish zone with some sort of gear or lure that makes it appear like something alive and edible. Fish, big fish, often eat it.

"All anglers are on a scale somewhere between 1 and 100 when it comes to being able to catch fish," Uncle Bud mused once. "No one is at 100; there's a lot of guys between level 40 and level 60. The ones who get past 60 and approach the higher levels are the guys who do a lot of little things right to not only find fish and hook them, but to make sure the fish stays on the line all the way to the net." In other words, to really fish with bait proficiently, it pays to sweat the details.

Gather and Prepare

Most bait used in the Great Lakes comes from a few different companies that net it in saltwater, flash-freeze it whole and in vacuum packs, or fillet it and freeze the fillets. One company, Familiar Bite in Amherst, New York, does the same with fresh-caught alewives that owner Walter Thompson nets, packs, and freezes himself. Familiar Bite also sells frozen herring.

Great Lakes anglers can also catch their own alewives, which Bud does each summer, with a Sabiki Rig. This is a light-line leader with six small hooks that are adorned with a bit of plastic or feathers to look like a tiny fish. A weight goes on the end of the Sabiki, and the whole rig is attached to a spinning rod combo and lobbed over the side of the boat into a school of alewives. The silvery baitfish actually bite the tiny flies, and you can catch up to six at once. Once caught, the alewives go quickly into a cooler with plenty of ice. It's not a bad idea to use slushy ice—some water added to cubes—so when the baitfish are flipping around in the cooler, they don't knock too many of their scales off.

When Bud is perch fishing, he always has a rod dedicated to Sabiki Rig fishing. When he sees a school of bait on the graph, out it comes. He often catches 50 or 60 of them in short order. He says it's vital to keep the alewives cold. By the time he gets back to his boat garage, the fish have expired, so he vacuum-packs them, 8 or 10 to a pack, and pops them into the freezer, whole and uncut by the fillet knife.

For herring, Bud orders trays of mid-size fish, Green and Blue Label size. Herring is categorized by its label. Red Label herring are the smallest and come 14 to a tray. They are fine for fishing whole or decapitated and placed in a bait head specially designed for a thicker bait. Green Label is the next biggest size, packed 12 to a tray, followed by Blue Label and the slightly bigger Gray Label, which are packed 8 to a tray. The biggest, Black Label, come five to a tray and are not widely used on the Great Lakes.

Bud likes Green Label; he prefers to buy it at a sporting goods store that carries it, so he can see its quality. When the eyes of the smaller herring are cloudy, Bud buys larger herring if they look better. He just trims it to fit in the heads and to the right size for sushi flies.

Instead of pre-cut herring strips, Bud prefers to start with frozen, whole bait and fillet it himself for bait heads and sushi flies. "It's labor-intensive to do, but it pays off," Bud says, explaining how he starts the process two days before he's going to use it. "There's a certain temperature the bait needs to be at to fillet easily. You don't want to wait until that fish gets soft before you fillet it because if it does, you better have a knife that's like a scalpel. You don't want it frozen and you don't want it thawed out, maybe a little more than halfway thawed to where you can bend it. Then you trim it down to size, whatever size of sushi that you want."

Bud fillets one side of the fish and sets the fillet aside. Then, unlike a fish-cleaning job to prepare fish for human consumption, he simply cuts the head off of the remaining side of the fish, giving him a second piece of bait with the backbone, ribs, and tail fin still part of it. This piece, with the tail, goes into the bait head. Bud trims the other, nearly boneless fillet (it might still have some ribs), into nicely shaped sushi for wrapping into a fly.

NOTE: The right side of the alewife or herring works best for most bait heads and should be the side that you leave the tail on with the backbone still in. That's because the fillet slides dorsal-fin-up into the head and the scale side is most visible, while the longer tab-side of the bait head and the hooks cover more of the unshiny, fleshy meat. This arrangement also allows the scale side to be on the outside of the rotation as the bait and bait head come through the water. Having the scale-side out creates more flash and attracts more fish.

After Bud has filleted 8 or 10 semi-frozen alewives and/or herring, making sure they stay cold, and being careful to not knock off scales, and reducing the bait's natural shininess, it's time to brine and scent them up for fishing in 2 days. This calls for two ingredients: non-iodized salt and herring oil. "I don't use the coarse salt, just plain table salt without the iodine. This is easier to shake onto the fillets, and I think the finer grain of salt gets absorbed into the fillets better. I lay the fillets, skin-side down, on a plastic tray and sprinkle salt on the meat side, which is face up. Then, I rub on some herring oil on the meat side of each fillet, and after that's all done, I turn them meat-side-down on the tray and sprinkle some salt and put some oil on the skin side. I let them sit, about an hour, somewhere cool, but not in the refrigerator or freezer. If you put the fillets in the fridge too soon, the herring oil hardens, like butter does, and I don't think it absorbs as well into the meat."

This preparation is important! The salt toughens the bait, so it stays pegged in the meathead or wrapped by the sushi wire. Without the salt, it would soon fall apart when trolled. After about an hour of sitting out in his cool boat garage, the trays go in the fridge. Bud then lets them sit and soak in the salty oil for a couple of days. When the day to go fishing arrives, he puts them into plastic Ziplocs.

Bud ties up all his own leaders for bait heads and sushi flies, and they're very similar. The materials are 40-pound test Seaguar Fluorocarbon, big No. 5/0 Gamakatsu Octopus hooks in the black chrome finish, and No. 1 XX Strong Gamakatsu Round Bend trebles, also in black chrome.

Bud, in typical meticulous fashion, first "pre-snells" the single hooks. "I put a three-wrap snell on the shank jammed right up against the eyelet," he says. "The end part of the hook wire that bends around to form the eyelet is sharp, so when you pull your snell tight against it, it can nick the fluorocarbon. I lost a couple of monster salmon that broke off right at that top single Octopus hook because of that. The three-wrap snell forms a cushion, so the snell knot that actually attaches the hook to the leader never touches that little rough edge. I haven't lost a fish because of a break-off there since I started tying the three-wrap snell."

Bud ties the leaders for sushi flies in much the same way, with the same-size hooks and the same 40-pound test fluorocarbon leader. The difference is that when he snells the top, 5/0 Octopus hook, he adds a piece of plastic coated, 22- or 24-gauge aluminum wire in with the snell; he just lays the wire longways against the hook shank and ties the snell. The wire holds the fillet in place—no hook actually pierces the meat.

"I do that and that wire is usually good for about three different baits until one end of it breaks off," said Bud. "I can still wrap the nose of the fillet with the other remaining piece of wire, but that will eventually break off, too. At that point, all I have to do is take about a 5-inch piece of the same wire and run it through the eye of the single Octopus hook and give it a twist to stay in place. That wire will work fine to hold the fillet for the sushi fly. Why do I bother snelling the wire in the first place? Because I'm anal, and I like things the way I like them. I'm so anal that sometimes I wish I wasn't so anal!"

With sushi flies, he puts the skin-side against the Octopus hook, flesh side outward, and wraps the nose of the fillet with the wire. This takes some of the flash away from the presentation, but the wire digs into the flesh and holds the chunk of fish in place better than putting the skin side out. His rigs have a couple of faceted beads between the single hook and the treble to add some color and flash in front of the dull fish flesh.

Bud also regularly employs "sushi squids." These are old-school plastics that were once immensely popular on the Great Lakes, but they are not real common anymore. Bud still likes them, getting special larger-size squids on his annual trips to Florida after the New Year. (NOTE: They are actually P-Line Squids, widely available in North America—Bud doesn't do a lot of online shopping.) He adds a tinsel fly with a plastic head that's designed to go under a squid body and is available from P-Line, Silver Horde and other manufacturers. This adds a bit of flash to the tail-end of the squid.

RUNNING THE BAIT

Bud has a special bait cooler that fits just right on the passenger side of his Grady-White, and it carries his arsenal of eight pre-rigged baits out to the fish. He modified the cooler to hold eight large, plastic cups of the sort you can get when you buy a 7/11 Store Slurpee. This keeps the baited up baitheads and flies from tangling with each other. Extra fillets in a Ziploc sit on ice in the same cooler for quick re-baiting. Incidentally, when re-baiting, Bud usually adds another squirt of herring oil to the fillet before it goes in the water.

So, you now have herring-oil-soaked bait, toughened by salt. Let's look at the different attractors and leader considerations with different delivery devices and ultimately explore Bud's all-bait spread. For bait heads, Bud likes the Shock Wave head from Church Tackle. This innovative design folds open and then snaps shut around the thick end of a fillet, which is held in place by spikes molded in to the head. These are nice because you don't poke a toothpick through to hold the meat in place. Bud also uses heads from Rhys Davis, which do need the toothpick, but he prefers the Shock Wave for ease of use. It doesn't bother him that the Church product is available in a limited number of colors.

"Any color works as long as it's white," Bud says of bait heads. Indeed, although he occasionally experiments with glows and other colors, when it comes down to tournament time and catching fish, white rules the spread.

He is also convinced that bait heads with stick-on eyes outperform bait heads without. "I really believe that adding an eye on each side of the head makes the bait look a whole lot more natural to the predator fish," Bud says.

NOTE: Bud always ties in a bead-chain swivel right behind the twinkie that's closest to the bait. The swivel lets the baithead move freely and avoids a twisted leader, which can lead to break-offs of fish.

Bud feels the same about flasher colors: white rules. That is, white rules, but other colors have consistent moments in the sun. For sure, when the day starts, his spread is full of white flashers and white bait heads. Once the sun gets good and high, he likes to switch a line or two to more translucent bait heads and flashers that feature UV finishes. If those rods start jumping, you can bet more UV goes in the water.

The All-Bait Spread

I am a big fan of the teachings of Dan Keating when it comes to setting a spread for salmon; considering the group dynamic and adjusting it to match the mood of the fish, whether that means stealthing everything up because the fish are neutral or putting together a power presentation that stirs things up with a lot of paddles when the fish are in the biting mood.

At first glance, Bud's all-bait spread, which he almost always uses in tournaments, diverges from the Keating philosophy. For one thing, Bud almost always has a flasher (sometimes a dodger) on every line. But, on second glance, you can see that Bud is trying to cover an extra large swath of the water with lures that are working fairly far apart from each other, with the exception of his two corner downriggers, which usually run with about 10 feet of depth separation and about 14 feet of lateral separation due to the width of the boat and the downrigger arms sticking out to the side.

He pairs bait heads with two main flasher and leader set-ups. First, he likes running a 11-inch paddle from companies such as Hot Spot and Dreamweaver. The leader for the big paddle usually is 5 to 6 feet long and features three "twinkies" spaced on the leader between the flasher and the bait head. These are basically tinsel flies to give the impression that the bait head and bait are part of a school of fish.

If the fish want big paddles with twinkies and bait, that's what Bud gives them, sometimes adding more on wire diver rods as well as copper and lead core behind boards. For sure, he starts his day on the water with paddles, twinkies, and bait on the center of his three Big Jon Brute downriggers. He runs the big paddle on a Secret Weapon Rig on his middle rigger. The three colors of lead core take the paddle down below the downrigger ball, and he wants this flasher, in the middle of his spread, to be the deepest. The center rigger also has his Fish Hawk Speed and Temp Probe on it, which relays speed-at-ball and the water temperature.

He then often runs smaller rotators with sushi flies or bait heads on his other two downriggers. The port corner might take an 8-inch Spin Doctor with a "sushified" fly, stretched 20 or 30 feet behind the ball and run 10 feet above the center downrigger line. He's a big fan of the "Blue Bubble" tape pattern for this flasher. The starboard-side rigger most often has another Spin Doctor—white with the greenish Mountain Dew tape or some other color.

With a sushi fly, Bud uses a leader behind the Spin Doctor rotator that is about 28 inches long. With a bait head and no twinkies, the leader is longer—in the 36-inch range. He sets the starboard rigger so it runs 10 feet above the portside rigger and 20 feet above the center rigger's ball.

Bud continues with the flasher/bait regime with his two diver rods and four planer board rods. Although he has four wire diver set-ups aboard, he almost always only runs two. The other two go into action if the diver bite heats up and nothing is coming on the board lines. Two boards come in and two other divers go out—but that's a rare scenario.

Normally, two wire divers—one per side—are all that run out of the *Uncle Bud*. He favors the biggest, heaviest divers available, using both Magnum Dipsy Divers and the No. 5-size Disco Diver from Lurk Divers. He doesn't get fancy with nor obsess about the color of these divers. They are almost always silver, which he feels helps attract fish—every once in a while they are white with crushed glow tape. He also uses long snubbers, 18 inches, behind the diver. His leaders are about three or four feet of 40-pound test Seaguar fluorocarbon. That might seem short for a leader but, consider that, with the 18-inch snubber, there are close to five feet between the flasher and the diver. Add in a five- or six-foot leader between the flasher and bait, and you have eight to ten feet between the diver and the fish. Make the leader any longer and you have more of a problem netting a big fish.

He sets the divers on the 3 setting, which maximizes how far they'll go to the side of the boat. He starts out setting the divers, so one is let out 25 feet more than the other, but then quickly adjusts them to the same depth if one catches a fish. For example, he might set the port diver 125 feet out and the starboard diver 150 feet out. If the port catches a fish, he pulls the starboard diver in 25 feet, so they both run at 125 feet out.

Moving out from the divers, Bud runs deep weighted lines, either copper or lead core, with shallower weighted lines on the far outside. These also have flashers and either baitheads or sushi flies on them, and he spreads them wide. "I almost always run a big, 11-inch white Bechhold Flasher with a bait head on the deepest planer board line," Bud says. "It has often been successful, which is why I keep doing it."

So that's his basic, nine-rod set-up: three riggers, two divers, and four lead core or copper line rigs out on boards, depending on how far down he is targeting. Just as he'll replace two board lines with two more divers if divers get hot and boards are dead, he pulls two downriggers—always the corners—and adds two more weighted planer board lines if the downriggers go stone-cold silent. He'll also add two divers and pull a couple of planer board lines if the board lines are stale and the divers are hopping. The one line that never gets pulled is the center downrigger with the Secret Weapon Rig on it, and that is as much because the SWR accounts for so many big fish as because that rigger has his Fish Hawk X-4 speed-and-temp probe on it.

Final Advice From Uncle Bud

Bud targets big kings. Big kings are his daily goal. Good, freshly-processed bait is one big factor that contributes to his success. The two other huge factors along with good bait are the right speed and putting lures into the right temperature zone.

"I like to be trolling at 2.2 mph at the ball," says Bud. "That seems to be the most productive speed, day in and day out." Equally (if not more) important is finding the right water temperature. Like Capt. Keating, Bud has found his biggest kings in water temperatures of 42 to 44 degrees Fahrenheit.

"That seems to be where they stay all day," Bud says. "In the morning, early, you'll often find them in warmer water and feeding, but once the sun gets up, I'm looking for that cold water, and I want to stay in and around it all day."

So, there you have it—almost the complete system that Bud uses to consistently get big kings to bite. To review, the better, fresher the bait is, the better it works. Good herring oil helps a lot. Keep those lures going the right speed in the right temperature.

Pretty simple, right? Yes and no. This chapter outlines what an angler should do to start consistently catching fish with bait. Read it, follow Bud's advice, and go fishing with the gear mentioned here, prepared the way Bud prepares it. It's highly likely you'll catch some big fish. You don't have to run an "all-bait spread."

By all means, follow Bud's advice on preparing bait. You can strategically run one, two or more bait rods in amongst a spread of standard presentations. Some of the best tournament fishermen and charter captains across the Great Lakes regularly weave bait in with other presentations. These rigs are run off downriggers, divers, copper, or lead core lines in amongst a spread of flasher/flies and clean spoons. Some anglers will also run "Calumet City Chicken" rig among a spread of spoons. This rig is simply a baithead and herring strip (soaked in herring oil) run clean.

We can all learn much from the wisdom Uncle Bud has acquired over the years. Remember what Bud said about all anglers being on a scale somewhere between 1 and 100? There are a lot more "little things" that go into improving your angling that Bud does that we all can learn from. Space was limited here, but you can read more about the "little things" that Bud does in my new book. It is loaded with details for effective bait presentations, great stories, photos, and diagrams to help illustrate the method behind the madness of Uncle Bud, and more details about bait presentations.

Look for *King Salmon Secrets From Uncle Bud* by Dave Mull at Amazon, www.innervikingtackle.com, and www.greatlakessportfish.com.

CHAPTER 13

Currents—Listen to the Lake

The Great Lakes are a dynamic system that wears many faces. I've often arrived at the lake only to find furious, angry waves tearing at the shoreline as if the lake were trying to expand its boundaries. Other days, the lake resembled the stillness of a country farm pond. Watching the mist ascend from the surface on calm mornings, I've often found it hard to imagine that the watery world below was in motion, yet, I've seen way too many days where the calm surface was but an allusion masking a world below filled with movement.

Currents are a mystery to many. Even though we cannot often see currents, we can measure their influence on three key areas—the water (water stratification), the fish, and our presentations, meaning our boats and trolling gear. First, currents influence the stratification process within each individual lake. They move masses of water within individual lakes, create upwellings and downwellings, and can raise and lower the depth of the thermocline. They also influence the development of the little understood sub surface Kelvin waves. Secondly, from the fish's perspective, currents dictate *where* baitfish and game fish school and influence fish temperament. Lastly, currents have a huge impact on our boats, presentations, and lures.

A thorough understanding of currents will help you to find fish like a seasoned charter captain. If you learn how to monitor the weather and wind prior to your fishing trip and match the current weather patterns with past seasonal fishing experiences, you will learn to anticipate *where* to find fish, before you leave the harbor! Another reason to dig deep into this chapter: you will have far fewer tangles!

This chapter will examine current formation and analyze types of currents. It will teach you how to measure currents, how to react to currents, and how locate fish. You'll also learn how to adjust your trolling speed, angle and the dimensions of your lure spread, pick lures, and to dial into fish. When you learn to read the environment and understand how your boat and gear respond to currents, you will catch more and larger fish!

THE BASICS

The Great Lakes are unlike any other body of water on Earth. Each individual lake is really big, as far as a lake goes, but they're not *that* big, as far as oceans go. Therefore, the lakes have some characteristics of the oceans (massive amounts of open water, currents, upwellings, downwellings, etc.), yet they retain some of the features of inland lakes (seasonal warming and cooling patterns, seasonal thermoclines, and fall turnover, to name a few). While all five lakes are connected, each individual lake should be viewed separately. Each lake features current nuances that are unique to its length, width, depth, and structure. Local currents are also impacted by bottom topography such as drop offs, reefs, humps, points, river outflows, and long pier heads.

Currents have a big impact on the water, the fish and our trolling spreads. Learning to interpret currents, and adjust your presentations, will lead you to fish like these!

Great Lakes' currents are predominantly wind driven. Surface currents are the most common current. These horizontally-moving currents directly impact secondary currents such as upwellings, downwellings, reverse currents, and vorticity waves. These currents are not permanent like oceanic currents such as the Gulf Stream. Because the wind in the Great Lakes frequently changes direction with every frontal passage, our currents constantly change. Every time the wind shifts directions, currents can change direction. The strength or speed of a local current fluctuates with the velocity and duration of the wind. A second force influencing currents is the Coriolis Effect. The Earth's spin gives all bodies of water in the northern hemisphere a clockwise rotation. Basically, the Coriolis deflects currents in the Great Lakes to the right.

The layers of water within each Great Lake are connected. Looking at the water column vertically, the layers rest on top of each other. A delicious, seven-layer birthday cake can help us understand this concept. Layers of rich, decadent chocolate cake are interwoven with butter cream filling. Each layer is distinctly separate, yet a part of the entire cake, so it is with the Great Lakes during the summer. The layers of the water column are stratified and separate because each layer holds water of a distinct temperature, but they are connected and part of the entire lake.

Surface currents tend to run horizontally. As a surface current pushes one area of water, that layer of water begins to move or *flow*. When one layer moves, it displaces the water down current. Sorta like the chain reaction of falling dominos.

To better understand the motion of a lake and to *see* how surface currents in one region of a lake can move at a different velocity and direction than other areas, visit www.glerl.noaa.gov. This site shows you the direction and velocities of surface currents as measured by satellite. This is a great tool to help you begin to understand how currents impact an entire lake. As you reference this site, you will quickly see that the current in one part of the lake often moves differently than in another area. This is because different winds will be in place over different parts of an individual lake. When you animate the chart, you can see how surface currents move. Local currents, generated by wind, will *push* a section of lake water that pushes the area down current and so forth. As you think about the area you are fishing, think about how the motion of the entire lake is affecting your region. From one week to the next, you will see how surface currents can move in different directions.

This way of thinking has revolutionized how I find fish. It was in early May one year when I first discovered the above NOAA website and began thinking about the greater influence of currents on the entire lake and the fish. This particular season was off to a slow start. The schools of coho, steelhead, and kings that dominate our spring fishery had failed to materialize along the southwest corner of Lake Michigan. The southeast corner of the lake—Michigan water—was on fire. We in Illinois and Wisconsin were taking a beating; if you caught three or four fish, you were the hero.

One evening, I heard that the fishing was slowing rapidly across the lake from us. This was a distance of about 100 miles. That evening, I randomly looked at the NOAA website and noticed that the surface push had shifted, and a strong current had set up flowing from the southeast to the northwest. This surface current looked as if it started off in southeast Michigan and moved directly toward the Illinois-Wisconsin border. A crazy idea crossed my mind. Since we had no bait or fish, maybe the current would push some of the bait and fish across the lake, and Winthrop Harbor anglers would start catching fish?

With this wild theory in mind, I started running great distances to the southeast. I started fishing deep, extremely cold water that no one had yet explored that spring. Guess what I found? Fish! The farther to the southeast I went, the more fish I caught. Here is what is interesting: the first day I ran offshore into the incoming push, I found small schools of fish. Each successive day, I encountered more fish. Each day, the schools moved farther and farther to the northwest. Since then, I look at this NOAA site every morning before running charters, and over time, through close observation, I've learned how currents coming from different directions each influence the water I fish.

No matter which of the Great Lakes you fish, you can access this web site (free!) and learn to apply the data to your fishery. You will be amazed at how much this will help you to find fish. You will learn which currents warm the water and which create upwellings and bring cold water in close. You will learn to identify which currents bring bait into your region and which currents shut down a fishery. Over time, you will become a better angler through your ability to analyze currents and their overall impact on your local fishery.

One last thought to keep in mind: currents can move schools of bait fish around. Alewives are weak swimmers and tend to get blown about by the currents. The salmon and trout can swim with the best of fish, but they will follow the alewives. If you have lots of baitfish in the area and the current shifts, you have to ask yourself, "will this new current push the bait somewhere else? Maybe to deeper water? Or down the shoreline?"

While Great Lakes currents can run in any direction, the strongest currents tend to run parallel to the shoreline. On Lake Michigan, the strongest currents occur on a north or south wind because of the great distance (also called "fetch") over the water that the wind travels. This has to do with the lake's north-south alignment and the fact that drop-offs roughly parallel the shoreline. Lake Ontario has some of the strongest currents because the entire Great Lakes watershed is flowing though the lake on its way to the Atlantic Ocean. While the winds drive the currents on Lake Ontario, there are two other forces at play. First, the Niagara River is continuously pushing a huge volume of water into the lake. Secondly, the St. Lawrence Seaway is pulling water out of the lake. On all the lakes, fish tend to school in bands roughly parallel to the shoreline.

Seasonal Overview—Water Dynamics

January on the Great Lakes is frigid! Ice coverage varies from lake to lake depending on the severity of the winter. Some years, significant ice complicates shipping, but in mild winters, pack ice drifts with the wind. No matter how much ice accumulates on the surface, the water column is fairly uniform in temperature—freezing cold!

Seasonal warming begins in spring as sunlight and warmer air gradually add warmth to the surface of the lake. This warming begins along the shoreline and transfers heat down into the water column and horizontally out into the lake. As a lake warms, the water begins to stratify in layers from

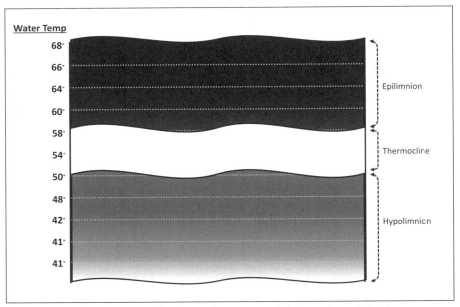

Understanding how water stratifies during the summer will help you locate fish. The warm water above the thermocline does not mix with cold water below. The thermocline is a layer of water that attracts fish and influences currents.

warm water above to cold water below. Warm water weighs less than cold water, so it *floats* on top of colder water.

From a horizontal perspective, the water column is layered. These layers vary in thickness depending on the winds, currents, and seasonal warming. As a lake stratifies, a zone of transition sets up. This distinct layer, called the "thermocline," is the dividing point between the warm water (62-degrees plus) above and cold water (less than 50 degrees) below. The layer above, the epilimnion, never mixes with the colder layer below the thermocline, the hypolimnion. The water in the epilimnion zone does not flow down into the hypolimnion zone and vice-a-versa. Ever since the invasive, filter-feeding zebra and quagga mussels proliferated, the upper layer epilimnion tends to be more fertile because sunlight promotes phytoplankton growth.

When fall's shorter days arrive, decreasing sunlight and cooling atmospheric temperatures lead to a gradual cooling of the entire Great Lakes. This is a gradual process, and at some point, the lakes go through their own, unique version of the *fall turnover* so familiar to inland fisherman.

Cold nights cool the surface layer. Cold water is denser than warm water, so it sinks down through the warmer layers below. This effectively mixes the water in a lake, redistributes nutrients, and ends the seasonal thermocline. The seasonal ebb and flow of a lake is now complete as a lake transitions into winter mode.

Common Types of Great Lakes Currents

The most common currents are *surface currents*. These wind-driven currents vary in direction, duration, and intensity. They are transitory in nature, and their intensity can change over the course of the day. A surface current follows the direction of the wind. For example, a west wind will create an easterly moving surface current. A south wind will create a northbound surface current.

Essentially, a surface current is created when the wind blows over the lake and *pushes* on the water. The wind sets a thin layer of the surface into motion. As this layer moves, it drags the layer beneath it, which drags the layer beneath it. This dragging and pulling motion extends down in the water column to the thermocline. At the thermocline, no further transfer of energy or motion occurs. The current above does not drag along the layer below the thermocline.

A thermocline might stop the downward migration of a surface current, but it also helps increase the speed of the surface current. According to research described in R. Mortimer's fascinating book, *Lake Michigan in Motion,* the thermocline acts as a *slippery* layer. When the wind blows on the surface and creates a surface current, the entire surface layer of water above the thermocline begins to *slip* on top of the thermocline. This *slippery* effect helps increase the speed of a surface current. As the wind picks up in the afternoon, the speed of the push will often increase by a few tenths of a knot.

Here's an example: during the morning, the wind is blowing out of the south at less than 10 kts. The surface current is less than 1 kt. In the afternoon, the south wind picks up to 20 kts. Now the current is moving at 1.3 kt. This is because the surface layer of water, sitting above the thermocline, begins to *slip,* and the whole chunk of water is moving to the north at a slightly faster rate.

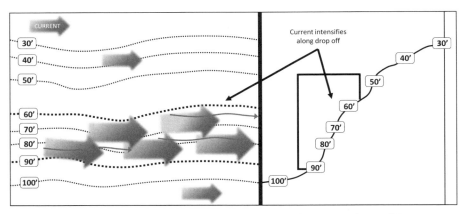

Currents are intensified along drop offs. Drop offs though out the Great Lakes are fish magnets. Interpreting how currents flow along drop offs will help you dial in your trolling speeds and angles.

Surface currents have seasonal nuances and are influenced by water temperature, air temperature, proximity to shoreline, and water structure. Research presented by Mortimer suggests that the intensity of currents on Lake Michigan is greater within 10 miles of the shore. Sharp drop offs that run parallel to the shoreline increase the velocities of both surface and sub surface currents on all the Great Lakes.

Mortimer also points out that larger waves give the wind "something" to grab onto and increase the velocity of the current. A surface current stays in motion as long as the wind is blowing. When the wind stops, the current will slow down but will often continue flowing at a greatly-reduced rate. When the wind shifts direction, the current follows suit. On Lake Michigan, when a strong northbound surface current is in place, it takes an extended period of north wind to overpower the north-flowing current and turn it around to a south-flowing direction.

When the entire water column is uniform in temperature in winter, spring, and late fall, the energy from wave motion is transferred throughout the entire water column. Practically speaking, when the wind blows on the surface, wave energy travels in a circular orbit and transfers energy both down into the water column and parallel along the surface layer. Water and nutrients can mix from the surface to the bottom. An un-stratified lake has fewer-currents at play as the entire water column tends to be moving in one direction. Your surface current will run throughout the entire water column. This makes dialing in productive trolling speeds much easier.

While surface currents directly impact the epilimnion layer, they indirectly create and influence a variety of sub surface currents including upwellings, downwellings, reverse currents, vorticity waves, and what I like to refer to as the sloshing affect. Remember being young, and sitting in a bathtub, and splashing water? As a child generates a wave in the tub, it moves and strikes the side of the tub. The energy from the wave bounces off the side and sloshes back across the tub. What do you think happens in a lake after a high wind event or intense lower pressure generated by a summer thunderstorm sends water racing to one side of the lake?

Reverse currents occur when a strong surface current runs into the shoreline. This forces water on the leeward shore down in the water column. This water begins flowing back out, below, and opposite the direction of the surface current. This current exists below the thermocline, and its velocity is often different than the surface current above. The intersection of a reverse current and bottom structure are great places to fish. They can also create upwellings. We used to think that a reverse current runs 180 degrees opposite the current above, but not always.

Upwellings are common on the Great Lakes and attract bait and game fish. Upwellings occur when an offshore wind pushes the warm surface water out away from the shoreline. As the surface water moves away from the shore, it is replaced by cold water flowing in along the bottom. The current is deflected upward in the water column. Upwellings bring cold water and nutrients from the deeper layers into shoreline regions and the upper layers of the water column. Upwellings also occur any time a cold-water current moving along the bottom hits a drop off and is deflected up.

Downwellings are the opposite. Extended periods of onshore winds push warm surface water into the shoreline. As the surface current hits the shoreline, it pushes the water along the shore down in the water column and out into the lake. With both upwellings and downwellings, you can see the interconnectedness of the entire lake in motion. Upwellings and downwellings move large amounts of water around the lake.

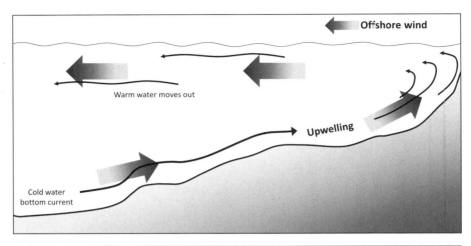

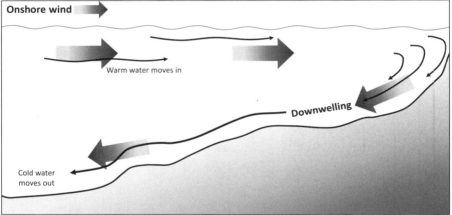

Upwellings and downwellings occur over the course of the summer. These events can significantly alter the location of the thermocline, and they can move baitfish and game fish into one area and seemingly chase fish out of another area. Understanding which wind regimes cause them, and how they affect the water off of your homeport, will help you catch more fish.

The Thermocline

The thermocline is a zone of transition and greatly influences where you will find Mr. Salmon and Mr. Trout. It is a boundary separating the warm water above from the denser, cold water below. This zone features a rapid temperature drop from low 60-degree water down to 50-degree water. The thickness of the thermocline varies greatly but generally is from 5 to 20 feet. Currents tend to form and run along this sub-surface break.

The thermocline is a feeding zone. Plankton that die in the epilimnion zone above sink down and settle or *float* on top of the colder, denser water below. This dead matter attracts zooplankton and baitfish such as alewives and young of the year perch. According to observations from divers, water clarity can vary greatly below the thermocline. At times, the colder water will be much clearer. When a thick thermocline is laden with dead matter, it can also filter out sunlight, making the realm below darker. Some have also suggested that the thermocline has an impact on sound vibrations as well.

The thermocline is not stationary, but it moves vertically up and down in the water column, depending on local wind regimes and currents. If a lake had no wind or currents, but just gradually warmed in summer, the thermocline would set up and simply settle deeper and deeper into the water column as warming extended from the surface down. While the overall seasonal warming trend forces the thermocline deeper into the water column, we must remember that winds and currents rake the Great Lakes. This can raise and lower the depth of the thermocline, especially within 10 to 15 miles of the shoreline. As you go out into the middle of the individual lakes, the water column is more stable.

The vertical location of the thermocline within the water column changes as you move in and out from the shoreline. For example, you may find the thermocline 100 feet down in 120 feet of water, but out in 240 feet of water, the thermocline might only be 60 feet down. Key variables determining the depth of the thermocline are wind direction and duration, proximity to deep water, local currents, and seasonal patterns.

Extended periods of offshore winds push warm surface water away from the shoreline and near-shore region. Cold water from the deep upwells and moves into the near-shore region. This will raise the thermocline up in the water column as you approach the shoreline. If the wind blows strong enough and long enough, the thermocline will move all the way into the shoreline. When this occurs, you will find ice-cold water along the beach. I've seen strong upwellings in the summer that have brought 42-degree water into the shoreline. While all upwellings are not this cold, it is common to have an upwelling bring 50-degree water to the shoreline in midsummer.

Extended periods of onshore winds will push warm surface water into a region. This forces the thermocline down in the water column. If an onshore wind blows long enough, it also forces the thermocline farther out into the lake. In this scenario, you might not find a thermocline until you move out past a certain depth. For example, let's say the thermocline was located 40 feet down in 100 feet of water. A week of moderate onshore wind brings warm surface water across the lake. As this mass of warm water moves into the shoreline, it forces the water along the shoreline down and out into the lake. This pushes the thermocline down in the water column and farther offshore. After a week of onshore wind, in our example, you might now find the thermocline 70 feet down in 100 feet of water. A second week of onshore wind might further drive the thermocline out to 140 feet of water.

As you move out into the lake, don't assume the thermocline will set up at one level and travel horizontally out into the lake at that level. This is especially true during summers that have constant frontal passages. When warm and cold fronts battle for control of a region, they feature many wind shifts. The constantly shifting winds confuse the water and result in an uneven thermocline. In this scenario, you will find that the thermocline has high and low levels as you move out into the lake. This is the result of water movement and mixing currents below the surface. You will find that the thermocline is higher in some areas and deeper in others as you move offshore. If you only fish a few times a month, you might find that the

This catch of kings was made when we dialed into a strong reverse current below, and large waves on the surface.

thermocline location is very different from one week to the next, based on local wind patterns.

MEASURING CURRENTS

One afternoon, I was struggling to get a bite. Seriously, I felt like I was on the Dead Sea. I was running out of stories to tell my customers who were consuming an ever-dwindling supply of *liquid courage*. I called my buddy Arnie who was about 8 miles north of me, and to my surprise, Arnie was kicking ass on the fish! Now I really had a complex! After all the routine questions we charter captains ask, Arnie asked me one revealing question, "Dan, how are your board (lead and copper) rods hanging?" Well, Arn, since you want to return to the 1980s to analyze my poor fishing performance, let me look. I looked back and noticed that the Walleye Boards on one side were pulling hard at a 45-degree angle, but the other side was a bit limp; there was less tension on the rods, and the boards didn't seem to be working as hard as the other side.

Arnie then told me that his planer rods were pulling hard on both sides. Bingo! Light bulb moment! Even though Arnie was only 8 miles away, the water was *moving* differently than the water I was fishing. Arnie and I were trolling the same angle, but the *pull* on my rods didn't match the pull on rods deployed from his boat. From that point forward, I tweaked angles and speeds until I had both sides pulling equally hard. We finally started catching fish!

How do you measure currents? Those of us who fished *back-in-the-day* simply looked at the angle and tension of downrigger cables, diver lines, and even planer boards to analyze currents and dial into the fish. The "old school method" can still provide intuitive anglers significant data on how currents are impacting their spread. In the preceding example, two very experienced anglers (Arnie and myself) with all the electronics in the world ultimately used the old school method to dial into the fish on a tough day.

Not everyone wants to fish like a caveman, and we do live in the twenty-first century. Can we reliably measure currents? Today, there are two popular methods to measure currents—GPS and sub-surface probes.

Probes such as the Depth Raider and Fish Hawk attach to your cannonball and relay data to a monitor on the dash. A remote probe, the Smart Troll, attaches to your cannonball or fishing line (such as a copper or dive planer) and sends a signal to a hand-held device. Both types of probes give you precise water temperatures and speed data at specific depths. If you don't fish on a regular basis, this data is invaluable!

Probes are simple to use. Most anglers run the probe on one of their downriggers. You can adjust the rigger probe as you fish and use it to build a mental picture of how the water is stratified. Once you've determined the temperature boundaries to set your lines, the probe will tell you your speed at the precise depth it is running. Many anglers will adjust their speed, at the target depth, to dial into the fish. Now, if you are running a variety of presentations across a broad vertical section of water, you will want to move the probe to each level to see what your speed is at each layer. You may find that your lures are moving along at one speed at 90 feet, but lures being trolled 30 feet down are moving at a faster or slower rate!

If you don't have a probe, it's easy to isolate and hold productive trolling speeds with a GPS. You'll want to pay close attention to two numbers: COG (course over ground) and SOG (speed over ground). The COG measures the angle that your boat is moving over the lake bottom (not through the water). The SOG tells you your boat's speed, as measured over the bottom of the lake, not through the water. Repeatability is a big part of catching fish, and the intersection of these two numbers is the key to dialing into a hot bite.

Here's how I fish: when setting lines, I note my COG and my SOG. For example, let's begin trolling on a 240-degree course at a speed of 2.4 kt. As the gear goes into the water, I watch how everything *looks*. After setting up, I hold the course and speed for 10 or 15 minutes. Does everything look good in the water? Is the boat *drifting* off to the side? Are the lines pulling hard on one side, weak on another? How's the tension on the divers or board rods? If things don't look right, I begin adjusting my lines.

If my lines look good and I'm not getting hits, I try slower or faster speeds, holding a 240-degree heading. If the fish are not biting or the lines still don't look right, I will begin to adjust the COG by 10-degree increments. After a course adjustment, I change my speed every few minutes, trying to dial into the fish. If I am marking fish, I get aggressive as I alter my settings.

Keep track of what speeds and angles you've tried until you find the productive path. Many days success is simply a matter of isolating the speed and angle. Once you start connecting with fish, hold your SOG and COG! An autopilot is helpful and allows you to focus on your presentations. If you don't have a pilot, ask Santa for a pilot, but if that doesn't work, keep a small notebook by the dash to mark down the productive angles and speeds. If you have to change course to boat a big fish, get back on the hot line as soon as you boat the fish.

Understanding the data your GPS provides will also tell you what the overall current patterns are beneath your boat and how they are impacting your lures and presentations. Here's how to analyze the numbers: every time you adjust your angle (COG), watch what happens to your SOG. Many times, when you change trolling direction, your SOG will increase or slow down. For example, let's say you are trolling at a 90-degree heading and your SOG is 2.1 kt. If you adjust your COG to 110 degrees, look at your SOG—did it change? For this example, let's say the adjustment to a more southeasterly heading caused your speed to drop to 1.8 kt. What does this data tell you? It tells you that a surface current is moving from a southerly angle. It also tells you that your speed at depth (where our lures are swimming) may have just slowed down when you turned to a more southerly angle. Even though you didn't adjust the throttle, your speed dropped. What do you think happened to the action of your lures at depth? Most course alterations require you to adjust your trolling speed.

Your COG might also be very different than your compass angle says you are moving. For example, you're trolling toward the west, but your compass says you are pointed on a 270-degree heading. When you glance at your COG, it says you are *moving* at a 310-degree heading. This discrepancy between the angle your boat is "pointed" and actually moving, as measured by GPS, tells you that a surface push is at play, and pushing your boat to the north. You need to ask two questions: what is this push doing to the water below and how is this angle affecting your lures at their trolling depth? When steering, use your COG to determine what direction you are moving. In the previous example, you would have to point your boat on a slight southwest heading, looking at your compass, in order to move straight west (270 degrees) over ground.

Here is another example that will tell you when a reverse current is at play. Let's say you are trolling north; the lake is calm with little or no wind, and your engine is idled back dead slow. Under these conditions, you know from experience that your SOG should be roughly 2.0 kts., but on this day, your lines don't look right. In fact, everything is hanging back. You glance at your GPS, and it says you are flying along at 3.1 kt. Your GPS is telling you that a strong surface current is moving from south to north. The surface push/energy of the lake where you are fishing is north bound.

This should lead you to ask several questions. If the surface is moving from south to north, how is this current impacting the water below? Is the water below moving in the same direction, or is there a reverse current below? If the subsurface current is different than the upper layers, at what level is the current changing speed or direction? At this point, you can drop a probe over the side to determine where the current break is, or you can learn to watch the angle of your downrigger cables and divers to tell determine at what level the current changes. For most anglers, a probe is easier—just drop it in 5-foot increments and note the speed-at-depth.

During the summer and fall, it is more common to have multiple or confusing currents beneath the surface. When the winds are strong and shifting directions every few days, I've seen days where there have been two or three well-defined current zones beneath the surface that are showing up on the sonar.

Further "big picture thinking" can be applied to the thermocline. If a strong current is at play, how will its interaction with the shoreline impact the thermocline location? All the layers of a stratified lake are connected. While the masses of cold and warm water may remain separate and not mix, we must remember that water in the Great Lakes moves in masses or chunks. As one mass of water moves, it is pushing on adjoining layers. This has a huge impact on the water we fish!

GPS helps you understand how all the layers of the water column are interacting. If you have a probe and GPS, learn to use both! Together, they will help you dial into the fish faster. Let me challenge you: fish one or two days a year without using your probe or GPS. It will force you to pay closer attention to the lake, gear, and fish. It may not be comfortable at first, but it will make you a better fisherman!

BOAT CONTROL—LEARNING HOW TO DEAL WITH WAVES AND CURRENTS

One question commonly asked at my salmon schools is, "do you troll with the current, into the current, or at an angle to the current?" While some great anglers fish exclusively one direction, relative to the current, I believe you can catch fish in a variety of directions, but you must control your boat in order to catch fish. A boat that is constantly surging makes it very difficult to maintain a steady speed and frequently leads to tangles. When your boat wanders all over the place, it makes it doubly difficult to determine productive speeds and angles.

Every boat fishes differently. A 36-foot Tiara fishes very differently than a 21-foot Lund does. Secondly, not all waves are created equally. In other words, different wind directions and velocities will produce waves of varying intensity, size, breadth, and duration. For example, along the southwest shore of Lake Michigan, a northeast wind has over 200 miles of open water to work with. This results in large waves—sometimes, really big waves! Not only does a northeast wind create tall waves, but they will be spread out. A wind straight out of the west produces short, choppy, tightly-spaced waves. Every wind regime produces a different wave texture or pattern.

Sometimes a two- or three-directional wave pattern occurs. If the wind has been blowing out of one direction for several days, the waves or swells will be one-directional. When the wind suddenly shifts to a new direction, it will create a chop, or a new wave pattern, on top of the waves, already in motion. If the wind shifts a third time, a third wave pattern will be added. Some people call this a confused sea; I have spent enough days in these conditions to know it can resemble spending the morning on the rinse cycle of a washing machine! Eventually, the wind will overpower the waves, and the wave patterns return to a one directional. In your home region, identify the nuances and wave textures that wind from all four quadrants produce. Incorporate that into your daily fishing plan.

Once you understand the types of waves each wind regime produces, your next step is to identify how your boat fishes best. Does your boat give you the most control with a following sea? A head sea? Some boats fish best quartering into a beam sea—when the waves are hitting you at a 45-degree angle to the bow. What is the point of all this? When you understand how your boat responds to various types of waves, you will learn which combination of lines to run, lead lengths, and other subtle nuances that greatly impact your productivity. You will learn where to begin fishing, based on setting yourself up for the best possible trolling path the waves will allow. Boat control will also help you minimize tangles.

If I'm not catching fish, I make frequent course adjustments based on my boat's angle to the wind and currents. I watch how my lines are running and look for the *hot* angle that will trigger strikes. This requires me to pay attention to surface and sub-surface current angles! Some days, the best troll will be parallel to the shoreline, which will have you trolling into the current or with the current. When currents running parallel to the shoreline are extra strong, you might find that a troll perpendicular to the shoreline, and the current, is more productive. Repeatability is a big part of salmon fishing, so remember, currents run the same direction under each wind regime. Therefore, remember what angles and speeds were productive when the wind and waves are out of a particular direction. Chances are, the next time you encounter similar wind conditions, the same speeds and angles will be productive.

When you encounter super-difficult conditions, fish to your boat's strengths. My buddy and excellent recreational angler Jim Klausing's last boat fished like a tank in a following sea. If the waves were larger than 3 or 4 feet, Jim didn't waste time fishing into the seas or at angles. He would run upwind an appropriate distance and spend the majority of his fishing time trolling with the wind. Not only did that maximize his catches, he and his crew enjoyed the day rather than fighting with the lake.

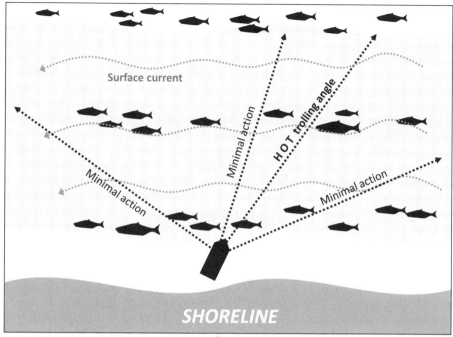

Great Lakes currents tend to run parallel to the shoreline. Likewise, fish school in bands running parallel to the shoreline. Finding the hot trolling angle is key to catching fish.

If your boat surges, doesn't slow down, or won't hold a straight course, you will want to invest in a sea anchor. A sea anchor is a large piece of canvas shaped like a funnel. The mouth is wide, and it narrows toward the end. They come in a variety of sizes that can be matched to small, medium, and large boats.

Sea anchors give you great speed control, help your boat track straight, and add stability to your boat as they minimize rocking motion. Once the anchor is deployed, you will have to troll at a higher rpm—this will help your boat track better as your prop is getting more torque in the water and, with an inboard motor, pushes more water past the rudder. Many days, the turbulence created by a sea anchor will attract fish into your spread. I have had many days where a rigger or diver run below the sea anchor is a hot rod. In the summer, this turbulence often draws fish out of temperature as I often set the downrigger below the anchor turbulence shallower than the other lines, and it catches loads of fish.

IMPACT OF CURRENTS ON TROLLING PRESENTATIONS AND LURE SELECTION

Another very important question to ask once you notice a current is at play is, *how is this impacting my lures and gear beneath the surface?* If no current above or below, your boat will theoretically troll in a straight course. Your downriggers, divers, planers, lines, and lures will be following in a more or less straight line. If no currents are at play, all of your lures will be going the exact same speed as your boat. Ahhh, life is good.

Unfortunately, these absolute calm, current-less days are rare. More times than not, you will be dealing with some form of current above or below. If a current is present, your lines may not be following directly behind your boat, and your lures may be doing some strange things. When the water below is moving differently than the water at the surface, your lures below may be moving faster or slower than your boat.

When dealing with challenging currents, fine tune your lure selection, lead lengths, and the horizontal and vertical relationships between all your lines. Here are some typical adjustments I make when dealing with a strong current: downsize your spread. It is easier to focus on fewer lines when you are not maintaining a full spread. This allows you to isolate productive speeds, lead lengths, and lure selection. It also results in fewer tangles, allowing you to really adjust and tweak your lines. I run my two boom downriggers either super short, 5 to 8 feet off the weight, or very long, beyond 75 feet. These two patterns will not tangle the other riggers or divers.

Wire divers are easier to run in a heavy current. I also spread my lead core and copper planer boards further apart to minimize tangles when fish are hooked. Also, when dealing with strong currents, run speed-tolerant lures that work at all speeds. Spin Doctors are great for this as are Super Slims and Michigan Stingers. Fewer lines, running properly, will catch far more fish than a lot of lines running poorly.

How Weather Impacts Fishing

After more than 30 years in the charter business, I've learned that my life, and my fate on the water, is closely tied to the weather. (Actually, I learned that after my first couple of weeks!) The weather influences daily sea conditions, and it is the driving force in determining *where* I will find fish on any given day. For this reason, I am closely tuned in to the weather during the fishing season. It's almost become a part of me—to the point my wife thinks I'm nuts. We'll be out to dinner, and I'll glance out the restaurant window, notice that the wind just changed directions, and randomly tell her that I'll have to run to a new area to catch fish on tomorrow's charter—all without thinking! Those who make their living on the water instinctively observe changes and overall patterns.

If you understand how weather influences migration patterns off your port, you will learn to anticipate *where* fish will be located and spend more time trolling where the fish are. Let's start simple: if the regional weather pattern is consistent with historical norms, most likely, the fish will follow their annual migration cycle. Salmonids tend to follow the same monthly patterns, year after year, as long as the weather is *normal*. Stable winds allow the thermocline to set up. Currents flow in one direction. Fish like stability and tend to form large schools under stable conditions. Fish are patternistic and predictable when the weather follows the same pattern day after day.

Weather impacts fishing! Fortunately, we got in before this showed up!

When unstable weather dominates a region, fish can get a little weird. Constantly shifting winds will scatter schools of game and bait fish. Swirling winds (when the wind keeps coming around the clock every few days) tend to mix the water up and cause currents to become confused or to appear random. Pockets of fish are very scattered and seemingly moving around randomly. Strong wind events disrupt established patterns and tend to break large schools up into smaller pods of fish. Any weather change can cause fish to move out of one area as they follow the currents seeking more favorable conditions.

Learn to identify how fish respond to instability off your harbor. Sometimes, the most extreme weather changes will drive the fish offshore to deep water. Many believe that deep water is more stable and fish seek out stability. The point is to learn where the fish move when adverse conditions seemingly shut down a fishery.

Fish react to daily weather changes, such as a line of storms or a frontal passage. When you run charters, you really can't choose when you go fishing. People hire you for a set period of time, and they expect you to produce fish, no matter what the weather is doing. Over the years, I've learned how fish respond to various weather changes. One of my favorite times to fish is a summer afternoon when a line of storms is approaching. Fish go absolutely nuts and feed aggressively as the pressure drops, the sky darkens, and the wind picks up. The front side of a weather change often triggers a massive feeding frenzy, which leads to wild action and huge catches.

The backside of a front, however, produces more challenging conditions. Often when the backside of a front takes hold, the sonar goes blank, and you would think there are no fish within 100 miles of you. What is going on? Sometimes, the fish do leave an area, but other times, especially if the currents have not changed, the fish seem to go through this dormant period. They might drop down to the bottom and evade sonar detection, or they might just be very skittish and moving out of our boat's path. Negative fish slowly come back to life. Many anglers just give up. I've learned that when conditions change it's often just a matter of tweaking your spread, adjusting colors, and patiently waiting out the fish. I've also learned that kings are far more sensitive to weather changes than steelhead, coho, and lake trout. If really wild weather shuts the kings off, it often makes more sense to target other species for a few hours or a day. Fish holding over deep water, in excess of 150 feet, are far less sensitive to weather changes.

One of the more challenging weather-related conditions is fishing after an upwelling has brought cold water into the shoreline. In years past, it seemed as if the salmon and trout always followed the cold water into the shoreline. Today, an upwelling event is just as likely to push fish to deeper water as it is to draw them into the shoreline. What is going on?

Upwelling events lead to a period of transition. The world beneath the surface has changed; the cold water that was deep has now moved up in the water column and in closer to shore. Fish can respond to an upwelling in three general ways. They may follow the cold water into the shoreline or shallows. When an upwelling brings nutrients and baitfish into shallower water, salmon and trout will follow the bait, but sometimes, even though conditions are ideal in shallow water, no fish are there. The water in the Great Lakes is much clearer than it used to be, so fish, especially kings, don't always like going into clear, shallow water. Fish might move into the clear, shallow water to feed at night and retreat to deeper water during the day.

Sometimes an upwelling produces a wedge-like column of warm water. Prior to the upwelling, the lake is stratified; a thermocline is set up, and the fish are all in their happy zones. An upwelling brings cold water in along the bottom, which hits the shoreline and moves up into the water column. This inward-bound, cold water forces warmer water, which previously occupied the entire water column from the beach out to about 3 to 5 miles, to move out into the lake. This chunk of warm water might be 50, 60, or 70 feet thick (vertically). As this *column* of water moves away from the shore, it pushes the previously stratified water further out into the lake. Any fish that are suspended, holding on the outside of the wedge, will be pushed further out into the lake. These fish have no idea that cold water is in along the beach.

Another upwelling scenario involves an area where fish were already present but were holding in warmer water of 54 to 60 degrees. When the cold water rolls in, these fish go into "shock" for a brief period of time. This dormant period usually lasts from an hour to half a day. Once they acclimate to the colder water, say 42 to 52 degrees, they become more active. Also, an upwelling can blow alewives or other baitfish out of one area and into another. Either way, the predators will follow them.

Weather greatly influences the currents, and as we now understand, currents move huge amounts of water around, sometimes changing fishing patterns overnight. Alewives and many other baitfish are weak swimmers and get blown around by the current.

When extended periods of steady winds set up, currents move large masses of warm and cold water around. We all know what can happen to a fishery with a sudden drastic change in water temp: fish can seemingly vanish, or miraculously appear out of nowhere.

Ultimately, extreme weather can lead to tougher fishing conditions. Anytime you face extreme conditions you will need to do some hunting to find the fish. Once fish are found, you need to camp out on the fish. Big wind events can concentrate fish. One autumn, we had a monster onshore wind event that drove the waves up and over Chicago's Lake Shore Drive. Following this three-day-screamer, we had to go out 8 miles (close to 200 feet of water) to find moderately clear water, but we found massive schools of kings and steelhead. Fishing was fantastic.

HOW THE WEATHER CAN HELP YOU LOCATE FISH—A NEW WAY OF THINKING!

Most people reading this book don't have the luxury of fishing every day. Most likely, you spend the majority of your time working and get to fish once a week or maybe a few times a month. Let's be honest: if you are on the water five or six days a week, you have a big advantage over the weekend warrior. Time on the water helps you dial into the fish.

Did you know that by watching the weather from your home or place of employment you can learn to identify *where* the fish will be? With a little knowledge, practice, experience, and a logbook, you can learn to make highly-educated guesses as to where you will find fish on those sacred days you get to go fishing.

Wind, season, and currents hugely influence where you find fish. Sea-

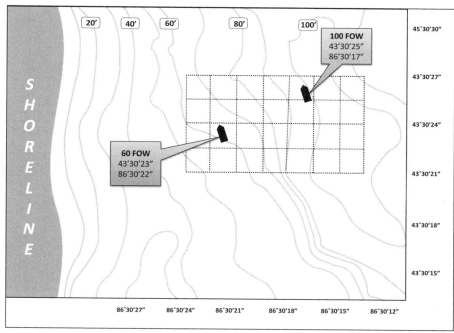

To better understand bottom topography, and how weather and currents influence fish location, in your mind, lay a lat/lon grid over the surface of the water. As you are fishing, learn to think about "where" you are, based on lat/lon numbers. This will give you a better understanding of the water.

sonally, fish have natural cycles, and they tend to follow the same general migration patterns year after year. With experience, we can pattern our fishing strategies toward these patterns. For example, chances are good that during July salmon and trout will utilize the same locations under specific wind regimes.

What does this look like? There are three parts to this system of fishing: how you view the lake, how you track the weather in the days leading up to a fishing trip, and how you apply past experiences and current weather trends to your fishing strategies.

First, recalibrate how you view the lake. Think of it like a grid. Most likely, you use GPS. A GPS allows you to isolate specific locations, seemingly in the middle of nowhere, based on numbers representing latitude and longitude. On the water, I think numerically. In my mind's eye, I lay a grid over the surface of the water and the lake bottom. I think about *where* I am based on my latitude and longitude position on that grid. I am keeping track of my location not by line of site (what I can see on the shore) but by my precise numerical location (lat/lon) on the grid. You've probably read posts on line or heard guys talk like this when relaying their position; they are identifying the water by Lat and Lon numbers.

This technique, or way of thinking, really makes the lake smaller. It helps you to familiarize yourself with structure. It will help you stay on top of fish. As you isolate favorite structures and areas that consistently produce fish, think of those regions in terms of numbers. It's not just a sharper drop from 80 to 110 feet south of the harbor; it is a precise geological feature at 30.22 north and 44.55 west line (for example). This way of thinking will make the lake smaller. It will help you isolate what regions are holding fish. As you start to associate precise areas with lat/lon numbers, you will begin to map out the features. Now, you will locate subtle turns in drop offs, areas where rock or hard bottom intersect muck, areas where deep water extends closer to shore, and other *spot-on-the-spot* features that are fish magnets.

As you begin mapping out the area off your homeport, a good topographical chart will help. Also, learn to use your plotter, and as you start marking spots, begin to draw out a map of the region. When I was younger, before we had all the modern navigation tools we now take for granted, I used to make maps of the water I fished. In a notebook, I would draw the structure, the way I thought it existed below the surface, based on hours of watching our old Vexilar paper graph and notating features based on our "relative" position. This helped me to understand what the topography looked like and how it might influence currents and fish movement. It helped me to catch a lot more fish.

The second part of this system involves how you view and track the weather prior to your outing. Monitor wind direction and velocity the week or two prior to your outing.

When you fish, keep a log of what areas (based on lat/lon) produced fish and note what the winds were like during the week of your outing. Next, keep track of what specific wind regimes (direction + velocity + duration) do to the lake stratification off your favorite port. Next, make notes on the water of what directions the surface and subsurface currents were flowing, following specific wind events. You will quickly learn which wind regimes force the cold water offshore and which winds bring cold water in close.

For example, are the winds onshore or running parallel to the shoreline? How strong and for how long have they been from a particular direction? Here's how to connect your observations to the lake. It's summer, and the winds have been blowing 10 to 20 mph into the shoreline. Chances are good that the thermocline will be pushed down in the water column, and you might have to head deep. If the winds are blowing offshore or at an angle to the shoreline, this may drive the fish higher up in the water column. It might move cold water closer to the shoreline.

Keep a logbook. With your new grid-like vision of the water, keep track of which areas (based on lat/lon) produced fish. What month was it? What was the prevailing wind direction for the week prior to your outing? Keep track of dominant wind regimes, how water was stratified, current directions, and where you caught fish. The fish will utilize the same regions year after year, based on season and local weather patterns. Currents will follow similar patterns under specific weather regimes.

Applying the data and knowledge is the third step. For example, it's June, and a northeasterly wind has dominated the week's weather. Last year

When strong winds and currents mix up the water, schools of fish will suspend offshore over deep, stable water.

or the year before, when a northeasterly wind blew for a week, you found fish in a specific area. Chances are good that fish will be in the same area again, based on the same wind pattern. Likewise, you can typically expect to find similar conditions for the currents, based on previous condition match ups. This methodology will save you tons of gas and time! You have to keep a logbook for a year or two, but it is worth it!

Off my port, if the wind is out of the northeast during June, I tend to fish a few specific areas. A completely different set of numbers will hold fish on a southwesterly wind. Each month can be different. When combined with the surface current chart, experience, and the logbook you will develop, you will find that the lake just got a whole lot smaller.

HOW TO MATCH STRUCTURE WITH SEASON, WIND AND SPECIES

- Think of the lake as a grid—overlay a latitude and longitudinal grid over the water and bottom topography of a region.
- Isolate key structure features based on their lat/lon positions.
- Monitor the wind and weather over the lake prior to fishing.
- Based on season, identify which areas (based on coordinates) fish concentrate in for various wind regimes.
- Determine current directions and velocities based on seasonal wind regimes.
- Glerl.noaa.gov/res/glcfs/glcfs.php?lake=

A FINAL WORD FROM CAPTAIN DAN

Powerful Fishing

My 9 year-old daughter Chloë does everything with gusto. From the moment she wakes and her feet hit the ground running, to the moment she lays her head on the pillow and drifts off to sleep, she's at full tilt. Playing soccer, practicing violin, or studying for a history test, Chloë knows one speed—*da da dat da da*—charge!

My family is planning our winter trip to Florida. Chloë, and her brother and sisters, can't wait to get down there! They love heading out in our small, 19-foot boat, in search of anything with fins. Whether heading out into the Gulf of Mexico in search of kingfish and tuna, or drifting the flats for the mixed bag, Chloë wants to be a part of the action.

You and I share that same passion, we are wired for the outdoors and fishing. Those who have not been infected by the bug don't understand what makes our pulse quicken as we walk the aisles of our favorite tackle store. They don't understand why we would subject our bodies to the beating of heavy seas or stand in a cold rain for hours, waiting patiently, hoping. Most likely, they do not understand the thrill that sends us into overdrive as we feel the pull of an unseen adversary on the end of our line. Yet it is undeniable—the passion in the heart of an angler pulls on his very being.

For me though, my passion went too far. Once I started chartering, my *hobby-out-of-control* got the best of me. Soon my goal was to catch the most and the biggest fish. Nothing else mattered: my passion became an obsession! The more fish I caught, the emptier it all became. I began to cover the pain and the emptiness with the things of this world. Despite my success on the water, I soon found myself adrift on the seas of life. Much like a 14-foot boat without an engine drifting miles from shore when a November gale blows in, I was lost, and had little hope of reaching the shore.

Can I ask you a question? It's the question I often ask when looking beyond the horizon. **Is passion deeper than the waters we fish?** Now, is it possible that passion is a clue, pointing us to look beyond ourselves, to the fingerprints of the One who created nature? Is our passion for the outdoors an invitation, pointing us to the Creator? Does this Creator want to engage with us?

I used to think this was absurd! I refused to consider such possibilities, stubbornly insisting on believing only what I could see and my own good works. Once I looked deeper, beyond the surface, I realized fishing and life are rather similar. Decades of fishing have shown me the value of trusting unseen realities. Time and again, my first impressions were proven wrong. At first I doubted the data my electronics revealed about the fish and water. No one could have forced me to believe in them, but years of experience have proven the value of sonar, GPS, radar, temp, and speed probes that show realities I cannot see. These tools gave me a deeper, fuller understanding of the waters I fished. They convinced me that maybe it was worth it to look beyond the surface of my first impressions and opinions.

It requires faith to be a fisherman, and it takes faith to navigate the modern world.

On the water, what do you really see? You know the drop off is there, you see it on the chart, but do you see it the way the fish do? Currents, we can measure them, and see their impact on our boats and lines, but do you *see* the currents? There are also the fish themselves. Looking across the surface we don't *see* the fish, but we know they are there. Fishing teaches you to see the unseen.

Looking deeper, beyond the surface, reveals that life is also filled with unseen realities; like magnetic north, satellites, the Internet, the global economy, the universe (it's really big!), and our own bodies. Our bodies are intricately designed and wonderfully made. It all works together even if we don't understand it!

On the water I overcame my stubbornness and learned to trust my

electronics. With experience, I learned to leverage the data they provided. My catches improved and I had far less tangles!

Off the water, I wished I had tools that could help me to see the unseen drop offs that I kept stumbling over, and detect the currents that were snarling the relationships of my life. When I was younger I had looked to religion, but too many negative experiences with churches and religious people had clouded my vision. It was out on the water where I met God. Through fishing, storms, and the *stuff* of life, God reached out to me through a handful of people and experiences.

I've shared much of what I've learned with you in this book. May I ask you one question? Is God real? If he is real you have to ask, "what kind of God is he?" Does he want to engage with you and lead you to a deeper life? In the same way that we have tools to help us *see* the unseen world below the surface, has God given us tools to help us *see* and *experience* Him?

I had doubts at first, like I did with technology. But once I gave these questions and "tools" a chance, some sources surprised me with their reliability. Once I trusted those unseen realities, the way I trusted North on the compass and my GPS, they surprised me even more with how my life began to change for the better.

I still tangle my lines on the water and to be honest, I still face choppy waters at home, and in my life. But I am no longer trolling blindly through the waves, unsure of how deep the water is, or which way the currents are blowing.

What I discovered changed my life in so many ways. Many things, however, still challenge the heck out of me, and honestly, I'm a work in progress. But I truly am enjoying life more than ever because the unseen realities of life are no longer a mystery.

I sincerely hope this book leads you to more fish, less tangles, and a deeper enjoyment of fishing and the great outdoors. Years of experience have taught me much about fishing, but there is one more tip I would like to leave you with. If you are curious about God, and his purpose for you, I know some reliable tools that will help you to understand the unseen realities of life.

I believe God created you and wants to reveal more of Himself to you, and to help you live your life with a Capital L. If you email me at bluehorizonsportfishing@gmail.com, I would like to send you a free resource. I wrote it especially for people like you and me. It weaves our passion for the outdoors into an honest, easy to read discussion about God and His world.

If your kicking the tires of this God thing, check out the following web sites. They are a safe place to explore questions about God and life.

www.everystudent.com
www.allaboutgod.com
www.cru.org/how-to-know-god.html

You can also check out what the Bible has to say, especially the Gospel of John.

Books, DVDs and Seminars by Captain Dan Keating

- *Great Lakes Salmon and Trout Fishing, The Complete Troller's Guide.* This book is foundational in the Keating series. It offers a logical, no-nonsense approach to the basic gear and tactics that are unique to salmon and trout fishing, 256 pages.
- *Keating on Kings, Great Lakes Chinook Tactics Way Beyond the Basics.* Many refer to this book as "The Bible of Salmon Fishing." In 256 pages, Captain Dan shares over 30 years of experience on how to locate and catch kings.
- *Angling Life, A Fisherman Reflects on Success, Failure and the Ultimate Catch.* A compelling page turner that offers valuable real life lessons. Tales of fishing, storms, adventure, and Dan's own shipwrecks are woven into a story that reveals deeper truths about life and our spiritual quest to connect with something greater than ourselves.

DVD's by Captain Dan Keating

- *Keating on Kings Part 1, Proven Tactics for Locating and Catching Kings* 75 minutes
- *Keating on Kings Part 2, Lure Selection and Advanced Techniques* 60 minutes

---

Books and DVD's are available at Amazon, your local bookstore or www.bluehorizonsportfishing.net

---

Book an instructional fishing charter with Captain Dan Keating aboard the BLUE HORIZON. This is a hands-on learning experience. Each outing is custom tailored to your needs. To book a charter email: bluehorizonsportfishing@gmail.com

Dan is a professional speaker who gives fishing seminars, motivational presentations and speaks at men's ministry events, churches, and schools. His authentic, down to earth messages are informative and well received. He also conducts Salmon Schools during the off season across the Great Lakes region.